Empire of Blue Water

Empire
of Blue Water

CAPTAIN MORGAN'S GREAT PIRATE ARMY,
THE EPIC BATTLE FOR THE AMERICAS,
AND THE CATASTROPHE THAT ENDED
THE OUTLAWS' BLOODY REIGN

STEPHAN TALTY

Crown Publishers New York

Library of Congress Cataloging-in-Publication Data
Talty, Stephan.
Empire of blue water: Captain Morgan's great pirate army, the epic battle
for the Americas, and the catastrophe that ended the outlaws' bloody reign. /
Stephan Talty. — 1st ed. Includes bibliographical references and index.
1. Pirates — Caribbean Area — History — 17th century.   2. Caribbean
Area — History to 1810.   3. Morgan, Henry, Sir, 1635?–1688.   I. Title.
F2161.T35 2007
972.904 — dc22
2006015273

ISBN 978-0-307-23660-9

Printed in the United States of America

Design by Leonard Henderson
Maps by Jackie Aher

10 9 8 7 6 5 4 3 2 1

First Edition

For Mariekarl

Contents

Timeline

1492: Christopher Columbus makes his first voyage to America.

1493: Pope Alexander VI issues his first papal bull, or charter, giving Spain dominion over all lands discovered and undiscovered in the New World.

1493–1550: Spain explores and colonizes the New World.

1519: The conquistador Hernán Cortés arrives off the coast of Mexico.

1540: Spain forbids any foreign ship from trading with its settlements in the Caribbean.

1544: Potosí's silver ore is discovered.

1586: The Elizabethan privateer Francis Drake raids Santo Domingo.

1588: The Spanish Armada is defeated.

1596: Francis Drake dies off the coast of Portobelo.

1621: Philip IV ascends to the Spanish throne.

1623: Thomas Warner takes possession of the small Caribbean island of St. Kitts, the first territory settled by a non-Spanish force in the West Indies.

1625: Charles I is crowned king of England.

1626: English settlers take possession of Barbados.

1628: The Dutch captain Piet Hein captures the West Indies treasure fleet, causing Spain to default on her loans.

1635: Henry Morgan is born in Wales.

1642: The first English Civil War begins, between the forces of Charles I and the armies eventually commanded by Oliver Cromwell.

1648: Thomas Gage's *A New Survey of the West Indies* is published.

1649: Charles I is executed.

1650: The sugar crop in Barbados is valued at 3 million pounds.

1651: The third English Civil War ends.

1655: The Hispaniola expedition conquers Jamaica for England.

1660: Oliver Cromwell dies. Charles II is crowned king of England.

1664: Morgan sacks Granada.

1664: Elizabeth Morgan, Henry's cousin and future wife, arrives in Port Royal.

1665–66: Morgan marries Elizabeth.

1667: The Treaty of Breda, signed by France, the United Provinces, and England, declares peace between the three nations.

1668: Morgan makes his raid on Portobelo.

1669: Morgan is granted his first tract of land in Jamaica.

1669: The *Oxford* explodes. Morgan changes his plan to attack Cartagena.

1669: William Godolphin arrives in Madrid to begin negotiations for a peace treaty with Spain.

1669: Morgan sacks Maracaibo.

1670: The Treaty of Madrid between Spain and England is adopted.

1671: Morgan raids Panama.

1672: Morgan is arrested and brought back to England.

1675: Charles II knights Morgan and appoints him deputy governor of Jamaica.

1676: Morgan returns to Jamaica as deputy governor.

1678: Morgan is appointed acting governor of Jamaica.

1678: Esquemeling's *Buccaneers of America* is published in the Netherlands.

1683: The Council of Jamaica suspends Morgan after a dispute with Governor Lynch.

1685: Morgan settles a libel suit with the publishers of *Buccaneers of America* after reading the English translation.

1688: Henry Morgan dies of dropsy.

1692: Port Royal is struck by a devastating natural disaster.

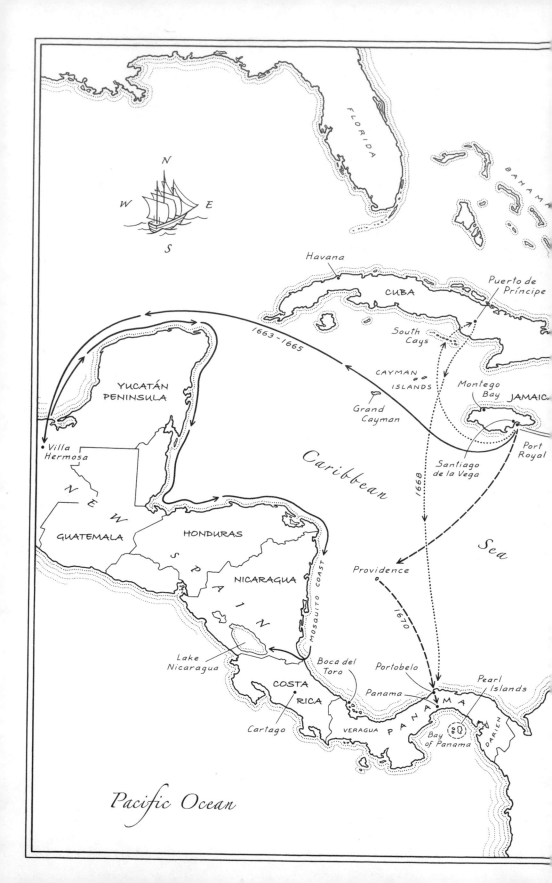

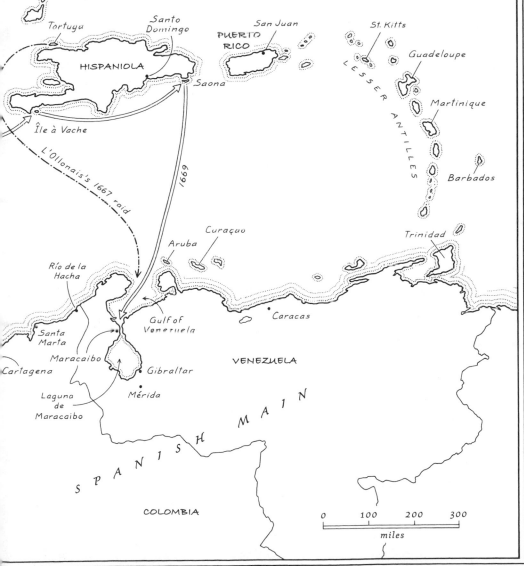

The Raids of Henry Morgan, West Indies, 1663-1670

————	1663-65 Attack on Granada
············	1668 Attack on Portobelo
═══════	1669 Attack on Maracaibo
– – – –	1670 Attack on Panama

Atlantic Ocean

Tortuga

Santo Domingo

San Juan

St. Kitts

PUERTO RICO

Guadeloupe

HISPANIOLA

Saona

Martinique

Île à Vache

L E S S E R   A N T I L L E S

Barbados

L'Ollonais's 1667 raid

1669

Curaçao

Aruba

Trinidad

Río de la Hacha

Santa Marta

Caracas

Gulf of Venezuela

Cartagena

Maracaibo

Gibraltar

VENEZUELA

Laguna de Maracaibo

Mérida

S P A N I S H   M A I N

COLOMBIA

0	100	200	300

miles

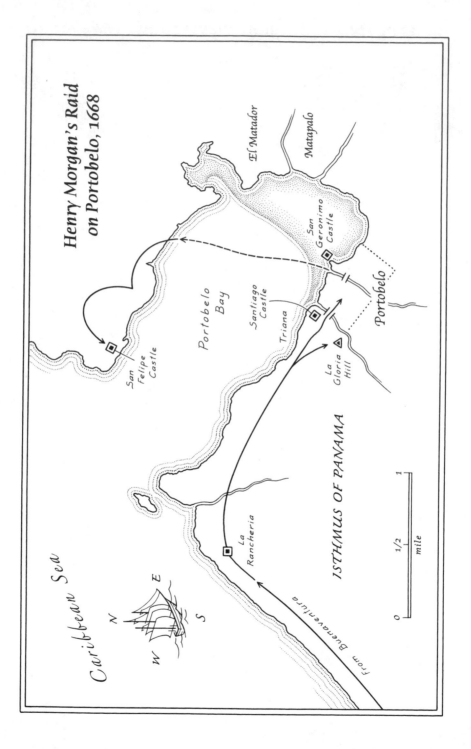

Henry Morgan's Raid
on Portobelo, 1668

Caribbean Sea

San Felipe Castle

Portobelo Bay

Santiago Castle

Triana

La Gloria Hill

La Rancheria

El Matador

Matapalo

San Geronimo Castle

Portobelo

ISTHMUS OF PANAMA

from Buenaventura

N
W   E
S

0   1/2   1
mile

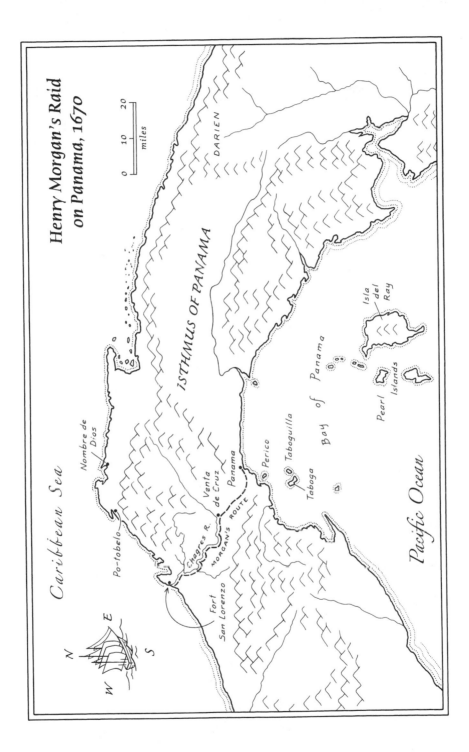

Henry Morgan's Raid
on Panama, 1670

0 10 20
miles

Caribbean Sea

Nombre de Dios

Po-tobelo

Fort San Lorenzo

Chagres R.

MORGAN'S ROUTE

Venta de Cruz

Panama

Perico

ISTHMUS OF PANAMA

DARIEN

Taboga

Taboguilla

Bay of Panama

Isla del Ray

Pearl Islands

Pacific Ocean

N
E
S
W

Impious was the man who first spread sail and braved the dangers of the frantic deep.

—AUGUSTUS

Empire of Blue Water

Introduction: The Lost City

To get to the lost city of Port Royal, you take the busy road to the Michael Manley International Airport, jostling on the crowded roads with the streams of cars and motorcycles and the taxis packed full of the people that flock to Jamaica from every corner of the world. At the airport entrance, the vehicles carrying the tourists, red and sated with sun, swing right toward the planes waiting to ferry them back to northern, less friendly cities. You continue straight. The faces in the other taxis (perhaps they know you from the hotel) turn and watch with concern as your van disappears down the half-deserted road. *Isn't he going home?* Everything for which the world comes to Jamaica—the Bob Marley Museum, the hotel pools—lies the other way. All that is at the end of this road is the ruins of a very old, and a very wicked, place.

Down the road a way sits the wrecked, overturned cockpit of a plane whose fuselage has completely disappeared, and past that a beached freighter lies stranded by some legendary hurricane. (The driver tells you it's been there since he was a boy, and he's easily thirty-five.) Beyond them the land on each side of the road narrows; the water creeps close to the road, and soon you are riding just a few feet above its gleaming, fretted surface. You're now traveling on the neck of the Palisadoes, the thin peninsula so tenuously attached to the Jamaican mainland that it has disappeared for generations at a time, whipped away by hurricanes, until silt from the ocean rebuilds it. It seems as if a good wave could wash right over it and cut you off from the world and that you would glide toward your destination over the blue waves.

A few miles down the road, you reach the limits of the old town. Across from a bus stop where Jamaican schoolgirls tease schoolboys as they wait for their ride home sits a small, iron-fenced lot overgrown with weeds; in the corner is a brass plaque. Most people not from here stop to read the words.

> Once called the "richest and wickedest city in the world," Port Royal was also the virtual capital of Jamaica. To it came men of all races, treasures of silks, doubloons and gold from Spanish ships, looted on the high seas by the notorious "Brethren of the Coast" as the pirates here were called. From here sailed the fleets of Henry Morgan, later lieutenant-governor of Jamaica, for the sacking of Camaguay, Maracaibo, and Panama—and died here, despite the ministrations of his Jamaican folk-doctor. . . .

There is a last, dark chapter referred to on the plaque, but that can wait. The quoted section is an admirable summary; the main facts are all there, if only a hint of their true drama. But if others, such as the Spanish, were given the chance to sum up Port Royal's history, there would be a different tone to it: blood, heathen orgies, midnight attacks, decapitations, routine torture, Spanish queens trembling with rage because of what had issued from this old port. The victors write the calmest prose, especially when they are English.

Just past the overgrown lot is a church, and walking toward it is a group of men and women dressed in seventeenth-century outfits. They can't be—but they are. *Pirates!* Or at least people dressed like pirates. As they get closer, you can pick up their accents and realize they are Americans; it turns out they are members of a pirate club, secretaries and office managers dressed in fantastically authentic period gear, the men in boots and doublets, a pewter drinking mug latched to a leather belt, the women with their breasts cresting out of their blouses. They've flown here on a pilgrimage to the home of Henry Morgan, the greatest of the buccaneers. We go together into St. Paul's Cathedral; inside are several pieces of loot—a chalice, plate, and other silver items—carried from the great raid on Panama by Morgan and donated to the church. One of the club members speaks up, a shy red-headed young man from Chicago, his face flushed with an urgent emotion. "Can I ask you a huge favor?" he asks the tour guide. "Can I just sit next to them?" He does, and his eyes look on them as a Christian would look at a splinter of the true cross.

Farther down the road is Fort Charles, named after the king who used the buccaneers as a stick with which to beat the Spanish. In the glass cases are items recovered from the old city: a stoneware jug from the German Rhineland; a Delftware cup; iron ankle shackles that would have once hobbled an African slave, brought here to serve on the vast sugar plantations, their dull circles seeming impossibly small. And here, in its leather scabbard, is one of the prizes of the collection: what the museum claims is Henry Morgan's comb. Into the leather has been carved a pineapple tree and the date 1677. Morgan would have been well into his second act by then, the marauder turned knight of the empire, hunting down his former mates and hanging them out on Gallows Point, not far from here. Schoolkids on a field trip stare dully at the comb—it doesn't seem very piratical—and then go tearing out the door. The museum is a shrine for members of the pirate club; the Brethren left so few physical remnants behind that they could almost be ghosts, and these are things they touched and used. But the artifacts, the maps on the walls, the words on the plaque, none of it can really capture the awful and wonderful things that happened here.

Port Royal lived a short, fast life. It was like Rick's Café in *Casablanca:* Sooner or later everyone came to the city. On its streets, slave traders, spies, and English dukes brushed shoulders with plantation owners and common whores like the famous No-Conscience Nan. But people such as these can be found in the histories of San Juan or Barbados. What makes Port Royal special is one group of people: the pirates. These were men who were intent on leading the freest lives imaginable and who thereby altered the fate of the New World through bloodshed and war until, after having brought the Spanish Main to its knees, they became disposable and were hunted down not far from here. The streets beneath one's feet became the crossroads of two empires—one being born, the other faltering—because of Henry Morgan and his men.

✤   ✤   ✤

The city feels like a place from which time departed centuries ago, if it even touched down at all; you get the feeling that it hurried across the bay to Kingston or skipped across the famous blue waters north to Miami. Even the colorful poster strung next to the fort entrance that proclaims EARTHQUAKE AWARENESS WEEK is out of date, the event having passed ten days earlier. In the larger Caribbean cities, they have real time, linked to Greenwich and the worlds of appointments and business. But the most important thing that ever happened here happened over three hundred years ago. That and the deserted streets, the hallucinogenic power of the heat, gives you the feeling that the second hand on your watch might be ticking backward.

It's only when you walk out to the water and step in and then bob gently on the shale gray surface that the story you have come to hear begins. As you take a breath and drop under the water, modern Jamaica—with its YA, MON T-shirts and the motorcycles and the tinny sound track of Bob Marley songs that plays over the island—falls away and you can almost inhabit the old bloodstained land. For if, as they sometimes do, a hurricane has swept away the silt and sand, not far out, below your paddling feet, streets appear and lead out into the depths. If you grab hold of a large stone the way the Indian divers did to reach the Spanish wrecks centuries ago, you could even drop down and walk the paths between them. The lost city is not really lost at all.

Here are buried the battlements of four huge forts, for this once was once the most heavily defended port in the New World. According to those who have seen it, the city is remarkably lifelike under the sand: The streets are recognizable, laid out exactly as they were centuries before. Coral growths have turned the cannon into spiky objets d'art; piles of roundball have been frozen into rusty pyramids. Below you are the walls of bordellos and merchants' mansions, their roofs gone, open like compartments in a jewelry box, and as you float down into one, you might find dinner plates or a clay pipe stamped with the fingerprint of the black artisan who made it and pressed his thumb into the soft clay as a maker's mark. If you are very lucky, you will reach down into the sand and come up with a souvenir. A blackened doubloon, a Spanish piece of eight, or even—and for this you would have to be as lucky as Henry Morgan himself—an emerald necklace from the Spanish mines of Colombia. If you do find a piece of treasure, pause for a moment before returning to the surface, where the only sound that will greet you is the rasp of the fishermen's outboard motors. With that piece of loot in your hand, you have come to the true beginning of the story, the reason white men came here at all. The search for immense riches is an old one, but here it did more than build mansions or set men at one another's throats. Here gold and silver transformed two enemies, sharpened their differences until they stood as competing visions of human society. Then the desire for the riches of the New World sent them crashing into battle to decide on a winner. Each wanted the wealth for different reasons, and each went about grabbing them in different, revealing ways. This particular story is unique to the boneyard you stand in, fifteen feet under the surface of the Caribbean Sea, a rich and vibrant city now fallen silent. Its present condition prompts two questions. What really happened in Port Royal? And what happened *to* Port Royal?

To find the answer, you must travel back over three centuries and look to the east.

"I Offer a New World"

In the winter of 1654, a newly commissioned frigate named the *Fagons* was dispatched from the ancient city of Portsmouth on a secret mission. Its journey was short; it sailed around the southeast corner of England into the quiet town of Deal. There on the shore waited the ship's only cargo: a forty-four-year-old Anglican rector named Thomas Gage.

It was rare in the Royal Navy of the time that a warship would be sent to pick up a single man, and a mere country pastor at that. But Gage was a unique figure in English life: A long-dreamt-of empire was about to be launched in part because of a book he'd written fifteen years before; the nation was preparing to send thousands of men to attack its archnemesis inspired by things that Thomas Gage, and he alone, claimed to have seen across the ocean. This mysterious man—no portrait survives to this day—was, as befits his role in this story, surrounded in life by controversy and black dread. He had ready access to the most powerful man in the country, Oliver Cromwell; indeed, the *Fagons* had been hastened around the corner of England "by order of the Protector" himself, and the Venetian ambassador wrote in a letter that Gage "had many secret conferences" with Cromwell in the months leading up to the ship's arrival.

Before and after the rector arrived, England's leader had been found studying maps of far-off places, and a globe of the world had appeared, without explanation, on his desk. All because of the humble Anglican.

Gage's past was crowded with ghosts; men had perished with his name on their lips. The rector came from a line of Englishmen who some considered saboteurs and infidels, while others swore they were the souls of Christian fortitude. Whether heroes or villains, the family had long since disowned Thomas; one sibling said he strove to erase every last memory of the man from his mind, while another wrote to a friend about "our graceless brother," whose actions "our whole family doth blush to behold." Thomas's father had cut off his inheritance years before, warned him never to return to England, even called him a lethal enemy, and Gage claimed that his older brother, a military hero, had made good on his father's threat and actually tried to have him murdered. All this resulted from Thomas Gage's years of religious intrigue: On his word, three men had recently been hanged, drawn, and quartered at Tyburn prison, a procedure whose savagery is not suggested by the surgical description of it. The *Fagons'* crew would not have welcomed Gage aboard the ship regardless of his past; religious men on a ship were a bad omen, as it was believed that the great storm maker Satan sent tempests across the oceans to drown them. The black-suited rector, the man who hanged his own friends, as the sole passenger? It couldn't be good luck.

As for Gage, one can only imagine his thoughts as the frigate appeared on the horizon, sunlight sparkling off the surface of its twenty-two new brass guns. His writing life was behind him, and he wouldn't live to record his thoughts on this, the most momentous voyage of his life. But surely he was flooded with memories; the ship was to take him back across the ocean to a place of his youth, a place that had disappointed him terribly and was yet now giving him a second chance at glory. As always when trying to dip into Gage's inner life, one must consider his appetite for power; the black sheep of an illustrious family, he hungered to make his name, and this would be his last shot. In the book that had launched this voyage, he'd written insouciantly to the leader of England, "To your Excellency I offer a New World." Actually, he meant *the* New World, and the appearance of the *Fagons* represented Oliver Cromwell's silent acceptance of the offer. As the ship touched the dock, Gage said his good-byes to his wife and three children; he would never see them again.

The ship headed back to Portsmouth, where a fleet was being fitted out for the expedition, an audacious spear that would be launched from the shores of England aimed at the vitals of a great world empire. No Englishman returned from its destination, or that at least was the legend: The enemy guarded its treasure house closely, and even natives from the nation that had conquered it needed to go through a long vetting process for permission to set foot there. But Gage had lived and explored in the forbidden kingdoms; it was said he was the only Englishman alive who had done so and came back to tell about it. Still, Cromwell was taking an extraordinary risk by trusting his expedition to the rector's stories: The descriptions of the ports, the fortifications, the soldiers whom the English fleet would soon face all originated within the memory of this singular man. As he sailed into Portsmouth harbor after a quick voyage aboard the *Fagons*, Gage would have looked at the ships spread across the harbor and the feverish activity—the dinghies ferrying men and supplies to the larger ships, the polishing of brass and repairing of rig and sail—with deep satisfaction. *I have done this*, he must have said to himself. *This is God's work and mine.*

✤   ✤   ✤

After a century of neglect, Portsmouth was again thriving under the expedition's demands. Its population of a few thousand people had sided with the Puritan Cromwell and his New Model Army against the forces of Charles I in the recent, savage civil war, and now it was being repaid in hard currency. The fleet of sixty ships was being repaired, outfitted, and manned (but not supplied with food, which would soon present a problem) in its docks. This meant a great deal of work in a time when the oceangoing vessel was one of the most technologically advanced machines Western societies produced; by the 1700s even small ships required the wood of hundreds of trees and carried three miles or more of rope. The port swarmed with activity, and the nautical grapevine hummed with a single question: *Where are they headed?* It was a major fleet; it must have grand ambitions. The most popular rumor held that Cromwell himself would arrive to lead the expedition on a surprise attack against Rome, seat of the pope, known to Protestants as "the Great Whore."

But when the signal gun was fired, echoing out from the town across the slate-colored sea, and the expedition's troops began lining up to board the ships, the natives changed their minds. The army of approximately 2,500 men emerged from their lodgings and were judged, and judged harshly: These were not the soldiers of Cromwell's New Model Army, the famous Roundheads, a force whose ferocity was matched by its discipline; to look at them, these men came straight out of the gutter. Cutpurses, drunks, "knights of the blade," incipient murderers. "I believe they are not to be paralleled in the world," wrote Major Robert Sedgwick, who would later command the men, or try to. "People so lazy and idle, as it cannot enter into the heart of any Englishman, that such blood should run in the veins of any born in England; so unworthy, so slothful, and basely secure: and have, out of a strange kind of spirit, desired rather to die than to live." But there was one man on the ships, anonymous as yet to history, who would give the lie to Sedgwick's words. In the space of eight short years, this brilliant leader would turn men like these stumblebums into what were perhaps pound for pound the best fighting men in the world. He'd boarded at Portsmouth or would join up later in the islands; the historical record is unclear. Perhaps he even brushed by Gage on the crowded deck as the fleet churned westward. His name was Henry Morgan.

Young Henry had been born in Wales in 1635 to a lesser branch of the illustrious Morgans, growing up in either the village of Penkarne or in Llanrhymney; Welsh genealogists remain locked in battle over which town can claim him. Henry was certainly kin to the great Morgans of Tredegar, members of the *uchelwyr* class, roughly translated as "the high ones." A family poet made the relationship between the main branch and the other families clear around 1661:

> *And so LanRumney yet must bend the knee,*
> *And from Tredegar fetch their pedigree.*

The only portrait of the young Morgan (now hanging at Tredegar) shows him as a plump-cheeked teenager, his chubby face framed by the rich brown curls of a wig. He looked like a dandy who might chase low-born maids and sponge off his father. Until, that is, you came to the eyes: They look out of the portrait coolly—appraising, measuring, uninnocent.

The place that Morgan came from would not have gotten him instant respect in London. Wales was considered a rustic outback, peopled by farmers and a few squires connected by complex lines of kinship. To the English the Welsh were "emotional, excitable people," wrote one historian, "whose taste for toasted cheese . . . was matched only by their devotion to their tedious native patois and their even more tedious pedigrees"; the cliché Welshman was a bumpkin "remote in his mountain fastnesses, surviving on cheese and leeks, surrounded by goats and unpronounceable names." The English had a great deal of fun with the Welsh, most of it related to cheese, but there was at least one area in which they showed respect: warfare. Milton called Wales an "old, and haughty nation proud in arms," and the Welsh were known to be crack soldiers. Morgan himself came from warrior stock; his two uncles, Thomas and Edward, were mercenaries who had left home to fight in wars all over Europe. When the Civil War broke out, Henry must have been told that the two brothers had chosen opposite sides to fight on: Thomas enlisted with Cromwell's New Model Army, and Edward pledged allegiance to the Royalists and King Charles I. As Thomas Gage had grown up hearing about martyrs and Scripture, Morgan grew up in a home filled with stories of war.

Edward Morgan fought close to home, as captain-general of the Royalist forces in South Wales, an important posting. Thomas Morgan was even more successful during the war. This "little, shrill-voiced choleric man" rose to become the right-hand man of Cromwell's most trusted general, George Monck, and was a key player in the attacks on Scotland and Flanders. He was wounded twice but survived to become one of the heroes of the war. Especially from Edward, who was posted close to Henry Morgan's home, young Henry would have learned the rudiments of siege tactics, artillery, and the leadership of men.

Judging from his later life, the young adventurer carried little of Gage's religious obsessions. The New World was for him a chance at riches and respect. He knew he was never going to earn them in the learned professions, as his meager education prevented those careers. "I left the schools too young . . . ," he'd later say, speaking of the law. "And have been more used to the pike than the book." A long wooden stick topped with an iron spike, the pike was a vicious weapon commonly used in the English Civil War, and pikemen were often stationed in the front line of an army formation, ready to bear the brunt of a cavalry charge. Anyone who wielded a pike had undoubtedly seen death up close.

The young warrior was traveling to the New World hell-bent on making his fortune and advancing the fortunes of his family. His name especially was precious to him; he'd later write, " 'God preserve your Honour' is and shall be the daily prayer of Henry Morgan," and he was famously tetchy about anyone who did not pay him the proper respect. The chip on his shoulder and the fact that he had so little schooling suggests that Henry Morgan did not grow up rich or coddled in Wales; the early exit from school could also indicate the extent to which normal life of the people there was thrown into chaos by the successive civil wars that engulfed England during his boyhood years. In any case, he'd joined the expedition with a burning desire to find the freedom to achieve his ends: adventure, estates, position. The last two were the same things that the lesser Morgans were forced to seek on bended knee from their more illustrious relatives. In the New World, the twenty-year-old Morgan was not going to bend his knee to anyone, unless it was to place it firmly on the neck of a Spanish officer.

Between these two men, Morgan and Gage—one dreaming of a religious empire, the other of gold and vast estates—you have rather neatly summed up the race for the New World.

   ✝ ✝ ✝

The people of Portsmouth watched as the ships sailed, still mystified as to what change this would bring in their nation's fortunes. In fact, only a chosen few knew the destination. The orders given to the commanders were sealed and not to be opened until the fleet was under sail. Thomas Gage, however, knew that the target lay to the west: on the island of Hispaniola.

The lands across the Atlantic had fascinated Western societies for centuries. The ancient Greeks believed that the spirits of their heroes left their bodies at the moment of death and traveled to the "Blessed Islands" that dotted the distant waters, to reside there forever. To the Englishman of the seventeenth century, the New World combined the wonders of Shangri-la with the remoteness of Neptune. It was a place of gobsmacking riches only hinted at by the laundry list of treasure the Spanish had extracted: a gilded ruby eagle, weighing sixty-eight pounds with enormous emeralds for eyes; the two Mayan orbs representing the sun and moon respectively, one made of solid gold, the other of silver, and both "as large as carriage wheels," with crisp images of the animals worked into the metal; the emeralds the size of a man's fist. They'd even discovered a mountain, Potosí, seemingly made wholly of silver, whose gushing-forth of ore served "to chastise the Turk, humble the Moor, make Flanders tremble and terrify England."

The New World that produced such wonders had been Spain's for many decades, ever since Pope Alexander VI stroked a line down the middle of a map of the world dividing the non-Christianized territories between Spain and Portugal. In 1494 the line of demarcation was shifted to 370 leagues west of the Cape Verde Islands, giving Brazil to Portugal and the rest of the lands, known and unknown, to Spain. England, France, and the Netherlands—the other players in the great game of empire—never agreed to the terms. In Cromwell's justification for his expedition to the New World, the division was called the pope's "ridiculous gift," while King Francis I of France remarked acidly, ""I should like to see the clause in Adam's will that excludes me from a share in the world."

Spain, however, had the power to enforce its wishes on all comers. It was an unlikely hyperpower, whose lustrous façade hid a faltering ability. But in 1654, as the leaders of the Hispaniola expedition, General Venables and William Penn, set out for the Americas, Spain was still a behemoth, the successor to Rome, and its control of the New World was largely uncontested. For its holdings there, the monarchy had enforced a policy of "no peace beyond the line," meaning that all territories beyond Pope Alexander's line of demarcation were not governed by European peace treaties. Spain and its enemies were to be considered in perpetual conflict in the Caribbean and the Spanish Main—the mainland of South and Central America. Although the Spanish kings declared this policy, the truth was that events in the West Indies would influence both relations between European nations and the treaties they negotiated.

Cromwell and his commanders wanted fervently to loosen Spain's grip on the riches of the Americas. Gage was their happy scout; his biography had become the blueprint for the invasion. But it also told a vicious tale all its own.

Thomas Gage grew up in a time of lethal battles between Protestants and Catholics. His family had been part of the Catholic aristocracy since the time of the House of Tudor; imagine the Kennedys in an age of virulent suppression of the faith and you have their profile. Distantly related to Sir Francis Bacon and Shakespeare, Gage's forefather Sir John Gage had been one of Henry VIII's brilliant circle of young, ambitious men; his star dimmed only when he did not fully support Henry's divorce from Catherine of Aragon, the flame-haired daughter of Ferdinand and Isabella of Spain. The resulting break with the pope, who denied the divorce, led Henry VIII to found the Church of England. The decision set Catholics and Protestants at one another's throats for centuries and became the crucial moment for the Gage family: their fortunes would now rise and fall with the Catholic faith in England. The internecine religious wars of the following decades often had a Gage among their cast of characters: Sir John was called back into service when the Catholic Mary rose to power; his son Robert and his wife hid priests in their Surrey estate, at risk of death; Robert's son was arrested for planning to assassinate the Protestant Elizabeth in the disastrous Babington plot, inspired by the pope's excommunication of Elizabeth and his offer of absolution for anyone—"cook, brewer, baker, vintner, physician, grocer, surgeon or other"—who would kill her. The conspirator was executed in September 1586 for high treason, setting a standard for family devotion to the faith.

This was the atmosphere in which Thomas Gage grew up: renegade priests from the Low Countries flung into secret hiding places at a knock on the door; forbidden masses celebrated in dripping basements; whispers, intense faith, deadly betrayals. His early life must have had something close to the feeling of the earliest Christians', and it clearly demanded a high degree of both character and devotion. But Thomas rebelled against it, leaving the Jesuit faith to which his family had devoted itself and joining a hated rival: the Dominicans. He was seeking the truth about God and man, and he believed he'd found it. Afterward he received a letter from his father saying "that I should never think to be welcome to my brothers nor kindred in England nor to him, that I should not expect ever more to hear from him, nor dare to see him if ever I returned to England, but expect that he'd set upon me even the Jesuits whom I had deserted and opposed to chase me out of my country." If one is to feel sympathy for Gage at any point in his increasingly sordid life, one might as well expend it the night he received his father's letter, when he sat disowned and nearly friendless in a foreign country. Thomas lay awake that night, unable to sleep, and wept at his father's words.

By age twenty-five, Gage was studying at a Dominican monastery in Spain. Soon he'd fallen under the spell of a commissary of the pope recruiting young friars for service in the Philippines. The Spanish had centuries before battled the Moors for control of Iberia and won; in their minds the Crusades were still a going concern, and they were sending friars and priests to the New World as soldiers of Christ. Gage signed up for the mission and sailed for the New World in 1625.

The promised land of the Americas turned out to be far different from what he expected. Instead of fighting for God's kingdom, he'd found the friars drunk and living like pashas. As he'd traveled through the empire, he'd seen up close how its religious men lived; here he writes about the disparity between how another order, the Franciscans, were supposed to dress and what they actually wore:

> The rules of the order of the Franciscans demanded that they wear sackcloth and shirts of coarse wool, and that they go bare legged, shod with wood or hemp; but these friars wore beneath their habits (which they sometimes tucked up to the waist, the better to display such splendor), shoes of fine Cordovan leather, fine silk stockings, drawers with three inches of lace at the knee, Holland shirts and doublets quilted with silk. They were fond of gambling, and acquainted with gamblers' oaths.

Everywhere he found the religious orders were feasting off the Indians, getting fat and rich; he called them *lupi rapaces,* "ravenous wolves." One young prior in particular, whom he met nearly straight off the boat, drove him wild. While his books of theology collected dust on a high shelf, this "gallant and amorous young spark" had a Spanish lute within easy reach, which he took down and strummed to a song about one of the local lovelies, "adding scandal to scandal, looseness to liberty." Gage was among the first witnesses to the corrosive effects of the New World's great riches on the Spanish and their divine kingdom. The truth was that the living faith of their forefathers had hardened into corruption, hypocrisy, and bureaucratic form.

Gage had spent twelve years in the New World, paid attention to everything he saw, and acquired a modest fortune from his dealings with the natives. On his voyage back to Europe, a Spanish mulatto pirate in league with the Dutch quickly unburdened him of the 7,000 pieces of eight ($350,000 in today's dollars) he'd so painstakingly filched, leaving Gage in despair. He'd returned to England in 1637 barely able to remember his English grammar; the relative upon whose door he knocked did not know him at first and said he sounded like "an Indian or a Welshman." Gage's father had been true to his word and left him unmentioned in his will; he was poor and Catholic in a war-torn country where the tide was turning toward Cromwell and the Protestants. Gage turned with it. In 1642 he was received into the Anglican faith.

And he'd become a Protestant warrior: He testified against his old Catholic comrades and helped the state convict them of high treason. The men faced an awful death: "that you be drawn on a hurdle to the place of execution where you shall be hanged by the neck and being alive cut down, your privy members shall be cut off and your bowels taken out and burned before you, your head severed from your body and your body divided into four quarters to be disposed of at the King's pleasure." (It was a method of punishment invented in 1241, to punish one William Maurice, a pirate.) In a display of true Christian fortitude, one of the men he testified against prayed for Gage's soul until the moment of his execution. The next year Gage gave evidence against two more priests and helped send them to their deaths.

But the reason that Gage was now sailing to America as part of an English invasion force was a book he wrote about his travel in the New World, *The English-American, or a New Survey of the West Indies,* first published in 1648 and then issued again in 1655 on Cromwell's orders. It was an immediate sensation. An introductory verse told why Gage's book would be different from others claiming to describe Spanish territories:

> *Those who have describ'd these parts before*
> *Of trades, winds, currents, hurricanes do tell,*
> *Of headlands, harbours, trendings of the shore,*
> *Of rocks and isles, wherein they might as well*
> *Talk of a nut, and only shew the shell;*
> *The kernel neither tasted, touched nor seen.*

Gage had tasted; in fact, he'd rolled the kernel around his mouth and savored its last bit of flavor.

At the time of the book's publication, Spain and England were locked in a contest comparable to the shooting years of the Cold War: two mighty powers, two ideologies, fighting for supremacy in faraway lands. Gage was England's Neil Armstrong, an astronaut who had journeyed unthinkable distances and returned to describe a new world. Of course, in this analogy the moon would have been colonized by Russia and fabulously rich in precious minerals; that added to the excitement that greeted Gage's book. *The English-American* was also a reconnaissance report, in which Gage not only gave detailed accounts of populations and local defenses but emphasized several main points: The Spanish had few fortifications; the native Indians and the Negro slaves would rise up with any invasion against their oppressors; and the Spanish were debauched and would be easily defeated. There was even a prophecy among the enemy that would help the invaders: "It hath been these many yeares their owne common talke," Gage wrote, "that a strange people shall conquer them, and take all their riches."

To help the prophecy come true, Cromwell pulled Gage out of his modest parish, away from the baptisms and the confessions of yeoman farmers. Something much more important awaited him:

Cromwell asked the preacher to write up a paper detailing how the Spanish empire in the Americas could be attacked and over-thrown. Cromwell had no intelligence service, no spies, to rely on: Gage was it. The rector quickly boiled down the relevant sections of his book, and Gage predicted that an invasion of Hispaniola, fol-lowed by Cuba, would result in the toppling of Spain's Central American kingdom—a vast, often impenetrable territory the size of France—within two years.

Twenty-nine years after he'd first sailed to the Americas, a very different Gage now traveled in a much larger fleet: 38 English ves-sels, carrying 2,500 men, journeyed out from Portsmouth. He was again on a religious mission: to exterminate Catholics from the New World and claim it for Protestantism. Gone was the heady inno-cence of his earlier voyage. These were not happy ships; the supply boats had not caught up with the fleet, and the men were already on half rations. They'd also learned to their disgust that they would not be allowed to keep any of the fabulous booty they expected to rake in on arrival at Hispaniola; and many believed that in fact the talk of invasion was part of a conspiracy and they were actually to be sold to a foreign prince as slaves on arrival. Mutiny was a live option; the ships were riven with anxiety.

The two commanders—Admiral Penn, in charge of the ships and sailors, and General Venables, in charge of the soldiers—were feuding over who led the mission. In fact, neither of them did; Cromwell's orders were high on ambition but regrettably short on precise command structure. It is a mystery why the Hispaniola expe-dition was so badly planned; this was England's first state-sponsored attempt at establishing an empire (the colonies in North America being private endeavors), and it was a hugely important moment in the nation's history. But the expedition was a shambles. It is not enough to say, as Sir John Seeley would later comment, that England "seemed to have conquered and peopled half the world in a fit of absence of mind." Cromwell was certainly distracted by domestic concerns, and he left the planning to a subordinate, only to send the

men off with a cheery message: "Happy gales and prosperous success
to the great enterprise you have in hand." But the stage was set for
disaster.

The Hispaniola fleet was meant to be the first strike in the
"Western Design," an ambition of English leaders back to the time
of Elizabeth, when privateers such as Francis Drake raided the
Spanish Main and pricked from Spain's mighty empire drop after
drop of blood. The Western Design called for England to conquer
and settle the New World as a Protestant colony where the Bible's
vision of a just world would be put into place. As a young man,
Cromwell had himself almost joined his Puritan brethren in their
voyage to Massachusetts; the idea of founding a new and pure land
had always had great appeal for him. Hispaniola was something
of a second chance. "Set up your banners in the name of Christ,"
Cromwell told an admiral. "For undoubtedly it is his cause." But
there were other advantages to an invasion: diverting the golden
stream of treasure into his own ledgers would free up Cromwell
from nasty budgetary battles with Parliament. Even Cromwell was
not immune to treasure fever.

The fleet stopped off at the islands of Nevis, Montserrat, and St.
Kitts and scooped up 1,200 more soldiers, then sailed on to Barbados to add 3,500 more, boosting the ranks to about 7,000 troops, an
awesome force in the sparsely populated New World. Many of the
fresh recruits were indentured servants so hopeless, so brutalized
by the routines of sugar plantations, that mere war seemed preferable. The English soldiers, themselves looked on as fourth-raters,
were not impressed by the recruits: "This Islland is the Dunghill
whereone England doth cast forth its rubidge," one sailor (most
likely the sailing master of Penn's flagship) wrote. The island's
blacksmiths churned out twenty-five hundred half-pikes—iron
heads fixed to eight-foot handles; orders were given out, along with
the password ("religion"). After waiting in vain for the storeships to
arrive, the commanders listened to Gage's advice and decided to attack Santo Domingo on the Spanish island of Hispaniola. Henry

Morgan would have received the news of the target along with the other anxious soldiers.

✦　　　✦　　　✦

On March 31, 1655, after many decades in the planning, the English spear finally landed—and was quickly blunted. The main body of troops went ashore thirty miles from the Spanish city in a maneuver, as historian Dudley Pope has written, "more suited to a comic opera" than a first strike at empire. The Negro slaves who Gage swore would run to meet them were nowhere to be found; instead the soldiers stumbled remarkably upon another white man, an old Irishman who had somehow ended up in this Spanish outpost, and press-ganged him into service. The hapless guide led the invaders around aimlessly for hours without bringing them any closer to their objective; the furious Venables had him hanged. When they did approach the Spanish fortifications, its soldiers, with indulgences around their necks granting them instant entry into heaven should they die fighting the English devils, peppered them with shot and ball. The ranks disintegrated; Venables hid behind a tree to escape the barrage, "soe much possessed with teror that he could hardlie spake." He soon retreated to Penn's flagship to commiserate with his wife as his troops retreated pell-mell from the slaughter. The soldiers set up camp on the shore, slapping away mosquitoes that slowly introduced malaria into their bloodstreams, and relieving their thirst with water infected with the organisms of dysentery and yellow fever. Troops began to drop left and right; a second attack days later was broken even more easily than the first. Twenty days after their landing, a retreat from Hispaniola was called, one that Penn and Venables would have dearly liked to continue all the way to Portsmouth. But they knew that Cromwell would be furious at the fleet returning empty-handed, and the Tower of London was not where they wanted to end their careers. The defeat at Hispaniola was Cromwell's first loss as a military leader, and no one was eager to give him the news without offering up a consolation prize. (When he did hear about the debacle, Cromwell was shaken: "The Lord hath greatly humbled us," he wrote.) The suggestion was made that the lightly defended island of Jamaica might appease the Lord Protector; and soon the fleet was headed there. The ships' burden was lightened by the loss of 2,000 men, all of whom lay buried or rotting on the shores of Hispaniola.

Jamaica was named after the Arawak Indian word *xaymaca,* "land of wood and water," and there wasn't much else there in 1655. The Arawak had succeeded the original Tainos and then been decimated by the ferocious, man-eating Carib Indians, who would give white men nightmares wherever they encountered them throughout the West Indies. Jamaica was one-sixth the size of Hispaniola, 146 miles long by 51 miles at its widest point, covered with thick jungle and raked by mountains rising to 7,400 feet. Columbus had found the island nearly uninhabited when he sailed into what would become St. Ann's Bay on May 3, 1494; he, too, was reeling from what he'd seen in Hispaniola—in his case, the graves of the settlers from his first voyage who had been slaughtered by the native inhabitants. With relief, Columbus named Jamaica "the fairest island that eyes have beheld," its imposing mountains often wrapped in a blue-silver gauze. (The view is not the same that greets the modern tourist approaching on one of the huge cruise ships—most of the trees and flowers now flourishing on the island were introduced by the English after the invasion.) The Spanish maintained a small garrison that had been attacked once before by the English adventurer William Jackson, who had rhapsodized about the island, "Whatsoever is fabled by ye Poets, or maintained by Historians, concerning ye Arcadian Plaines, or ye Thessalian Tempe, may here be verified and truly affirmed, touching ye delight and plenty of all necessarys conferred by nature upon this Terrestrial Paradise, Jamaica." His men asked to settle there, and when they were refused, twenty-three of them ran off to the Spanish as deserters, the first Englishmen to fall under the island's spell.

What also distinguished the island was its crucial position along the Spanish treasure routes: Jamaica lay at the choke point between the Central American collection spots—where silver, gold, and gems from the empire were gathered—and the sea routes to Spain. The English, through no skill of their own, had stumbled on a strategic windfall. By taking Jamaica they'd be able to cause havoc with the stream of gold that helped sustain the Spanish Empire. Penn and Venables landed on May 10; by May 11 the capital had been taken and the governor was headed deep into the jungle. It was an easy victory: The total population on the island was only 2,500, and many of these people were farmers. Venables negotiated with the governor, who returned five days later to obtain food for his troops and to arrange for the Spanish to leave Jamaica for the Spanish Main (although some holdouts remained). The articles of capitulation were so detailed in their demands for treasure and slaves that the Spanish said "they read like an inventory drawn up by heirs in disagreement." The Indians had marveled at the greed of the Spanish; now it was the Spanish's turn to marvel at the Puritans.

The English set up their colors and tried to begin the work of settlement; land was parceled out, patrols organized. But the diseases that had stalked the soldiers in Hispaniola returned, and the hungry men stood little chance against infection. Soon Jamaica resembled a "very Golgotha," in the words of one soldier: "Poor men I pity them at the heart, all their imaginary mountains of gold are turned into dross." Major Robert Sedgwick, who was sent out from England to take charge of the settlement, found the troops in worse shape, he thought, than any group of English fighting men in the history of the nation. "Many dead," he wrote tersely, "their carcasses lying unburied in the high-ways, and among the bushes to and again; many of them that were alive, walked like ghosts or dead men, who as I went through the town, they lay groaning, and crying out, 'bread, for the Lord's sake.' " The men ate dogs and iguanas, snakes and rats; when they fell dead, the dogs then ate the men. They were hit by dysentery, the plague, "phrensies and madness," and mysterious infections that caused a man to swell to the size of a barrel. When the soldiers were mustered in November 1655, it was found that only 3,710 of the original 7,000 were still alive, and many of these were already failing;

eventually 5,000 Englishmen would lose their lives on Hispaniola and Jamaica.

The invasion of Hispaniola was simply the latest front in an age-old religious war. But the vast riches of the New World and the men who sought them were about to transform the battle into something different. The man who would lead England was already on the scene: the twenty-year-old Henry Morgan. Morgan somehow survived the horrendous pandemic that swept through the English ranks on Hispaniola and Jamaica and learned firsthand several valuable lessons he'd never forget: how not to lead troops in the New World, how not to attack a fortified Spanish position, how not to enlist the local Indians to your cause, and how not to share power between commanders. When word of the Jamaican conquest reached the Spanish territories in Mexico, the church bells rang in sorrow. With this intrusion the Antichrist had breached the walls of the promised land. In the coming years, Henry Morgan would make those bells toll again and again. He was the genius of the next battle: a clash of worldviews made bloody by the treasure that lay beyond Jamaica.

But there were soon ominous signs that Port Royal held its own dangers. In addition to the tropical storms and hurricanes that swept over Jamaica, the English settlers reported that the ground beneath their new settlement shook regularly with tremors. The Spanish could have told them about another phenomenon that visited the coasts of the New World: the *maremoto,* or tsunami. The first recorded *maremoto* in the New World had smashed into the several towns along the shores of Venezuela, one wave surge so powerful that it demolished a naturally formed dike and severed the peninsula of Araya from the South American mainland, drowning many Indians in its wake. The Spanish heard stories of the monster wave when they conquered the area decades later. In 1530 they witnessed their own tsunami, which struck various points along the South American coast. "The ocean rose like a miraculous thing to see," said one report, while another spoke of a massive inflow of black, fetid salt water that smelled strongly of sulfur. The water surged twenty-four feet

and destroyed a Spanish fort and may have drowned people as far
away as Puerto Rico.

Modern scientists could have told the English settlers that the
Caribbean averaged some kind of tsunami event once every twenty-
one years. In a sense the clock on Port Royal was ticking from the
moment Morgan first set foot on Jamaica's shore.

The Tomb at the Escorial

As Morgan prowled the jungles of Jamaica, forty-five hundred miles away in Madrid, a dark mood prevailed. Not since Rome was in its twilight had there been such odd scenes in a court that ruled the known world. The atmosphere was embodied in the somber person of King Philip IV.

At fifty, Philip had the long Hapsburg face; he was tall, with wounded eyes caught indelibly by the master painter Velázquez in his portraits of the king. An ex-sportsman and libertine who had spent his youth cavorting in the fleshpots of Madrid, he now required that all the grandees at court who wished to address him wear black from head to toe. He was stone-faced; famously, he'd smiled only three times in public. He was not naturally this way; in other circumstances Philip might have turned out very differently. The sadness that seemed to emanate from his royal person was less personal than historical. A tremendous weight was pressing down on Philip: The empire he'd inherited was tearing apart before his very eyes, and he felt powerless to save it. In fact, he believed—and here one runs up against the incredible narcissism of the Spaniard during the nation's golden age—that his personal infidelities had caused every one of Spain's recent disasters. It was as if his body were a map of the empire, and every eruption and desire that twitched through it caused upheavals and defeats from one end of the kingdom to the other.

On the hot days of that spring and summer, as the news of Jamaica's fall made its way to his court, Philip could be found at the Escorial, the palace built by his grandfather on the slopes of the Sierra de Guadarrama outside of Madrid. Constructed in gratitude for the victory over the French at Saint-Quentin in 1557, it contained art galleries, a library, a college, and a monastery. But Philip was not studying the masterpieces that were hung on the gallery walls, though they were magnificent and featured the faces he knew so well, those of his own family of Hapsburg kings; instead he could be found in the mausoleum, where he'd recently had the bodies of his ancestors brought together and placed in the marble pantheon. Courtiers gossiped about the long hours Philip spent there; he emerged, they reported, with his eyes red from weeping. But for Philip the hours spent alone in the dark, cool tomb were his new pleasure. "I saw the corpse of the Emperor, whose body, although he has been dead ninety-six years, is still perfect," he wrote to a friend, "and by this it may be seen how richly the Lord has repaid him for his efforts in favour of his faith whilst he lived." Still, the bodies of his illustrious dead comforted him less than one empty space; he spent hour after solitary hour kneeling on the stone floors, staring into the slot where his own body would lie. "It helped me much," he admitted. How he envied the dead, who could not be humiliated by events and whose bodies had ceased to rebel against them. How, in his quiet moments, he wished to join them.

Philip held in his hands reins of power that with a single twitch could unsettle the lives of men and women across the globe; it was an empire nearly two hundred years in the making, which now held in thrall millions of people of many different cultures. Sir Walter Raleigh ticked off the things Philip's forefathers had overcome: "tempests and shipwrecks, famine, overthrows, mutinies, heat and cold, pestilence and all manner of diseases, both old and new, together with extreme poverty and want of all things needful." The Spanish had conquered them all and saw themselves as the new Israelites, chosen by God to drive the Moors out of the Iberian Peninsula and then to reclaim the world for Christ. A Catalan author in the sixteenth century wrote that the Spanish Castilians believed "that they alone are descended from heaven and the rest of mankind are mud," but in some ways they could hardly be blamed. How could a thinly populated backwater like Spain become the first global superpower since the Romans if God didn't have a hand in their victories? What were the spurting riches of the New World but God's reward to His faithful? How could Cortés have conquered the Aztecs with 550 men? It was absurd! And hadn't a visionary told King Ferdinand, the co-founder of the nation, that he wouldn't die until he entered Jerusalem in glory, a prediction Ferdinand fervently believed? A skeptic looking at the remarkable series of conquests would have to say there was something at work that could not be explained by armaments, management style, or weak opponents. The variable x, to the Spanish, was God's will. Machiavelli marveled at how Ferdinand had transformed himself from a "small, weak king" into the "greatest monarch in Christendom."

And Spain had extended that monarchy to the New World. When Spain's explorers—native or not—discovered a new territory, they did what all such men did: clambered to the shore, jabbed a pole with a fluttering banner atop it into the ground, and declared the land the property of their monarch. But in the Spanish case, the statement was literal: Mexico, Peru, the islands of the Caribbean, and all of Central America belonged *personally* to the current king or queen of Spain. They were not annexed but taken as legal birthright; the long-absentee landlord had arrived to claim his ancestral home. When some locals were found, they'd be read (in Spanish, a language the natives could not understand) a long proclamation called the Requerimiento, which began with the creation of the world and showed how the pope had granted rights to all the piece of land the conquistadors were now standing on. The Requirimiento was in effect a property deed with a history going back to the beginning of time, and it had to be read before the property passed into the hands of the Crown and before the conquistadors could launch the inevitable attacks on their listeners. "This monarchy of Spain," wrote Thomas Companella in 1607, "which embraces all nations and encircles the world, is that of the messiah, and thus shows itself to be the heir of the universe."

*　　*　　*

The voyages of Columbus were the expression of an ambitious and forward-thinking monarchy, the conquistadors embodied a warrior spirit that reveled in adventure and accepted hardship as a test, but the empire was the result of gold and silver. Without the ore that poured forth from the mines of Mexico and Peru, Spain would have remained a modest European power and not the world-altering behemoth it became. The discovery of the Americas' wealth transformed the world economy and Spain's place in it. The amounts are staggering: between 1500 and 1650, approximately 180 tons of gold flowed through the official port of Seville, so much that the entranceway that connected it to the royal palace where Philip IV impatiently awaited the arrival of his treasure was known as "the Golden Doorway." Gold animated the dreams of the explorers, conquistadors, merchants, and pirates, but it was the 16,000 tons of silver (worth at least $3.7 billion in current dollars) that Spain extracted from American mines that allowed for uniform coins to be made and distributed throughout the world, revolutionizing (in fact, one might say, creating) the global economy. In 1535, Spain decreed that a mint be established in Mexico City, and a year later the production of rough silver cobs began, using crude dies and a sledgehammer and then, in 1732, a minting machine. During its useful life, the mint produced 2.68 billion silver coins; merchants and common people were soon using them for buying everything from a bushel of corn to a shipload of Chinese ceramics. Even in the American colonies, the Spanish piece of eight was more popular and plentiful than were

English notes; the currency issued by the Continental Congress were denominated in "Spanish Milled Dollars." Fueled by a universal currency, worldwide trade exploded, and the gold and silver streaks arced across the oceans like sparks from a Roman candle. Ships from the Atlantic seaboard to Shanghai and everywhere in between traded on the new commercial sea routes, exchanging pieces of eight or silver ingots for Colombian emeralds, French muskets, and indigo from the ancient woods of the Caribbean. "The king of China could build a palace with the silver bars from Peru which have been carried to his country," wrote an official in the Philippines. The value of the treasure taken from the Americas during the Spanish reign ranges from $4 to $6 billion *in unadjusted dollars;* its present-day worth would be many times that.

By the time that Penn and Venables sailed, however, the Spanish dream of universal monarchy was growing confused and dark. Fernand Brandel called the empire of Philip II *"un total de faiblesses,"*—"a total of weaknesses"—and by the mid-1600s they were everywhere to be seen. The reasons were many and complicated, but in the end Spain was radically overextended: Every mile of territory that was conquered had to be pacified, guarded, supplied, administered, and, once any treasure was carted off, made self-sustaining. As the decades passed, it seemed that everyone was benefiting except the Spanish: The Crown was forced to borrow huge amounts from the Genoese financiers who underwrote the galleon fleets; when the ships returned from the New World, brimming with escudos and pearls, the majority would be parceled out to lenders across Europe, leaving only a small percentage for the Crown's actual operating costs. "Everything comes down to one thing," sighed Philip II. "Money and more money." The king's 1584 income was estimated at 6 million pesos; his debts totaled nearly 74 million. By the time of Philip IV, the kingdom was in even worse shape. Foreign affairs absorbed a staggering 93 percent of the budget. The kingdom was dependent on the treasure of the West Indies to support its empire, and Philip's European armies waited for the galleons' arrival to march. On October 4, 1643, the king wrote a correspondent that the silver fleet had arrived and the money had instantly been used "to dispose my forces." Other times he tied the galleons even more closely to the fate of Spain. "We are expecting hourly, by God's help, the arrival of the galleons," he wrote, "and you may imagine what depends on it for us. I hope that, in His mercy, He will bring them safely. . . . It is true, I do not deserve it, but rather great punishment; but I have full confidence that He will not permit the total loss of this monarchy. . . ." Any disturbance in the flow of gold could threaten the very existence of the empire.

The treasure of the New World had acted like a steroid on the empire, expanding it beyond its natural dimensions. And the king depended on it like a drug. Jealous of the source, he wouldn't let non-Spaniards set foot in the Americas or trade with their inhabitants. The empire ballooned, but the Spanish mind closed in on itself. Religious fervor hardened into ceremony; the vast bureaucracy stifled ambition; a rigidly hierarchical society replicated itself in all its colonies. To take only the humblest example of the iron bureaucracy that ruled men's lives in the empire: In Panama or Havana, poor men needed state-approved licenses simply to beg on the streets. No human activity escaped the hand of tradition and state control. The empire had shut itself off to the idea of flexibility and change.

As their fortunes slowly darkened, the Spanish increasingly felt that God was rebuking them, just as the Bible told them He had the Israelites when they failed to take the promised land of Canaan. The glory days had been an *engaño*, a trick; the Spanish believed they'd gone from being God's darling to his bewitched plaything. No one felt the curse more than Philip IV. When news reached Madrid that Jamaica had been lost, Philip was convinced he'd doomed the nation. "The news fell upon Philip like an avalanche," wrote one historian. "Panic spread through Seville and Cadiz, and curses loud and deep of the falsity of heretics rang through Liars Walk and the Calle Mayor." England had successfully been kept out of direct conflict with Spain for decades, but now they'd obviously cast their fortunes against their ancient enemy. And the fact that they'd done so in the West Indies, the source of the bright stream of gold and silver that helped sustain the empire, signaled a new opening in the struggle. England had placed itself perfectly "to obstruct the commerce of all the islands to the windward with the coasts of the mainland and of New Spain," an officer of the court acknowledged. "The fleets and galleons will run great risk in passing Jamaica."

Philip tried to maintain his stoic façade in court, but when he wrote to one correspondent, his true emotions came pouring out. His deepest fear, the complete collapse of the empire, would be a distinct possibility if England really entered the fray and seized the American treasure:

If this should happen it would be the final ruin of this realm; and no human power would be able to stop it: the Almighty hand of God alone could do it; and so I beseech you most earnestly to supplicate Him to take pity upon us, and not to allow the infidels to destroy realms so pure in the faith. . . . Blessed be his holy name!

3

Morgan

O n   t h e   i s l a n d   o f   J a m a i c a, Philip's inheritance was not yet lost to the English. A killer's game of cat and mouse was under way. The Spanish holdouts had retired to the mountains, and the English held the shore and the new town of Cagway; beyond that was enemy territory. To English boys from Coventry or Dover, everything past the tree line or the small town was terrifying: when they'd slept on the shores of Hispaniola at night, the sound of the giant crabs emerging from the ocean and scuttling across the beach had shot them bolt awake; it sounded exactly like the clatter of bullet cartridges on an infantryman. And then there were the fireflies that were mistaken for the lit fuses carried by soldiers to light their muskets. Convinced that the Spanish soldiers were closing in on them, they stayed tense, trigger-happy until dawn. Even after they'd lived on the island for weeks and begun to grow accustomed to its sights and sounds, the beauty of the place turned sinister at night, when the oddly humanlike jabbering of the monkeys crescendoed with birdcalls and unidentifiable screams (animal? human?) to a deafening roar. For all along they knew that their true enemies — the former slaves — were watching.

Gage had been wrong: The blacks had not turned against the

Spanish; they'd disappeared into the jungle and become excellent guerrilla fighters. "They grow bold and bloody," Major Sedgwick wrote, "a people that know not what the laws and customs of civil nations mean, neither do we know how to capitulate or discourse with them, or how to take any of them." The soldiers could not even find their hiding places and were forced to send to England for hounds. The malnourished survivors of the invasion sent patrols into the bush to smoke out the last of the resistance; when they went in numbers, they were safe. But when hunger tempted a lone Englishman to walk out of the cleared settlement where his mates stood guard with muskets, into the trackless jungle, different rules applied. Tempted by the fish in the streams or the hope of capturing an iguana or guinea hen, a soldier might head out into the bush, then stop and listen. The jungle emitted a stream of snaps, low calls, whirls, and clicks; he understood none of it. He went on. All along, the black guerrilla was tracking him soundlessly, to English eyes a shadow among shadows, sensed but not seen. When the famished soldier at last let down his guard to chase a lizard or hook a fish, something would flash in the corner of his eye, and a machete would cleave his skull from the crown forward.

Each side knew the stakes. When the English search party would see the vultures circling above and find their dead mate, the mutilations would be gruesome. Officers suffered worse fates: Captured and force-marched to the other side of the island, they'd be interrogated under torture (with methods learned from the masters of the Inquisition), then shipped off to the salt mines of the Main or the dungeons of Cuba, to which death was often preferable. (One captured English soldier told the Spaniards what they wanted to hear: that the Jews of Flanders, recently allowed into England, had financed the invasion—a complete falsehood.) The black guerrillas captured by the whites might face a punishment similar to that dealt out to disobedient slaves on Barbados, reported by an Englishman. The "rebellious negro" was chained flat on his belly and fire was applied to his feet until he was gradually burned to ashes while still alive. Others were starved to death with a loaf of bread hanging just out of reach, and they were known to gnaw the flesh off their own shoulders before dying. It was in this atmosphere that Henry Morgan came of age as a soldier.

His deliverer—the man whose life had brought Morgan to Jamaica—did not live to see his rise. Thomas Gage succumbed to disease early in 1656; in the records of the Admiralty, his widow successfully applied for back pay in the amount of one pound 6 shillings and 8 fourpence, his last appearance in the ledgers of English foreign affairs. At the end of his book that had led the English nation to the shores of Jamaica, Gage had compared himself to one of the spies sent into the land of Canaan, Moses's emissaries who had gone in search of the promised land and returned to describe a place filled with milk and honey, with clusters of grapes so large that two men had to carry them. (Gage did not mention that they also told their people of the strongly fortified cities and that "the land through which we have gone as spies is a land that devours its inhabitants.") He saw himself as the scout for the great Protestant empire soon to rule the New World, and perhaps even a martyr, like his Catholic ancestors. "I am ready to witness with the best drops of blood in my veins," Gage wrote. "Though true it is that I have been envied, jealousied, and suspected by many."

One would be naïve to take him at his word; our last glimpse of Gage brings us closer to his true character. It finds the ex-friar serving as the interpreter for the English commanders as they negotiate the surrender of the Spanish. Surely Hispaniola had been an appalling embarrassment for him; his sunny predictions had cost lives, and he was forced to witness his fellow Protestant crusaders falling left and right. But in the Spanish report on the invasion, he has recovered from any embarrassment, and we find him yelling at the *sargento mayor* of Santiago de la Vega (later Spanish Town) about insufficient supplies, basically lording it over his old compatriots. The writer's dislike of the man comes through; he describes Gage as a man full of "noisy menaces" who "took the habit of Saint Dominic . . . and, ordained a priest, returned to England and fell from the Faith." When the Spanish claimed that Jamaica belonged to them, having been granted to them by Pope Alexander and occupied for 140 years, Gage shot back that Cromwell had taken the island for the English and that "not right, but might of arms gave them possession," tossing in that the pope had failed to snatch away Henry VIII's realm when the king turned against him and adding "other blasphemous, licentious words." At this the Englishmen began laughing.

Gage had come to the Americas in search of a religious crusade, but he little realized that the war he was relishing would take a far different shape: It would be a confrontation not between two traditional faiths but between two radically different visions of men and society. Cromwell's "banners of Christ" had been folded up and put away; in their place would come the flag of the pirates, whose way of life was utterly foreign to both Catholics and Protestants. Port Royal would not mark the beginning of Spain's replacement with another theocratic empire. The town and its pirates would follow another path, one focused more intensely on the individual than on the kingdom of belief.

The English eventually hunted down the remaining guerrillas, and the invasion fleet dispersed to ports back in Europe. Some of the former soldiers settled down to lives as farmers; it was immediately clear that the island's soil was rich, perhaps as rich as that of the fabulous moneymaker, Barbados. Still, in the early years the ex-soldiers and the other adventurers who were making the real money had turned to a new trade: privateering.

Privateers were sailors from one nation who had been given permission by their monarchs, contained in documents called letters of marque—also called letters of commission, or simply commissions—to attack and capture enemy ships. Licensed marauders of the seas, they ranged from pirates simply looking for a tissue of legal protection to men who thought of themselves first and foremost as patriot soldiers. A pirate had no commission; he usually attacked anyone and everyone he came upon, regardless of nationality, and he was hanged on sight if captured and given no protection as a prisoner of war. Privateers were supposed to share their "purchase" (treasure) with the nation they represented; the English owed 10 percent to the lord admiral and 6 to the king. Pirates kept what they stole. Privateering was invented by a cash-strapped Henry VIII of England, who had no navy to attack the French (it having been sold by Parliament to pay his debts); he came up with the idea of issuing commissions to three private captains for the purpose of causing havoc with French shipping. Privateers were completely respectable; nobles often signed up when in a financial pinch.

Piracy was much older and threaded through the history of all seafaring nations. Julius Caesar had been captured by pirates off the island of Pharmacusa and spent thirty-eight days gambling and declaiming his own verses with the corsairs; he joked that when he won his release, he would come back and crucify all of them, which the pirates found hilarious. When he'd bought his release, he quickly borrowed a fleet of ships, tracked down the pirates, and crucified them. St. Patrick was seized by pirates, who sold him as a slave in Ireland. On his return from his battles with the Turks, the ship of Miguel de Cervantes, later the author of *Don Quixote*, was intercepted by Barbary pirates, and he spent five miserable years as an Algerian captive, repeatedly attempting to escape.

Who were the pirates of the West Indies? They were an assemblage of runaway slaves (the famous maroons), political refugees, disaffected sailors, indentured servants whose masters had tossed them off the plantation, hard-bitten adventure seekers, the flotsam and jetsam of the New World. They will play so vital a part in the coming battles, and they shared enough common characteristics and experiences, that it will clarify things to profile a typical pirate/privateer. There is enough information on the privateers who served under Morgan to give us a detailed composite picture of an average member, drawing from the experiences of various members of the Brethren of the Coast, as the pirates and privateers of the Caribbean were known. We shall call him Roderick.

Roderick was nineteen years old, short (five foot four being a
common height in those days), English (as most of Morgan's men
were), and unmarried—in one survey of Anglo-American pirates
from 1716 to 1726, only 4 percent had taken a wife. He was blue-
eyed, lean, and quite strong for his size. Roderick had grown up in
Dover, one of the great seaports of England, which were veritable
factories for sailors and pirates. He went to the docks not only out of
tradition (his father and grandfathers had earned their living on the
water, rolling into their hovels after six long months away with tales
of Morocco and Corsica) but because he had an itch for adventure
and newness. He looked with astonishment on friends who became
clerks or cobblers. One English sailor wrote that he "always had a
mind to see strange countries and fashions," while another said that
his mind was "engrossed with voyages, the longer and more dangerous, the more attractive." By signing up as a sailor, Roderick was already marking himself out as a breed apart. But when his merchant
ship, undermanned by the owners in order to save money and pack
more trade goods aboard, was spotted and captured by a pirate ship
on its way to Barbados in 1660, Roderick faced a dilemma. He and
his mates were brought out of the hold, marched up on deck to face
the outlaw crew, and offered the chance to join up. They'd heard
many tales of real-life pirates in the waterfront dens; who could resist
the story of John Ward, a working-class English boy who had sailed
off to Algiers, converted to Islam, assembled a pirate flotilla that
could rival the Venetian navy, captured ship after ship loaded with
spices and treasure, and built a palace of alabaster and marble where
he lived out his life in unimaginable luxury? But the men who were
lined up across from Roderick were more frightening than romantic.
One had his eye shot out; another was missing an arm; a few had fa-
cial scars obviously left by a Spanish cutlass. They could hardly be
called white men anymore, so blackened with the sun was their skin,
so crisscrossed by their surprisingly delicate tattoos. The flint-
lock pistols on silk strings that were their permanent accessories
and their most prized possessions hung gaily around their necks, and

their outré clothing—silks, damasks, and velvets in eye-smacking colors—announced the fact that their latest victim had been a French merchantman. Their captain gave a short, surprisingly persuasive speech. "We sing, sweare, drab, and kill men as freely as cakemakers do flies," he boasted. "The whole sea is our empire where we rob at will." Any man who joined up would get an equal share. All could vote on their missions and their policies. Toward the end he mentioned briefly that they'd be taking the ship's carpenter, whether he was willing or not, as they'd lost their last one on a raid against a coastal town on the Spanish Main. But everyone else was free to choose.

Roderick considered. His life on the merchant ship was dull and underpaid; the captain whipped the men occasionally when he drank to excess. The nautical life had not yet matched his conception of it; Roderick wanted greater excitement and greater rewards. He looked down the line of crewmen and saw two other men step forward, and with sudden conviction he strode across the twelve feet of planking that separated sailors from pirates. He had just made a sizable leap: from law-abiding citizen to hunted criminal. You could go no further astray in the seventeenth-century world, except perhaps by proclaiming yourself a child of Satan or killing a man, and the new pirates would get ample opportunity to do the latter. The pirates looked at him as he approached their line, and the captain nodded slightly. Roderick turned and stared down at the deck, unable to meet the eyes of his former mates. He'd just left everything he knew.

The Spanish had helped create this petri dish of malcontents. If they'd allowed legal trade with their colonies and opened up their cities in the New World, these vagabonds would most likely have been incorporated into a thriving economy and become respectable workers in the region's booming industries. The hard cases among them would have been hunted down by the English and French authorities and punished for interfering with trade. But the Spanish resisted—for them, trade was not a virtue in itself but only a tool to achieve the worldwide divine kingdom. By hoarding the riches and preventing these men from finding a place in the world, Spain slowly built its own perfect enemy, an enemy diametrically opposite in almost every respect.

Roderick and the West Indian pirates had a special ancestor: the *boucaniers*. These outcasts got their name from *boucan*, the process of smoking strips of beef obtained from the cows that ran wild on Hispaniola (brought there by the Spanish in a failed attempt at raising livestock), which these hunters would shoot, butcher, and then cure expertly over a pit fire. The tangy, preserved strips of meat could be traded with passing ships for everything a man needed. The *boucaniers* found their way to the forests of Hispaniola in the early decades of the 1600s, a diverse assortment of political refugees, religious refugees, escaped Negro slaves, outright criminals, and disgruntled or abused servants. They were Scotch, Irish, Dutch, French, and mulatto, and they were all radicals in one respect—they rejected everything a good bourgeois looked for in life. Last names were not to be used; some had pasts they did not wish to discuss. (With one stroke they dissolved everything a Spaniard worked toward his whole life.) Women were not allowed into their camps, on pain of death; instead the cow killers paired off with matelots (literally, "bedmates," but used to connote friendship) for lifelong, probably sexual, relationships. The *boucaniers* used flat stones for plates and hollowed-out calabashes for cups. They shared everything; no one had more food, liquor, or ammunition than the others. These backwoods communists topped off their lifestyle with a very basic appearance: They wore homemade suits fashioned of cow skins that were covered with layers of dried blood so thick that it looked like black tar.

What they'd created was a male fantasy of escape from all civilizing influences: women, heritage, children, and money. No one had power over them; living on the far-flung edge of Western civilization, the *boucaniers* were freer than almost anyone else in the world. This gift they'd give to their inheritors, the men with so many names:

pirates, buccaneers, filibustiers, corsairs, and the more decorous privateers. The Spanish looked on the buccaneers and their inheritors
as vermin. They were godless, without culture or meaning to their
lives. Their system was no system; it was as if they were savages
who had freely chosen to reject all that the Spanish held dear. And
they were trespassing on the divine kingdom. So the Spaniards
hunted them.

When the Spanish soldiers began to track them down like the
cattle they survived on, many of the buccaneers fled to wide-open
ports where another kind of living awaited them. The island of Tortuga attracted many of the French buccaneers, while the Jamaican
town now named Port Royal in honor of the new king of England,
Charles II, became another destination. In the five short years since
the English had arrived, Port Royal had been transformed from a
killing ground into "the wickedest city in the world." Privateers had
turned Cromwell's new city on a hill into a Sodom and Gomorrah. It
was a thriving outpost of English civilization and a serious annoy-
ance to the Spanish, two of Cromwell's objectives when he sent the
expedition out from Portsmouth. But, spiritually speaking, it was a
disaster.

Roderick, our representative pirate, gaped at it when he first arrived in 1660. The town had 4,500 white residents and 1,500 Negro
slaves. There were eight hundred houses eight years later, three hundred more than its competitor, New York, with more taverns and
brothels than the rest of the English colonies combined; forty new
licenses for drinking houses were issued in the month of July 1661
alone. And it was so rich that, in 1662, the government proposed
building a mint on the island, to melt down and coin the piles of silver and gold plate that the privateers were bringing in. Port Royal
lived and prospered not by an English proverb but by a Dutch
one: "Jesus Christ is good, but trade is better." When Roderick
strode down from the docks, he saw a town bathed in the light of
the Jamaican sunset, its shops and houses thrown into relief by the
big blue mountains hovering behind them, its streets covered with a

layer of golden sand and coral dust that cushioned Roderick's steps as he made his way toward the bars that lined the waterfront. He could not believe how smartly dressed the local merchants were. Riding through town in fine carriages pulled by six horses, jeweled rings on their fingers and shod in shiny leather boots, they were the equal of Dover's richest gentry. Port Royal had the romance of a civilized oasis about it. But then Roderick walked toward the pirate haunts such as the Bear Garden, which looked like any of the rough joints you might find in Portsmouth or London. There was a blast of singing and shouting as he passed by the open door. Lingering there, he saw that bets were being thrown down at the cockfight pit dug right into the tavern's sandy floor. Pirates spilled past him into the night air and invited a local man, at gunpoint, to have a glass of rumbullion, a potent grog. Down the street others had carved a hole in a wine barrel, and local whores were taking their turns dancing in the spray. It looked like the kind of place where a thug off a corsair ship might murder someone whose face he didn't like or where you might come across a newly arrived privateer having his way with a prostitute in an alleyway off the harbor.

There was one difference from his home in Dover that Roderick noticed immediately: Here the pirates seemed to own the place. Never before had he seen bad men act as if they were the law.

In Port Royal the privateers were commanded by Christopher Mings, whom the great diarist Samuel Pepys had described as "a man of great parts and most excellent tongue among ordinary men." The son of a shoemaker, Mings had climbed his way through the ranks from cabin boy to captain by sheer force of will. In 1659 he led a privateer expedition against the Spanish Main, taking and pillaging in succession the towns of Campeche, Coro, Cumana, and Puerto Cabello. At Campeche his subordinates (who may have included a young Henry Morgan) advised a sneak attack by moonlight, but Mings scoffed at the idea as being beneath an English seaman; he sailed into the harbor in broad daylight, with his trumpeters sounding the attack and his drummers beating a martial tune.

The fort fell in the first attack, surprise or no surprise. And when he returned to Port Royal, Mings's boats were brimful with Spanish loot, estimated at a value of 1.5 million pieces of eight.

It is notoriously tricky to give present-day equivalents for seventeenth-century money, but a very rough estimate can be obtained. The math goes like this: In the late 1600s, four pieces of eight were worth about one English pound. One English pound in 1670 would be worth £115 today. And £115 British today equal $204 U.S. So divide that $204 by four (as it took four pieces of eight to equal one pound) and you have $51. That's how much modern buying power in the local Wal-Mart a single piece of eight might get you. Or you can forget all that and just think of a piece of eight jingling in Roderick's pocket as worth $50 or more.

In today's dollars Mings had just snatched $75 million. It was an immense fortune, and it surged into Port Royal's taverns, goldsmith shops, and merchant houses. The only entity that didn't profit from the raids was the English government: When Mings refused to give the lord high admiral his share, he was sent back to England for trial.

Mings returned to Jamaica in 1662, having been freed by an indulgent Charles, who was grateful for Mings's support during the bad days of the Civil War. The raiding began again. Next on his list was Santiago, the second-largest city in Cuba after the jewel of Havana, too strong even for the privateers. The mission was to be Henry Morgan's initiation into the trade: He was the captain of one of the twelve ships that sallied forth to try their luck against the Crown's forces. The fact that he'd already achieved the rank of captain suggests that Morgan had proved his talents as a soldier during the guerrilla wars and that his talent for leading men—and making alliances with those richer or more socially prominent—was already evident. Morgan's family and their illustrious military history also probably earned him a foot in the door, reputation-wise. But everything after that he earned himself.

On September 21, 1661, Morgan and the other adventurers were given a hero's send-off, with wives, whores, and merchants lining the shore to cheer the boys away. It was the middle of hurricane season, which runs from June to November, and the ships tacked to Negril in Jamaica and then headed north for Cuba at three knots. Off the coast the fleet encountered a surprise: a ship already anchored near a cay, commanded by none other than Oliver Cromwell's scapegrace nephew, Sir Thomas Whetstone. Whetstone's background was not unusual for a gentleman pirate. The Restoration of Charles II had brought with it a return to pleasure, and Whetstone had thrown himself into the whirl of parties and plays, spending wildly; he was soon being hounded by creditors. Luckily, he'd sided with the Royalists and not his uncle during the Civil War, and King Charles had released him from debtors' prison with a loan of £100, with the understanding that he'd recover it on the high seas. Charles did not grant him a commission, however, so he was operating as a full-fledged pirate. His crew was almost entirely Indian, natives who had been forced off their land by the Spanish. They were out for more than treasure. Whetstone and his Indian crew soon joined Mings's expedition.

A council of war was held aboard Mings's forty-six-gun ship, *Centurion,* and a final battle plan was worked out. Santiago was a defender's dream: The port sat on a bay accessible only through a long, thin channel, sixty yards wide at its narrowest, with high cliffs towering on either side. At the entrance to this channel stood the Castillo del Morro, a major fort whose guns could easily reach any ship attempting to sail through the gap. Another battery of guns sat at the cliff's foot, just below the Castillo, adding more firepower. And in this age of sail, the winds at the mouth of the channel were notoriously tricky.

For the seventeenth-century sailor, winds were animate creatures, the physical manifestations of minor demigods and demons. Roderick believed they lived on mountain summits or in the hollows of caves, awaiting their orders to go and blow up a storm or hasten a ship to its destination, orders given by their commander, the great North Wind. The South, East, and West each had its own personality, as did all their various subalterns, from North by Northwest down to harbor breezes. Seamen imagined that the winds led sailorly lives; shouted into action by the blustery voice of the North, they'd go out, whip up a hurricane, then retire exhausted to the top of an Alpine peak for a game of cards or some storytelling over rum punch. These gales had feelings: They could be offended, wounded, or flattered, and sailors often called out to them encouragingly as they passed. Each had its own peculiar sound, which the mariner claimed to know by heart: lazy murmurs, keening gusts, voices angry or mournful. It is a testament to the loneliness of the seas and how much power wind had over the sailor's life.

The breezes off Santiago were chaotic and difficult to predict, so the men decided on a direct attack up the mouth of the channel. Capricious or nonexistent breezes slowed the fleet's pace, but on October 5, the men spotted the Castillo del Morro, towering over the entrance to the bay. By now the fleet had swelled to twenty ships with late arrivals from Port Royal, and the captains used telescopes to gauge the action of the wind at the channel mouth. Old hands who had sailed this way before knew that at dusk an onshore breeze would kick up; Mings decided to use it.

He swept the fleet in to the village of Aguadores at the mouth of the San Juan River, two miles from Santiago. The Spanish, who thought the attack would have to wait until the next day, were startled to find riders arriving from Aguadores saying that the English were pouring off their ships onto the rocky shore. By nightfall Mings had landed 1,300 men without losing a single soul. The privateers lit fires and waited for morning. At Santiago the troops were put under the command of Don Cristóbal Arnoldo y Sassi, a well-connected Spanish-Jamaican who had led the Jamaican guerrillas in their battles with the English invaders. Perhaps the governor hoped for some of the guerrillas' success in picking off the English; but this was to be an old-fashioned frontal attack. The next morning the English marched to Santiago and, just after sunrise, sent wave after wave of musketeers toward the castle. The Spanish broke in short order, with Arnoldo leading the retreat. The privateers spent five days looting the town, taking anything that could be resold for the tiniest sum, down to the iron fixtures in the church. During the whole operation, Mings lost only six men to enemy fire, while twenty succumbed to sickness. When he sailed into Port Royal on October 22, the crowds along the shore erupted in celebration. Roderick and the boys flowed off the ship and straight into the taverns. By now our nineteen-year-old privateer was an experienced binge drinker. The pieces of eight jingling in his pocket promised weeks of nonstop carousing. He'd killed his first man at Santiago, a Spanish musketeer he'd shot in the face with his pistol, now tucked safely into his leather belt. Roderick would spend all he'd earned on rum and women, but Morgan, although it is likely he dropped a few cobs in the taverns, husbanded most of his share for the future. His plans were grander than Roderick's.

The raid on Santiago was a preview, in miniature, of Morgan's expeditions to come, which shows how much he learned from the irrepressible Mings. One more expedition to Campeche, which netted the privateers fourteen Spanish ships in addition to the usual assortment of trade goods and silver plate, and Morgan was ready to set out on his own. Privateering was confirmed as a business proposition: Fabulous riches lay strewn across the length and breadth of Central America, and Mings had proved that the rabble London had flushed out of its sewers and its army ranks could take it when motivated. Now the English blade had been placed at the jugular that fed Philip IV's empire. Soon Morgan would begin to press it home.

❧ ❧ ❧

In London the man who had set the invasion of Jamaica in motion was gone. Cromwell had died in 1658, and his Puritan revolution seemed to dissolve like morning fog. In his place came a far different man, Charles II, whose biography was touched early and often by piracy. The new king's father, like many of the Stuarts, had married a Catholic, Henrietta Maria of France. This had enraged conspiracy-minded Protestants like Thomas Gage, who were always prone to rumors of papist plots to take over the country. When she was pregnant with Charles II, Henrietta had sent to France for a Catholic midwife. Her dwarf and dancing master were sent by sea to retrieve the woman but were captured by pirates and delayed past the blessed event. The man in the street rejoiced: Charles II was guided into the world by faithful Protestant hands.

At his birth, fortune-tellers predicted that Charles would be drawn to mathematicians, merchants, learned men, painters, sculptors — and sailors. Astrologers foresaw a man with a "mincing gait," a high-pitched voice who would be lucky in both marriage and war. Charles's father once stated that "the state of the monarch is the supremest thing upon earth: For kings are not only God's lieu-tenants, and sit upon God's throne, but even by God himself are called Gods." His son, however, came of age in a much more uncer-tain world. He had to fight for power from his exile in France, flitting in disguise through enemy ranks, endangered and hungry. He'd even turned pirate for a brief moment when he sailed up the Thames and held merchant ships for heavy ransoms to raise money for his armies. Cromwell's death in September 1658 opened the way for Charles II to assume the throne, and he'd be the monarch whose court would be enriched and scandalized by Henry Morgan's raids. He brought the Restoration to England, and with it a spirit of debauchery of which Morgan and his boys would have approved. By his return to the throne in 1660, Charles was a canny, passionate man with few illusions; in the marvelous description of one historian, he was "life-bitten."

Charles inherited a monarchy with few assets and many lurking enemies. The main players in Europe were at war with each other for most of the seventeenth century, seeking dominance and riches, but only four were vying for colonies in the West Indies: France, En-gland, the United Provinces, and Spain. During Charles's reign France was the rising power, rich and led with supremely cynical bril-liance by Louis XIV. Spain, despite her recent military losses, was still Spain; it was difficult for the English, who had been raised on tales of her immense power, to believe she was really as depleted as she seemed. The United Provinces (the modern Netherlands) were tough and resourceful and had a powerful navy that was increasingly able to challenge any of the European fleets. And England was dependent on its West Indies privateers to do the work of empire. Other countries of varying degrees of potency—including the behemoth Austria (the Holy Roman Empire), Sweden, Italy, Greece, and Russia—were not active in the Caribbean arena, while Portugal was preoccupied with Brazil. In the mid- and late seventeenth century, European nations switched allies constantly in their bids for domination on the Continent and in the New World. Religious affinities and popular opinion meant little in this furious grab for power: Protestant kings would ally themselves with Catholic monarchs one year and then switch sides the next. The colonies of the New World were chess pieces in this ever-changing game, to be milked for money to fight European wars and to trade away if absolutely necessary.

So when Charles went looking for a bride, it was power and not love that he sought. Eager for cash and new markets, Charles gazed longingly at Portugal, who wanted desperately to have England as an ally. Only recently freed from the iron grip of Spanish dominion, Portugal held rich colonies in the East; it dominated the vital trade in spices that went back to 2600 BC, when Egypt's rulers fortified with hot pepper the diets of the workers building the pyramids of Cheops. Portugal was weak, and if it collapsed, its rich possessions might fall into an ally's waiting hand, giving England lucrative assets around the world: "Bombay as the mart for the trade of all India, . . . Tangier as a centre for the commerce of the Mediterranean, and . . . Jamaica as the key that would unlock to England the great Spanish treasuries in America." Besides which, the Portuguese had placed a well-funded spy in Charles's court, and he distributed bribes high and low. Spain reacted with panic to the threat of an English-Portuguese alliance, but Philip IV had little money to spare for greasing the palms of Charles's men. Portugal was offering the fabulously rich Catherine of Braganza, daughter of their monarch, while the daughterless Philip (again hampered by the mortality rate of his legitimate children) countered with the ruler of Parma's daughter. But many doubted whether he'd be able to deliver the huge dowry he promised.

Jamaica was a pawn in this great game. When Charles was in exile, he'd signed a secret agreement with the Spanish to return the island and crack down on the privateers if Philip IV, his friend and fellow debauchee, would supply him with 6,000 troops. But once he returned to power, the giveback seemed inadvisable. Merchants were doing a busy trade with Jamaica, and they were furious that he'd think of returning the island to the Spanish. From an island full of renegades and drunks, Charles began to see Jamaica in a new light: as "the navel of the West Indies," "a window on the power of Spain." Philip, on the other hand, kept bidding up the price for the return of it; he was desperate to regain his inheritance.

But the Portuguese bribe, and the promise of more to come, won the day. Charles would keep Jamaica and accept Catherine; in 1662 he announced his engagement. Catherine brought not only her plain and retiring person but also Bombay, Tangier, and £300,000 (approximately $61.5 million in today's dollars) to the union. The announcement caused a "great passion" in Madrid; the breach with England was now official. There were even rumors that the fleet Charles sent to retrieve his bride would double the insult by intercepting the galleons from the Americas and ransacking them. It wasn't true, but the gossip only pointed up Spain's nervousness. The empire seemed under attack on every front.

Having decided on holding Jamaica, for the next ten years Charles did little to govern it. When the Council of Jamaica shipped back a copy of its new laws for approval, the document was mislaid— for a decade. The "fit of absent mind" continued; policies often shifted with the winds and with whether a pro- or anti-Spanish adviser was in favor in Charles's court. The pirates and their Jamaican allies would have a relatively free hand to roam the Caribbean, with one edgy eye on London but with a remarkably free hand to strike at will.

✤   ✤   ✤

Charles's snatching back of the Jamaican offer was another disappointment for Philip IV. His torments only intensified as he grew older and in 1661 were capped by one overriding concern: a male heir. If he did not produce one, on his death Europe would be plunged into a war of succession and his empire would be carved up by his enemies, his family's legacy scattered to the winds. Philip felt that by denying him a son, God was mocking him, the great seducer, the man who had illegitimate children stashed all over Madrid. How better to illustrate that fact than the fates of the royal sons, starting with Baltasar Carlos, who had died one after the other? How could his bastard sons thrive while his heirs withered and died? It was clearly a message: God would not allow any product of Philip's legitimate pleasures to survive, as punishment for his darker ones. To say, as one writer has, that Philip was "possessed of the greatest capacity for sexual pleasure recorded of any modern monarch" is unprovable, but he'd certainly rank high—and yet not one of his heirs had made it to adulthood. In 1661 his last surviving legitimate son lay dying.

In the early days of that January, the monarchy was desperately striving to save the last boy, three-year-old Felipe Próspero. One religious leader had led a pilgrimage of devout Spaniards to the convent of the Barefoot Nuns, praying for the boy's survival. The bodies of revered saints were moved from sacred site to sacred site in an attempt to appease God; the incorruptible corpse of San Isidro, whose body miraculously had never decayed, was laid beside Felipe's crib, as were the ashes of San Diego Alcalá. But it was all in vain. On January 11, the boy passed away and plunged his father into fresh despair. Philip wrote to a friend, his mind divided between two calamities:

I assure you that what has most exhausted me, much more than the loss of my son, is to see clearly that I have vexed God and that he sent this punishment to castigate my sins. Pray to Our Lord that He may open my eyes, that I may perform His holy will in all things. . . . There is nothing new in the English situation.

There was only one hope left: Months before, Philip had deliberately slept with his queen, Mariana, one last time as an insurance policy against Felipe's death. Now she was pregnant, and a few days after the death of Felipe she went into labor. The eyes of Europe—certainly of its monarchs in France and Vienna—were turned toward Madrid as the fate of Spain was decided.

As Mariana prepared to give birth, she was brought to the Tower Chamber, which had been made ready for her. Around the room had been carefully placed the royal family's most sacred relics: There was a Roman nail from the cross, three thorns from Jesus's crown on Golgotha, an actual fragment of the cross. The relics represented the physical connection between Jesus and his heirs on earth, the Spanish monarchy. As the contractions came quicker and quicker, Mariana was bled. And then on Sunday, November 6, the news came: It was a boy, Carlos Próspero. The French king instantly sent his spies to check on the health of the child. The Spanish court proclaimed him "most beautiful in features, large head, dark skin, and somewhat overplump," but the French communiqués painted a much different picture: Carlos was so small and tender that he was placed in a box of cotton. "The crown was firmer on his head than the ground now beneath his feet," one spy reported. But Philip was satisfied. "Our Lord was pleased to give me back the son he had taken from me," he wrote. With an heir, however fragile, in place, Philip had fulfilled his last duties to his ancestors, and his spirits improved.

The news did not. The raids of Mings's privateers were just more in a continuing stream of bad omens: droughts, plagues, and a disastrous loss to the Portuguese army in 1665. A possible cause was uncovered when the authorities raided a suspected counterfeiter's house and found secreted away two plates; on them was engraved a heart pierced by an arrow and the words "Philip IV son of Philip III and Margaret" on the first and another man's name on the second, along with some biblical verses and the chilling words "Thou are mine and I am thine." Witchcraft was suspected, and the investigation went on for months, with the woman who lived at the house interrogated by the Inquisition. Delving deeper into the sorcery, Philip's court priests confiscated the small bag the king had always worn around his neck to keep him safe. Instead of the relics it was believed to hold, inside were a portrait of Philip pierced with pins, a book of charms, and other tools of the devil. Convinced at last that they'd found the source of Spain's disasters, the ecclesiastics burned the contents.

But the true devils lay to the west. Henry Morgan was beginning his career in earnest.

4

Into the Past

In November 1663 the twenty-eight-year-old Morgan finally set out on his own to test his mettle against the Spanish Empire. Along with three other captains, he left Port Royal and sailed for Central America bound for New Spain (current-day Mexico). Most likely the crowds were thinner for his departure than they'd been for Mings's: Morgan was not yet a name to conjure with in Jamaica.

What kind of ship Morgan commanded is not known, but privateer and pirate ships were often specially modified by the raiders to suit their purposes. In the weeks before the mission, Roderick, who had joined up with Morgan, worked with the other privateers to get the ships ready; the first order of business was to rip out the wooden bulkheads in the holds, which were used in merchant ships to keep barrels and trunks from sliding. Cabins—first class and steerage—were gutted, creating an open space belowdecks, for reasons both practical (to accommodate the large number of men these ships often carried) and philosophical (pirates were democrats and decreed that no man should have better quarters than the next). Carpenters would reinforce the deck to support extra cannon and cut slots in the hold for guns or mount them fore and aft as "chasers," cannon that could be fired on anyone trying to pursue or escape them. Aboveboard, the forecastle and any superstructure behind (in seaman's terms, "abaft") the mainsail was removed, as were the cabins ("roundhouses") in the stern, creating a clear deck ideal for boarding vessels or stashing excess numbers of privateers, captives, or booty. Finally, the rig of the converted vessel could be altered by stepping the mainmast aft, for increased power in the wind. Pirates adored speed; an extra knot could mean the difference between riches and hanging. Like grease monkeys cackling as they dropped a supercharged V-12 into their father's vintage Olds, Roderick and the other Brethren took a stock mercantile vessel and made it into a thing built to fly.

Onto their customized ships, the privateers loaded *boucan,* water, hard tack, and their most valuable possessions, prized above women and even Spanish gold: their muskets. The long, broad-butted muskets and the pirates' skill with them were so essential to their success that one must pause to linger over these unique seventeenth-century creations. Like Lewis and Clark heading into the vasts of the western territories, the privateers depended on their firearms for their very lives; Lewis and Clark needed them for killing buffalo, the privateers for killing men. They bought them from French and Dutch traders who plied the waters of the New World, and getting a good musket and a pair of working pistols would have been one of the first priorities for a buccaneer. They paid small fortunes to obtain them, using any seed money they'd brought with them from the Old World, from their wages as indentured servants, or from selling *boucan* or animal skins; there were a dozen ways to get the necessary cash. They cleaned the guns obsessively and would slit the throat of anyone who dared touch them.

The pirate musket was an objet d'art, often originating in the shops (one might almost say studios) of the great French gunsmiths: Brachere of Dieppe and Galin of Nientes. Mass production of firearms would not be perfected until the middle of the eighteenth century, when interchangeable parts were produced and assembled into a piece. So the privateers and pirates carried one-of-a-kind matchlocks (in which a burning taper was placed into a pan of gunpowder) and the later wheelocks (in which a metal wheel spins against a flint, causing sparks to fly and touching off the powder, a technique supposedly invented by Leonardo da Vinci). The finest of these heavy iron guns were considered near counterparts to Renaissance paintings and sculpture. On a typical French musket, you might find the hammer shaped into the form of a leaping dolphin, while on the blued barrel would be etched intricately worked portraits of gods such as Jupiter and Mars throwing thunderbolts or reclining on billowy clouds. Producing these firearms was a complex process involving a designer, a stockmaker, a barrelsmith, a metal carver, an inlayer, and an engraver. To achieve the scenes that made the French guns distinctive, the craftsman would work much as a sculptor like Leonardo would, his chisel and chasing tools guided by his free hand as he pounded shapes into the cold metal. The craftsman was a metallurgist who had to know how to forge metal, reduce it, soften it to a working consistency, harden it, then "clean it white," shining it until it gleamed like porcelain. Gunsmiths also strove for lightness; due to their innovative design, the French-produced wheelocks were lighter than their competitors on the Continent, a wonderful attribute when you're carrying a weapon on twenty-mile marches through Central American jungles. Ironically, the buccaneers, whom many regarded as civilization killers, carried into battle an instrument that was at the forefront of Renaissance artistry. A Spanish soldier sometimes had to face off against the privateers with an outdated arquebus, which was less accurate than the long-barreled musket, a crucial disadvantage when trying to pick off a buccaneer. The musket gave the pirate a distinct tactical advantage.

The Spanish monarchy's grip on the lives of its settlers extended even to firearms. The rather shocking truth was that the Crown strictly limited the amount of weapons that could be imported into the New World by private citizens. The only weapons legally available were the ones supplied by the government in Madrid, which often took the best ones for its soldiers in Europe. Ensuring that the weapons that were shipped to the New World reached the soldiers at the other end meant trusting in a long supply line, where greed or simple necessity might mean that the muskets disappeared. Like a mistrustful parent, the Crown wanted to control the firepower that guarded its treasure. This official fear of private enterprise at every level meant that the Spanish would often face Morgan with only a few decent muskets equivalent to what the buccaneers carried. The Spanish settlers could and did trade with the illegal Dutch and French merchants who trawled their shores, but they could not always pay the prices that the privateers could for a musket in working order, and so they often went without. Morgan didn't depend on London for his guns; if he had, the Welshman might never have won a battle.

Roderick, now twenty-two, had quickly learned the value of having a good musket. He'd bought his from a Dutch trader who had come through Port Royal, borrowing some of the purchase price from his mates and getting the rest out of his stash from the Mings expedition. He was hoping to earn enough to pay off his debtors (he'd run up a tab in several of the taverns, for meals and rum, and with a certain prostitute) with a solid payday from this modest expedition. And he was enjoying the newfound respect he got on the streets of his adopted town. Tradesmen and merchants nodded to him; townspeople gave him a wide berth when he was blind drunk on rumbullion. Perhaps it was actually fear and not respect, but Roderick would take it. He was no longer a scrub boy on a merchant ship; he was the protector of Jamaica and, more important, a customer with the potential for fantastic future earnings. He'd come up in the world.

As he sailed out to make his fortune, Henry Morgan was much changed from the cherubic Welsh boy in his early portrait. He was now lean, broad-shouldered, and bronzed by the Jamaican sun. He wore his beard short and pointed, in the style of Sir Francis Drake, and around his forehead tied a scarlet kerchief. In later expeditions he'd carry a wig among his things, in case he was called to accept a surrender from a Spanish noble. Captains liked to dress well, in the

manner of English gentlemen: In 1722 the captain "Black" Bart
Roberts was described as being "dressed in a rich crimson damask
waistcoat and breeches, a red feather in his hat, a gold chain round
his neck with a diamond cross hanging around it." But Morgan's
working clothes would have been much less glamorous: a cotton
shirt, breeches, leather boots. He was dressed for war.

Here on the eve of Morgan's first expedition is where one John
Esquemeling (or Alexander Exquemelin, another variant that has
come down to us) enters the story. The details of his life—in fact, his
very identity—are incomplete, but it's clear he was a surgeon who
accompanied Morgan on some of his raids. Some believe that "John
Esquemeling" was a pseudonym for Hendrik Barentzoon Smeeks, a
surgeon who left his hometown of Zwolle in central Holland to
serve aboard a merchant ship with the Dutch East India Company,
during which service he shipwrecked, landed on a boat that sailed to
Java, and eventually ended up at the French pirate port of Tortuga,
where he came into contact with the Brethren. Others believe that
he was in fact French, from the town of Honfleur, and had sailed to
the West Indies as an apprentice before learning his trade and hook-
ing up with Morgan. Whatever Esquemeling's true background, out
of his exploits came a memoir, *The Buccaneers of America,* published in
Holland in 1678 and then in many subsequent translations. Esquemeling's reports are sometimes contradicted by the Spanish accounts, but he knew Morgan and fought under him, and if some
parts of his book smack of embellishment, key passages are verified
by Spanish accounts, by Morgan's reports, and by other sources.
His stories of the buccaneers almost single-handedly created the pirate craze that obsessed Daniel Defoe and enchanted Robert Louis
Stevenson and gave birth to the image of the pirate as cruel, wild,
and free.

Buccaneer expeditions followed a routine. The privateers would
first meet over a bowl of rum punch on the captain's flagship. (Refusing a drink would often bring "a Man under a suspicion of being
in a Plot" against the Brethren of the Coast.) The first order of

business was fresh meat, especially tortoise. What the buffalo was to the American settler in his wagon train, the tortoise was to the pirate: Without the sustenance that animal provided, it's unlikely that the buccaneers could have achieved half their victories. They could distinguish among the four species common to the West Indies and knew their breeding grounds intimately. "The choice of all for fine eating is the turtle or sea tortoise," wrote one visitor to Jamaica in 1704. "The flesh looks and eats much like choice veal, but the fat is of a green colour, very luscious and sweet; the liver is likewise green, very wholesome, searching and purging." Pork was also a favorite, and to get it the buccaneers would hit Spanish hog yards in the middle of the night. "Having beset the keeper's lodge, they force him to rise," Esquemeling tells us of Morgan's fledgling fleet, "and give them as many heads [of swine] as they desire, threatening withal to kill him in case he disobeys their commands or makes any noise." Having seen to their rations, the Brethren would then call a second council, where the central issue was "what place they shall go, to seek their desperate fortunes." The men would often suggest towns they'd raided before or toss out a piece of secondhand information on weak defenses, lazy sentries, warlike mayors, a particularly large stockpile of silver. Finally a target would be agreed upon, and the real drinking would begin in earnest.

One cannot help but compare the process to the situation aboard the Royal Navy ships that brought Morgan and so many others to the islands. On the Hispaniola expedition, the men were so uninformed and demoralized that many of them believed that their commanders were going to sell them as white slaves. They were given no incentives to fight, and they fought terribly. They were allowed no share in the prizes, and so they didn't seek them. As a merchant seaman, Roderick had gained nothing from the successful completion of his mission; with the Brethren he could earn a different kind of life.

Roderick had joined a uniquely democratic institution. Back in England he'd heard odd stories about the Levellers, who had recently proposed universal suffrage (except for those under twenty-one years of age, servants, those on charity, and a few other categories). The Levellers believed that men were citizens who could be ruled "no farther than by free consent, or agreement, by giving up their power each to other, for their better being." To the average Englishman, this was madness, "utterly revolutionary and even frightening." The Levellers were crushed for talking about these ideas, but Roderick was beginning to see that the average pirate would have garroted you had you tried to deny him his basic rights. He lived in a democracy where the most important decisions were often made from the bottom up; it was a tradition that would save Morgan more than once. Nothing like it existed in the Spanish colonial system.

Once they had a confirmed destination, the buccaneers agreed to the articles that governed the ship for the duration of the voyage. Too timid at this point to speak up, Roderick watched the proceedings from a distance, his back pressed against the ship's wall. He soon learned that the captain was in charge only when the crew was fighting, chasing a ship, or being chased. The rest of the time he got no more respect than his peers. There was an election for the quartermaster, who would look after the rights of the pirates, take command of any prisoners, settle disputes, and all in all act as a "trustee for the whole." The pirates voted on how many shares of treasure each pirate would get. The captain got five or six shares to the common pirate's one; the master's mate got two; the cabin boy one-half. Skilled tradesmen were well compensated: The carpenter who'd be responsible for fixing any breaches of the hull from cannonballs or storm damage was often was paid 150 pieces of eight; the surgeon and his "chest of medicaments" got 250. Men of both professions were so sought after that pirates would sometimes attack merchant ships just to steal away their shipwright or doctor, who was then forced into piracy.

The most extraordinary clauses in the articles were the ones addressing the "recompense and reward each one ought to have that is either wounded or maimed in his body, suffering the loss of any limb, by that voyage." Each eventuality was priced out:

Loss of a right arm: 600 pieces of eight
Left arm: 500
Right leg: 500
Left leg: 400
Eye: 100
Finger: 100

Some articles even awarded damages for the loss of a peg leg. Prostheses were so hard to come by in the West Indies that a good wooden leg was worth as much as a real one. And other ships posted rewards for bravery: The first man to board an enemy ship or throw a grenade into a fortification would walk away with extra pieces of eight. "In case wee should meete with any strong opposition in any place . . . ," one set of articles read, "the first man entering such place or places shall have 20 pounds, alsoe he that first displays his colores in such place . . . 20 pounds; as alsoe to all those that carry ladders, for every ladder soe carried and pitched upp against the walls . . . 10 pounds." Generous medical insurance, incentive pay, and employee control: Most modern American corporations would not match the pirates' articles until well into the twentieth century, if then.

The articles were a savvy psychological document. Each clause not only gave the ordinary pirate a voice and a stake in the mission but it sharpened their incentive to win, which would benefit the leaders even more than the common buccaneer. The pirates understood what drove men, and they used that knowledge as a tool of battle. Pirates did not get paid a yearly salary or pensions for long-term service, so they had to maximize their earnings during raids.

Its articles firmly established, the tiny fleet sailed northwest, skirting the tiny Isle of Pines off the west coast of Cuba, and then headed due west toward the Yucatán Peninsula. What today would be a modestly interesting sail for a yachtsman with a GPS system was in the mid-1600s a journey into blankness, only here and there illuminated by a known landmark or a familiar current. Speed was determined by dropping a piece of wood onto the sea's surface and measuring the time it took to reach the stern. There were no charts to guide Morgan, no way of measuring longitude. Navigation in the New World was an art that drew on ships' logs, lead lines (for measuring the ocean's depth), collective memory, and gossip. Dead reckoning was also a primary tool; sailing due east or west from a "deduced" position (or "de'd" in the log, thus the term "dead reckoning") was a reliable method: Sail due east from the Canary Islands and you would arrive at Africa's west coast; sail west and you would find yourself in the Bahamas. But this kind of knowledge built up over decades; the West Indies had few such routes available to the captain. In the Gulf of Honduras, ships that had become hopelessly lost in the foul weather were reduced to listening into the night for the splash of migrating tortoises, the only thing that could lead them to land. Ships' pilots prayed fervently to the Holy Virgin for guidance through a nest of reefs. Most pirates could attest to the truth of what a French soldier bound for the New World wrote in his journal, "Now we saw nothing but sky and water and realized the omnipotence of God, into which we commended ourselves."

Morgan's first foray into Spanish America retraced the expedition of Hernán Cortés in 1519, and he knew as little about the territory he was invading as Cortés had. The longhaired, woman-loving conquistador had sailed around the Yucatán Peninsula with twenty-two boats, artillery, cavalry, swords, arquebusiers carrying their fire-belching matchlocks, twenty women, and a crew of 600. The Spaniard was hailed by the native inhabitants, the Mexica, as the god Quetzalcoatl, who they believed was returning from the sea, where he'd disappeared millennia before on a raft of serpents. Cortés was in search, of course, of gold, colonies, and converts, but he'd also been charged with the duty of mapping the shores of Mexico and reporting back on the inhabitants of the territories, who were rumored to be "people with large, broad ears and others with faces like dogs." Cortés found the Mexica to be incredibly hospitable and rich in gold and gems; their emperor, Montezuma, welcomed the white man with

honeyed words: "O our lord, thou has suffered fatigue, thou has endured weariness, thou has come to arrive on earth." But the conquistadors wanted to rule the Mexica, and inevitably they and the Mexica
soldiers, fortified by rations of psychedelic mushrooms and peyote,
went to war. The natives lost thousands, the Spanish hundreds, and
Cortés finally prevailed after a series of battles that changed the face
of the Americas forever. Morgan sailed into a world altered by
swords, guns, and horses. But he and his men were in fact inheritors
of the days when Spaniards were daring, independent thinkers
who could earn their fortunes through war. If only Philip IV, back
in Spain, could have recaptured that ethos, his kingdom would be
protected.

In his report on the expedition, Morgan wrote that once the
buccaneer ships had passed the western tip of the peninsula, they
tacked southwest into the Bay of Campeche, using the lead line to
avoid the shallow cays and reefs that make the coastline a mariner's
nightmare. Their target was Villahermosa, the capital of Tabasco
province. It had been founded in 1596 by the Spaniards and was a
thriving trading post and settlement; how many people lived there
was unknown, but it was a formidable target for the small force led
by Morgan. The expedition's lookouts watched for a telltale plume
of brown in the brilliant blue water, indicating that a nearby river
was pushing its silt as much as twenty miles out into the bay. The
second such sighting told the men they'd found the Grijalva River,
which would take them to Villahermosa. The ships anchored, and
107 men disembarked, leaving aboard a skeleton crew, and headed
for Frontera, a small town three miles upriver. Here they came
across the local Indians, a moment of high tension for any invader:
On Cortés's journey the conquistadors had stumbled on an Indian
altar "covered with clotted blood," the site of many human sacrifices.
But the buccaneers soon learned that the Indians detested the Spanish and would be happy to join the expedition as guides. Their new
allies had bad news, however: Marching the fifty miles straight to
Villahermosa would be impossible. The banks of the river were

dense swamps for twenty miles on each side, snake-infested and impassable on foot. Jumping into boats would get them to the capital quickly, but the advantage of surprise would be lost; surprise was necessary not only as a military tactic as it was to prevent the townspeople from digging holes and hiding their silver plate or running off to the countryside. So the English were forced to follow the Indians into the bush for a grueling three-hundred-mile slog that took them around the outer edge of the swamps and away from any settlers who might alert the town to their approach. By the time it was over, Morgan had far exceeded the famous trek of Sir Francis Drake across the isthmus ninety-one years earlier; in fact, he'd travel approximately thirty-seven hundred miles, the distance from Los Angeles to Caracas.

Villahermosa was many hundreds of miles away from the pirate haunts of Port Royal and Tortuga, and its citizens believed that distance ensured their safety. Towns might see ten or twenty years of peace before a horde of buccaneers suddenly appeared on the horizon one day. Guards slept at their posts; the roundshot (small cannonballs) for the cannons rusted in the soft night air until they'd no longer fit into the mouths of the guns. Keys to chests full of gunpowder hadn't been seen in a decade. Vigilance under the hot sun was a challenge few commanders could meet. So when Morgan's men burst into the town square, the Spanish defense collapsed; Morgan reported that he quickly took and plundered the village. The pirates searched the houses for plate and jewels, gathered a few hundred prisoners, and headed back to their ships. But when they arrived at the river's mouth, Morgan's heart must have dropped: He saw that his ships had been captured by a contingent of Spanish soldiers, who now attacked with three hundred men. Aiming their muskets with care, the privateers cut down the enemy one after the other, quickly repelling their charge. The Spanish retreated and sailed off. Morgan had not lost a single man, but his only means of returning to Jamaica was gone.

The young Welshman was now stranded hundreds of miles from

home with no transportation, little food, and a passel of violent men under his command. In modern terms it was as if he'd crash-landed on the dark side of the moon. It was a precarious moment. Countless other buccaneer armies would disintegrate under such circumstances in the coming years; the history of the West Indies is littered with their pathetic stories, which often followed a similar plot: a minor setback, dissension, mutiny, breakup, starvation, or death from Spanish guns. Like soldiers caught behind enemy lines, Morgan and his men would now have to improvise, and quickly. Roderick was horrified at their situation; merchant ships sailed known routes and resupplied at regular intervals. But here it seemed as if they could die in the sun and no one would ever know. Roderick had come face-to-face with the realities of pirate life: There was no support network and no safety net.

As Morgan debated the options, two Spanish barks and four canoes suddenly sailed into view; Morgan's troops pounced on their owners and commandeered the vessels. The canoes were of a type forty feet long and powered by a basic sail, paddles, and muscle; the privateers leaned into their strokes as they churned back to the Yucatán Channel, a five-hundred-mile journey, all against a one-knot current that added twenty-four miles to every day's distance. The privateers were now living off the land: They had to find water and food and keep a sharp eye out for the small towns that dotted the coast. When opportunity presented itself, they attacked. At a place called Río Garta, the privateers "with 30 men . . . stormed a breastwork there killing 15 and taking the rest prisoners." Morgan was not running back to Jamaica; in fact, he was becoming more aggressive. It would become an emblem of his expeditions: *Always act as if you have the upper hand, even if you don't.*

The men grew more confident with every skirmish with the Spaniards; a force of their size and sharpshooting skills would have little to fear unless they came across a significant garrison or a large body of hostile Indians. And there was even something reassuring in encountering Spaniards, who were at least a known quantity out here in Indian territory. These were the ancient lands of the Aztecs, and even in the 1660s the place had a dark history, a past made up of rumor and hearsay that prevented lesser men from venturing there. Who knew what lay around the next bend in the river? Thomas Gage had reported on a menagerie kept by Montezuma and filled with unspeakable things:

> The hunters were maintained in that house because of the ravenous beasts which were also kept in the lower halls in great cages made of timber, wherein were kept in some lions, in others tigers, in others ounces, in others wolves. . . . There were also in another great hall . . . snakes as gross as a man's thigh, vipers, crocodiles which they call caymans, of twenty foot long with scales and head like a dragon; besides many other smaller lizards and the other venomous beasts and serpents. . . . To these snakes and the other venomous beasts they usually gave the blood of men sacrificed to feed them. Others say they gave unto them man's flesh, which the great lizards, or caymans eat very well. . . . the floor with blood like a jelly, stinking like a slaughter-house, and the roaring of the lions, the fearful hissing of the snakes and adders, the doleful howling and barking of the wolves, the sorrowful yelling of the ounces and tigers, when they would have meat.

The buccaneers safely passed by old Mexico, Morgan would later report, turned the northeast corner of the Yucatán Peninsula, and headed south along the coast, crossing the Gulf of Honduras. When they came to the Isle of Rattan, they rested, took on water, and prepared for a raid on Trujillo on the mainland coast. Trujillo had become a destination for epic journeys. Over a century and a half before, Christopher Columbus, on his fourth and final voyage to the New World, had anchored in the nearby Bay of Trujillo and made his first landing on the American continent here. His men said the first Catholic mass ever celebrated in the Americas. Later Cortés had arrived in Trujillo after a ghastly march from Mexico City overland through nearly impenetrable jungles. Now Morgan added his name to the list, as his men crashed into the town, quickly stormed the fort, carried away everything of value, and for good measure snatched a Spanish vessel.

Next in their sights was Monkey Bay, 450 miles due south, off present-day Nicaragua. To get there Morgan followed Columbus's route along the dangerous, rock-toothed shoreline that now forms the coast of Honduras. Downpours could be torrential; on Columbus's voyage the sky was the color of mist and merged with the sea at the horizon, making navigation difficult. Rain, sky, and ocean all turned the same color. The precipitation had come down in solid sheets, so the explorer could not see the other ships in his fleet, which covered only six miles a day. Columbus wrote that his sails were torn, that their anchors, shrouds, hawsers, and launches were stripped away. He'd never seen a storm "so terrible, that lasted so long." The privateers swept around the belly-shaped coast and dropped down to Monkey Bay, where they recruited nine Indian guides who were not friendly toward the Spaniards. Granada lay at the far end of the huge inland Lake of Nicaragua; to get there they'd have to paddle up the San Juan River in their canoes. The men traveled by night, surprise still their best weapon, and slept hidden in the underbrush by day; they forded three falls where they had to carry their canoes, covering 111 miles before the river brought them to a "fair laguna, or lake, judged to be 50 leagues by 30, of sweet water, full of excellent fish with its banks full of brave pastures and savannahs covered with horses and cattle." The grazing cows soon began dropping to the report of muskets, and the men enjoyed "good beef and mutton as any in England." After feasting on the herd, the men approached the town, "hiding by day under cays and islands and rowing all night." On the fifth night, they reached the outskirts of the city of Gran Granada. Founded in 1524 by Hernández de Córdoba, Gran Granada was a rich commercial outpost that just might, the buccaneers hoped, still contain some of the golden Aztec treasures that had astonished the conquistadors. The town was twice as big as Portsmouth and boasted seven stone churches, colleges, monasteries, and, more important, seven companies of cavalry and militia. But Gran Granada, like so many others, was unprepared for the buccaneers. What astonishment Morgan's band must have caused when they marched into the town square, overturned the great guns, captured the sergeant-major's house, which doubled as the town's armory, locked "300 of the best men prisoners" in the great church, and went on a major spree. The privateers had been children's stories told to wayward boys to frighten them. But now they swept in, real as life, with over a thousand of the local Indians, who, believing themselves liberated, joined in with the plundering and were on the verge of executing the Spanish prisoners en masse until Morgan reminded them that the English would be leaving and the natives would have to live with their colonizers when they were gone. The knives were stayed, and Morgan and his men collected their loot, headed back to their ships and set their course for Jamaica. Roderick counted his takings and was satisfied: He could pay off his debts, rent a better room, and look forward to more weeks of carousing back in Port Royal. It wasn't just the money—it was the feeling of entering the town with as much cash in one's pocket as the richest merchant, of being able to look anyone in the eye, hard if he liked. Money made the man in Jamaica; it didn't matter who your father was or what you had done in the Old World. Roderick's estimation of himself was rising by the week.

Each of Morgan's raids was remarkable for a different reason. His first was a feat of navigation and improvisation: He'd covered thousands of miles across portions of the globe for which no good maps existed, made alliances with Indians, learned to trust their advice, survived the loss of his vessels, and brought his men back safely and much richer. The Spanish had proved less of an adversary than sheer geography, and in fact Morgan had studiously avoided attacking the power centers of the empire: Havana, Cartagena, Panama. But he'd rampaged at will through the length and breadth of the empire. The sheer number of miles he'd covered demonstrated how the Spanish Empire had been distorted by the search for treasure: It was a collection of distant towns strung out over a huge continent. It had not been created with defense or sustainability in mind, only exploitation. What excitement Morgan must have felt as he set course for Jamaica: He'd just proved to himself that the empire was vulnerable to smart, driven men like himself. If he could mold the Brethren to his will, he'd be as rich and as respected as any of his illustrious kin. The West Indies were his for the taking.

Reports filtered back to Madrid about Morgan's feats in territories previously thought out of reach. Morgan began to acquire the name that would pass the lips of terrified colonists for years to come: *El Draque*. The Spaniards were beginning to believe he was the reincarnation of the dreaded Sir Francis Drake.

5

Sodom

When word reached Port Royal in the fall of 1665 that Morgan was on his way back in, the townspeople were amazed, having considered the men lost at sea or long dead in some wretched jungle. The buccaneers had been gone two years. Morgan, now only thirty years old, sailed triumphantly into the port, dressed in the spoils of war: new stockings, fine Spanish knee breeches, and a jerkin taken from the grandees of Granada. He sailed in a commandeered Spanish vessel, itself symbolic to the eager English faces that lined the wharves of a victory over Madrid's minions. His face was weathered and tanned by the long days under the sun, with that salt-lashed glow that sailors have after months at sea. He was now fabulously rich; he'd gained unique experience in the voyage and perfected the sea-to-land raid that would become his specialty; he'd naturally assumed command of the men as his skills as a soldier rose to the fore. Morgan had remade himself in the wilds of Honduras and come back a new man.

On his return the Welshman found that his luck was still good. His uncle Edward had been named lieutenant governor of Jamaica, a reward for his service in the Royalist cause. The cash-strapped and recently widowed Edward had arrived on the island on May 21, 1664, with his two sons and three daughters. His eldest daughter had died during the voyage, having succumbed to the great killer, not the Spanish but disease, "a malign distemper by reason of the nastiness of the passengers." Jamaica was continuing to fill up with settlers, and the government was not picky about the class of folk who accompanied Edward. And installed as governor was one Sir Thomas Modyford, a former Barbados plantation owner and politician. In many ways Modyford would play the supporting role to Morgan in the coming years. They were an intriguing pair: Modyford the consummate politician, crafty, subtle, the author of ingratiating letters to his masters in London that, on second reading, were loaded with spiked resentment and canny forays. Morgan's intentions were voiced out of the mouth of a musket, but Modyford was an artist of diplomatic subterfuge. He was the colonial administrator par excellence, furiously working to extract every inch of latitude he could from his English superiors while at the same time conducting a freelance war on the Spanish enemy that threatened his livelihood and his home.

The Morgans were delighted to see their semilegendary cousin, who must have been a figure of romance to them, the embodiment of the dashing buccaneer; his friends and followers had regaled them with tales of Morgan's adventures. The Morgan daughters stood out from the usual female company of Port Royal as well; this was a town where a whore could graduate to being a planter's wife, if she played her cards right, so scarce were white females on the island. Proper girls were sent back to England to find proper boys to marry; the roughnecks of Port Royal had to make do with what was left behind. Henry's cousins had lived in upper-crust society in Prussia most of their lives, having fled England when the Puritans won out over their Royalist brethren, and had returned to Restoration London just in time to revel in its gaiety and social froth. They could gossip about the king's dalliances and talk about the latest plays: John Dryden's comedy *The Wild Gallant* (1663) had fizzled, while the king's own troupe of actors, the Gentlemen of the Chamber, had inaugurated the opening of Drury Lane with a drollery called *The Humorous Lieutenant* (1663). Talk of culture and royalty must have been like champagne bubbles in Morgan's nose; in Port Royal the only musical entertainments were choruses of drunken sluts and pirates down by the waterfront. When Henry fell for the eldest remaining daughter, Mary Elizabeth, he did not waste time in making his feelings clear. He risked his life for money, but he didn't want to marry for it, as Elizabeth's father was by no means rich. This was clearly a love match (and, as a union between first cousins, not as controversial as it would be today). Elizabeth accepted, and all that was left to do was to get the approval of Colonel Edward, who was off fighting the Dutch on the island of Statia. Then, a month and a half after Henry had sailed back into the harbor, news arrived: Statia was taken, but Colonel Morgan was dead. "The Lieutenant-general died not with any wound," his second-in-command reported, "but being ancient and corpulent, by hard marching and extraordinary heat fell and died." The islands often required a season of acclimatization; the colonel had gone out too fast and too hard.

There was also news of a change of opinion on the privateers. The Spanish were furious about the privateers like Morgan, "much dejected," one English official reported, "at hearing of our hostile carriage toward them, which has wholly ruined their trade." In the eternal minuet of European alliances, Charles was now wooing the Spanish as allies and trying to head off war with France and the Dutch, so he ordered that his Jamaican subjects stop their raids on all parties, which to the islanders was like an open invitation to every nation to attack them at will. If the privateers could not get commissions in Port Royal, they'd look to the French island of Tortuga to get permission to attack Spanish targets. The commission business can get confusing: Dutch or French privateers might carry English commissions against the Spanish. English privateers could sail with Dutch or French commissions. So long as *someone* was at war with Spain—the richest and most desired target in the West Indies—you could get a license to attack them. The letter didn't have to be from your native government; the privateers were soldiers of fortune, even if men like Morgan preferred to sail for their home country.

Thomas Lynch, a rich planter and an advocate for better relations with Spain, doubted that the 1,500 privateers could be reined in without five or six warships. "What compliance can be expected from men so desperate and numerous," he wrote, "that have no other element but the sea, nor trade but privateering?" The Spaniards were not the only ones threatened by the flourishing of the buccaneers; some in Port Royal were beginning to realize that the lure of gold was empowering the worst instincts among them. Here, unlike in England, there were few institutions to restrain the power of the Brethren. The old class structures meant little in Port Royal; nationalism, which could get the rabble of London primed for a war, was important, but in the final analysis it was trumped by gold and opportunity. The peculiar circumstances of life on the Caribbean frontier were molding a new kind of mind-set: that of an autonomous, geographically mobile, highly confident, heavily armed bandit-hero with few ties to nations or systems of belief.

A certain Jamaican, one Mr. Worsley, made that point in a letter that described the situation of the merchants and planters on the island. Mr. Worsley was convinced that the French were wooing the buccaneers to their side and that one day the townspeople of Port Royal would come to regret their alliance with the murdering bands. Like the townspeople in a Hollywood western who hire the disreputable, ex-alcoholic gunman to protect them, Mr. Worsley (and many like him) were secretly appalled by their guardians, and he wrote that if "such a crew of wild, dissolute and tattered fellows" had become so accustomed to preying on people, they were liable to turn on their own. The very individuality that made the pirates such marvelous fighters made them sorry material for a civilized society. And the treasure of the New World empowered them, made them stronger than decent men. As it turned out, Mr. Worsley was right to worry. The day would come when the traders of Port Royal would see the pirates turn away from the Spanish devil and, cutlasses raised, advance slowly toward their merchant allies.

What Worsley recognized was that the pirates were a kind of supervirus: They represented an extreme form of predatory capitalism, where the strongest, who produced nothing, preyed on the weak, who were forced to give up the goods they'd made or extracted from the earth with great effort. The merchants favored a milder form of trade, with some rule of law and payment for what was taken. But to dislodge the Spanish system they were forced to introduce the most virulent form of their own social code and watch it wreak havoc on their enemy's economy. The problem was that, once set loose, such a virus could not be controlled. That was the merchants' worry: that their experiment might lead not to a profitable trading network with the Spanish colonies but a complete breakdown of social order, in which men stopped obeying the rules of a market economy, went renegade, and pillaged and killed to make their profit. It was the risk you took when you invited men like Roderick to protect your interests.

But for now the town was booming. Huge warehouses were built on the harbor and packed with animal skins, logwood, sugar, and tortoiseshell. Three- and four-story homes, built of brick, stood shoulder to shoulder beside the mean huts that had previously served as shelter. A fine stone cathedral, the pride of the town, shot up. The English ignored the Spanish style of building: low-slung houses with thick wooden poles driven deep into the ground, giving the buildings a low center of gravity and anchoring them into the earth. The Spanish had learned that the unstable island required such a building style, but the English rejected this architectural folklore entirely. They were interested in re-creating England here in paradise and claiming their place in a way everyone would understand. Their heavy, rigid homes went up all over Port Royal, and their warehouses and civic buildings didn't deign to recognize the local conditions: Stone piled on top of stone, that was the look. All of it was built on a layer of loose sand only thirty to sixty feet deep, beneath which lay coralline limestone and rough gravel brought to the area by glaciers during the Pleistocene era beginning 1.8 million years ago. It was not a solid place to build a city, but Port Royal lived for the moment.

Worrying, too, was the region's continuing susceptibility to tsunamis, described by the Spanish as "seaquakes." Spanish explorers reported discovering rich pearl beds near the Venezuelan island of Cubagua in 1499, but forty years later they were gone, and it is believed they were wiped away by an earthquake and tidal wave. Three ships a hundred miles off the coast of Honduras had felt the ocean shake beneath them so violently that they thought they'd hit a shoal. Convinced that "the sea was against them," the fleet sailed for home. There were tales of cities destroyed, of residents looking out and seeing the sea mounted higher than the land, of towns moved to the slopes of mountains to avoid the rampaging waters.

There are different types of tsunamis: teletsunamis, caused by events remote from the affected area (such as a distant earthquake across the ocean); landslide tsunamis, caused by debris plunging into the sea after a mass movement of earth; self-explanatory volcanic tsunamis; and tectonic ones, generated by the sudden shifting of plates and crustal blocks underneath the sea. The first type was rare in the Caribbean; it wasn't until the Lisbon earthquake of 1755 that we have a recorded example of a tidal wave sweeping across the Atlantic for seven hours to pound the coasts of South America. Jamaica was protected from most teletsunamis emanating from the Atlantic by the massive bulks of Cuba and Hispaniola, which acted as buffers. But it was highly vulnerable to the last three.

❖ ❖ ❖

In Madrid the final act of the Hapsburg dynasty in Spain was about to begin. Philip IV was failing: Nephritis pained him constantly, and his writing hand was now paralyzed. When a comet flashed across the sky in late 1664, many took it as a sign that Philip's end was near. All eyes fell on the heir, but Carlos II had inherited his father's bad luck in the form of debilitating sickness: He was weak, feeble-minded, with a massive, lolling head, his famous Hapsburg jaw so out of alignment that he could not chew his food, his body racked by fevers and mysterious pains. The Hapsburg mania for finding mates among their own, which kept power within the clan, had once been their signature; it was said that the family triumphed through marriage, not war. But in Carlos the tactic had produced a near monstrosity. It wasn't enough that seven of his eight great-grandparents descended from a single female ancestor; she had, in addition, to be mad.

Her name was Juana, a plump-faced, intelligent, unusually well read daughter of Ferdinand and Isabella of Spain who had married Philip I and bit by bit grew obsessed with him. In his absence she'd fall into a kind of trance, staring dully into space and breaking out into fits of hysterical screaming. Soon the windows of her room were barred, and even her parents locked her away in a strong castle when she came to visit. When Philip died, she succumbed to her other world completely; she began a funeral march unlike any other before or after in the annals of royal madness. Philip's heart was removed and sent home to Flanders, and his body was packed into a coffin. But Juana refused to relinquish him; instead processions of men with torches, armed guards, and chanting monks preceded the coffin as the queen journeyed from castle to castle through her realm. Juana never let the coffin out of her sight, and every day she'd open it and inspect the body for any signs of renewed life; disappointed, she'd kiss Philip and close the lid once again. Women along the roads were kept out of view; Juana believed they could still tempt Philip away from her. The macabre procession went on for weeks.

One day Carlos would grow obsessed with death as well. But first he had to survive the toxic genes bequeathed to him by his ancestors.

As the future monarch struggled to live, the Crown mobilized every tool in its power. A team of thirty-one wet nurses was mobilized to suckle him; they had to be between twenty and forty years old, with breasts of a certain size, decent and good-natured, and neither Jewish nor Muslim. Candidates endured a long and tedious examination of their family tree before being allowed to give Carlos the teat. All the while the Spanish court kept up the pretense that he was a robust child, but Louis XIV, who was married to Carlos's sister, had his doubts about his brother-in-law (even suspecting that Carlos was really a girl disguised as a boy). He sent spies to confirm them. One after the other was rebuffed, until the French ambassador finally laid eyes on the heir. He immediately reported back that the boy "appears very feeble, he has a rash on both cheeks, . . . his head is covered with scales." The French diagnosis would always be more accurate than the Spanish.

But Philip had fulfilled his final obligation to Spain; an heir, such as he was, was in place. As the end approached, he'd wished his son a happier life than he'd enjoyed. He did not seem to fear death; when it was asked whether the peripatetic bodies of the saints—miraculously preserved remains of Catholic holy men, which were believed to have healing powers—should be brought to his sickbed, he'd indicated they should not be moved: no extraordinary measures, as it were. When Don Juan José de Austria (no relation to the famous lover Don Juan), the only one of his bastard sons he'd recognized, arrived from his exile, Philip would not see him. "Tell him to go back to Consuegra," he'd said wearily. "It is time now for nothing but death." (This insult would burn with the proud Don Juan and cause years of trouble for Spain.) For Philip, death was not such an unhappy prospect. The curse had been passed on to Carlos; he could do no more harm to Spain, and God could do no more harm to him. When he died on September 17 and was carried to his place in his beloved Escorial, he passed on to his son a number of enemies and only a frail peace with England and its privateers.

If Carlos had been robust and strong-minded, his story would have been different. But his pale, deformed face was an invitation to conspirators, and soon they were gathered around him. His mother, Mariana of Austria, was appointed queen regent and given effective power over the affairs of state. Her closest adviser was Father

Nithard, a Jesuit despised by the common Spaniard because he was Austrian. Carlos's illegitimate brother Don Juan was constantly plotting to oust Mariana and gain control over Carlos.

The young king was the incarnation of his battered country, his weak constitution an accurate mirror of what he inherited. Corruption was so common that it was not even perceived as corruption; it was just the way things were done. It permeated the kingdom: Posts in the government, on the all-important galleons and elsewhere, were sold to the highest bidder. One college in Navarre paid handsomely for the right to confer medical degrees on its graduates, even though there wasn't a single professor of medicine on the faculty. "The son of a shoemaker hates that occupation," one government official wrote. "The son of a merchant wants to be a gentleman, and so on with the rest." Rank was all: Some members of the titled classes avoided going to hospitals during the plague epidemics because it could have meant a slight to their honor; they found death preferable.

This attitude extended to the New World. A captain-general sailing to Cuba or New Spain would pay the Crown for the privilege, then make back his money and more by selling off positions to crew members. The Americas-bound ship was a microcosm of what Spain had become: A typical one would include a veedor, or legal counsel, who would see that all the king's laws were obeyed even in the middle of the Atlantic Ocean; there were eight gentlemen-in-waiting for the captain, four trumpeters, and a master of the plate, responsible for cataloging every piece of treasure brought on board and for delivering it to the Crown's representatives on the ship's return; there was a constable, a captain of arms, and the all-important notary who would affix his stamp to every piece of paper that the expedition produced. (The Archivo General de Indias in Seville, which stores the archives from the Spanish Empire in America, holds over 80 million documents.) There were even ships, called *navíos de aviso,* or "advice ships," that hauled nothing but dispatches from Spain to America and back again. Copies, duplicates, triplicates — entire boats full of paper! Compare that to the average pirate ship, where every last ounce of extraneous material was tossed overboard in the name of speed, and you get an idea of the two worldviews that were about to do battle in earnest.

The differences were striking: The pirates were radical democrats; the Spanish, monarchists; the pirates prized daring and risk taking, while the Spanish prized conformity, and those who improvised often found themselves rotting in a squalid Madrid prison. The pirates were possessed by "an insatiable desire for riches"; the Spanish wanted power and honor. The pirates were often castoffs and godless heathens; the Spanish believed themselves to be God's chosen ones. The pirates were commanded by Henry Morgan, who rose from nothing; the Spanish followed Carlos, the heir to the Hapsburg dynasty. The pirates were individualists; the Spanish represented a fantastically complex system. The pirate's world was closer to our own; the Spanish lingered in a medieval dream.

The final confrontation between the two was now being held in check by London; Charles II had ordered that the privateers "desist those hostilities upon the Spaniards and other neighbours, as much disturbing the settlement of that plantation." The king was being disingenuous; he did want to avoid turning Jamaica into "the Christian Algiers," the worldwide headquarters for sea raiders, but reining in the buccaneers was actually a sop to his new allies. The island was a thorn in the side of Spain, and he needed Spain now. And so the privateers were called in. Town criers preceded by drummers went through Port Royal and two smaller towns reading the king's directive. Many of the Port Royalists reacted with bitterness; the king did not seem to realize that they were living on a frontier where, on any given day, a Spanish, Dutch, or French ship could appear on the horizon and disgorge hundreds of soldiers or pirates, who would then proceed to plunder your house, rape your women, and squeeze your eyeballs out of your head (a favorite torture of the time). The king's directive provided no funds for beefing up the island's militia and no Royal Navy ships to protect the harbor. The lack of commissions was driving away the privateers, the only thing that kept the island safe.

The Spanish colonies did not sit back and wait for the English. In the same way that Modyford repeatedly beseeched his English superiors, the governors of the different territories kept up a constant stream of entreaties to Madrid, asking for ships, soldiers, and funds to arm them. There was a fleet in service called the Armada de Barlovento, or Windward Squadron, which in theory was permanently stationed in the West Indies. But, as always with the Spanish, the distance between "in theory" and "in reality" was large: Seven ships had been redirected for domestic use before they ever made the trip. And Spanish administrators were waiting impatiently for the other six to arrive in their waters and hunt down the Brethren.

Governor Modyford found that the revoking of commissions had the predicted results: The privateers drifted off to the Windward Islands, where they went pirate completely (attacking without commissions) or cadged letters of marque from the Portuguese or French. Modyford hanged a few of the locals who went out buccaneering without permission, but he pardoned more. He tried to entice them with commissions against the Dutch, but the privateers saw the Hollanders as fellow Protestants; it was difficult to get up a lusty hatred when contemplating a mission against them. Besides, they were not as rich as the Spanish. The trade that mushroomed from the privateers' taking was shrinking, and Modyford could not even get answers to his frequent letters to Lord Arlington, his superior in London. He'd been given permission insofar "as should seem most to the advantage of the King's service and benefit of the island," but knowing the détente with Spain, he did not want to set Morgan loose on the Main.

By 1666, things were getting desperate. The Port Royal Militia, which had boasted Henry Morgan as one of its first leaders, had only 150 men, down from 600 the year before; even a modest Spanish force might conceivably take the island back. On February 22, Modyford called a meeting of the island's council for the purpose of replenishing the militia. They agreed that the only way to achieve it was to start granting commissions against the Spaniards. The council gave many reasons that this would be a good thing for Jamaica: It would stimulate trade with New England; it would help the small farmer, who provisioned the privateer fleets; and, lest we forget what Jamaica would become, "it hath and will enable many to buy slaves and settle plantations." The last justification was the most pressing: The Spanish, the council claimed, "continue all acts of hostility, taking our ships and murdering our people." For this, the buccaneers were the only answer. "They are of great reputation to this island and of terror to the Spanish," the council declared.

Modyford had sent a scout to entice back some of the disaffected pirates, and though "much wasted in numbers, many being gone to the French," they agreed. The governor was still being careful, however, and issued a commission to raid the Dutch island of Curaçao. In charge would be the elected admiral of the Brethren, Edward Mansfield. Henry Morgan was not listed among the men recruited for the mission; Modyford had put him in charge of the Port Royal Militia and the defense of Jamaica. The Welshman was busy building the massive Fort Charles, at the entrance to Port Royal Harbor, and replenishing the ranks of the garrison.

Mansfield and his men set out for Curaçao, but once the Brethren were under way, his crew announced that "there was more profitt with lesse hazard to be gotten against ye Spaniard which was there onely interest." The buccaneers decided to switch their target to Cartago, the capital of Costa Rica, but were soundly defeated after a long, starvation-haunted march, during which the different nationalities began bickering. (The contrast with Morgan-led expeditions could not be clearer.) With his men exhausted and famished, Mansfield knew that attacking a Spanish town without permission would be trouble. Attacking a Spanish town without *taking* it was worse: London tended to look with more favor on illegal missions that were at least successful. Desperate for a prize, the marauders turned toward two islands and a long-held dream: a pirate republic.

Providence and its smaller sister island, Santa Catalina, had been one of the first English colonies in the Americas, settled by Puritans from Bermuda and England in 1630. They lay almost halfway between Port Royal and the Spanish town of Portobelo, where the silver fleets came to fetch the king's treasure every year. Providence would be a perfect home away from home for the pirates, perched as it was within easy striking distance of the Main's lucrative cities. Santa Catalina had a less savory attraction: It was the home of criminals, adulterers, and women of disrepute sentenced to a term of exile away from their home cities in Panama or New Spain.

Pirates had always dreamed of having their own country, unsullied by civilian interference. Madagascar would become a pirates' haven in the late 1690s; its hidden coves, pliant local women, fresh water, and supplies of citrus fruits (essential in battling scurvy) contributed to making it a paradise, and its close proximity to the Red Sea and Indian Ocean guaranteed a steady supply of treasure. "Gone to Madagascar for lymes" was a common expression among the Brethren. Other republics would follow. Calico Jack Rackham and the legends of a later generation took over the island of New Providence (in the Bahamas) in the early 1700s and erected a tent city packed full with thousands of pirates. The island's democratically elected officials let the pirates do what they wished: whore around, hide out in the island's countless limestone caves, and drink themselves unconscious, to feel the first stabs of bright sunlight through their eyelids as they lay on a deserted beach after a night of carousing. It was paradise. The cliché was that pirates did not dream of going to heaven when they died, they just dreamed of going back to New Providence.

In his quest to found such a haven, Mansfield easily took the island, killing only one Spaniard. He sailed back to Jamaica to report on the consolation prize, and Modyford immediately sent out reinforcements to secure the island. But Mansfield's small victory had set in motion a series of tit-for-tat adventures that grew exponentially in scope, until four years later the Spanish would find Henry Morgan assembling the largest pirate army ever seen in order to storm their oldest city on the continent.

Spain decided to draw a line in the sand of Providence. The viceroy of the province of Panama, Don Juan Pérez de Guzmán, called a council of war on hearing the news of the island's capture. In a split vote, the council determined to "retake [Providence] from the pirates, the honour and interest of His Majesty of Spain being very narrowly concerned here." Two ships sailed from Portobelo on July 7 to reclaim the island, which Mansfield had now left in the care of his lieutenants as he sailed back to Jamaica. The 517 men on board gave the Spanish a ten-to-one advantage over the fit English soldiers on Providence. After slamming one of the ships onto a reef, the Spanish commander sent a party onto the island to demand surrender, to which the English gallantly replied that they "preferred to lose their lives" than give back the land. The Spanish soldiers poured onto the island and were met with odd-sounding volleys: The English at one of the forts had gone through all their ammunition and were now cutting up the church's organ pipes and blasting them out of cannon at the advancing troops. It was a valiant defense of a practically worthless piece of rock, but in the end the English saw that the numbers were against them and gave up.

Now one will begin to see why the hatred between Spanish and English ran so deep and why men often fought to the death in the Caribbean. There was no Geneva Convention, no articles of war, to govern what happened next. Sir Thomas Whetstone, the ne'er-do-well nephew of Oliver Cromwell and speaker of the Jamaican House of Assembly, along with the island's new English governor and an army captain, were to be sent to Panama in chains. Under the terms of the surrender, the rest of the surviving soldiers were to be sent to Jamaica. But the Spaniards double-crossed the soldiers, and they were carried to Portobelo, where jailers packed the thirty-three men into a small dungeon and chained them to the floor.

They were forced to work in the water from five in the morning till seven at night, and at such a rate that the Spaniards confessed they made one of them do more work than three negroes, yet when weak with want of victuals and sleep, they were knocked down and beaten with cudgels, and four or five died. Having no clothes, their backs were blistered in the sun, their shoulders and hands raw with carrying stones and mortar, their feet chopped, and their legs bruised and battered with the irons.

When the news of the men's fates reached Jamaica two years later, it would stoke the hatred even more.

There was one other result of the Old Providence episode: Mansfield had returned to Jamaica after he'd captured the island and requested more men and matériel from Modyford, to hold it as an English possession. Modyford didn't wish to commit more forces than he already had and so turned the admiral down. A disgruntled Mansfield had set off for the corsair island of Tortuga to drum up some reinforcements, but there, in Esquemeling's wonderful phrase, "death suddenly surprised him, and put a period to his wicked life."

The position of admiral of the Brethren was now vacant. It would soon be filled by the young upstart Henry Morgan.

✳   ✳   ✳

In Europe the musical chairs were changing again and the waltz's beat quickened. Alliances were being remade at a dizzying pace. France declared war on England in January 1667, but it was a conflict contained mostly to the Continent and to the islands of the Lesser Antilles. Then, on May 23, England finally signed the Treaty of Madrid with Spain. Eleven years after Jamaica had been taken, the queen regent was still refusing to let it go: The treaty did not formalize the English takeover, in fact did not even mention it. The island was still in play; the war in the West Indies would continue. But Charles's mind that summer was focused suddenly on the Dutch, who in June 1667 sailed up the Thames, burning ships and blasting forts as they went. It was a humiliating loss for a maritime nation, with scenes of panic along the famous river and people fleeing down roads into the country to get away from the Dutch.

Charles's extravagance had set the stage for the defeat; spending on masques and jewels left little money for the navy, and now England had paid the cost. There were whispers, of course, that the Catholics had somehow sold the country out; there were always whispers. But the old standby could not absorb the rage of the English people. Outside Westminster, Samuel Pepys heard shouts of *"A Parliament! A Parliament!"* England needed time to recover and to rebuild its navy; on July 31, 1667, the Treaty of Breda was signed between the United Provinces and England. By the end of that summer, Charles II was at peace with Denmark, France, Spain, and the Dutch.

As Europe calmed itself, Jamaica was catching fire.

6

The Art of Cruelty

In Port Royal, Modyford was trying with every tool in his arsenal to hold his island together. The merchants were furious that the Treaty of Madrid did not give them legal cover to sell their goods to the Spanish colonies. Spain had again given the upper hand to marauders like Morgan instead of tradesmen like themselves. The slave traders railed that there was no provision for an *asiento*, or a contract for their lucrative trade. The planters bitched that the privateers continued to suck away their disgruntled workers. And the privateers clamored for commissions. The waters off his shores teemed with wild-eyed men, Spanish navy ships, and Dutch corsairs. And London told him to keep the peace. Modyford calmed his superiors with assurances that he would, "as far as I am able, restrain [the privateers] from further acts of violence towards the Spanish, unless provoked by new insolences." Even now Modyford was hearing rumors and mumblings of a new Spanish confidence after the recapture of Providence. Returning traders spoke about activities in Cuba: troops being mustered, a fleet being readied. Jamaica was said to be the target: Spain was finally going to take it back. Having assured London that he'd restrain the privateers, Modyford did just the opposite. He and the council issued Henry

Morgan a commission for reconnaissance work, to sail to Cuba and "take prisoners of the Spanish nation, whereby you may gain information of that enemy to attack Jamaica, of which I have had frequent and strong advice." Modyford needed solid evidence of war preparations on the Spanish side to justify any future battle plans; without them his hands were tied. Up to this point, Morgan's official status in Jamaica was as a colonel in the Port Royal Militia, the citizen soldiers who were on call to defend the island against any attack. Modyford elevated him to "admiral" of the militia. It was at this time that Morgan was also named to the top rank of the Brethren of the Coast. He was a double admiral, of both the legal and the shadow forces that guarded this lonely outpost of English civilization.

The word went forth that Morgan was assembling a fleet, and privateers appeared out of the coves of Tortuga and the bars of Port Royal, including his old friend John Morris, the Jamaica-based privateer who had sailed with Morgan on the first expedition and about whom little is known except that he became the admiral's right-hand man. Pirates rarely planned their missions in port. The message would be broadcast that an expedition was afoot, and a rendezvous point was arranged. The leaders informed the men how many pounds of gunpowder and bullets they needed to bring, where the ships would assemble, and on what day they should set out. Morgan chose the South Cays off Cuba, where they'd be protected from the ocean waves that could snap an anchor chain. One by one the other ships appeared over the horizon; by the deadline at the end of March 1668, there were a dozen ships and around 700 men ready to sail. These were not grand vessels: Many of them were single-masted open boats that had planks of wood laid over them to provide shelter from the sun and from water seepage into the provisions. They had no cannon or superstructure. Often they were glorified longboats designed only to get the pirates from Point A to Point B. The largest ship in the fleet, the Spanish-built *Dolphin*, belonged to Morgan's compadre John Morris and carried eight cannon and just 60 men at capacity. Roderick was aboard the *Dolphin*. He looked thinner than he had on his arrival in Port Royal after the first raid. Like most of the Brethren, he'd blown through his share of the booty with astonishing speed and had cut back to one meal a day. Morgan's call-up had been a godsend.

Had Morgan known what was out there waiting for him, he might have demanded bigger ships. Modyford's informants had understated the danger. The long-awaited Armada de Barlovento, the fleet of six vessels designed to protect the Spanish Main, had finally arrived in the New World after decades of bureaucratic death matches between the Council of the Indies and the navy. "The only reason that forced Her Majesty to convene the Windward Fleet again," wrote a Spaniard from Mexico, "was the great destruction caused by the enemy pirates. The enemy is hostile and has destroyed the commerce of the region." The armada's arrival instantly changed the balance of power on the open seas. These were not the usual Spanish galleons, their decks cluttered with trade goods, bales of silk dresses stuffed into spaces where guns should have gone, their crews facing the interference of lawyers and notaries. These were heavy warships bristling with cannon, manned by competent soldiers, and far superior in firepower to any pirate ship in the world. They were even commanded by an admiral, Alonzo de Campos y Espinosa, who had been given one and only one mission: "to clean the coasts of the Indies of the pirates which infest them." Henry Morgan was not public enemy number one for the Spanish quite yet, but he was climbing toward the top of the list. And if he and his small ships ran into the armada on the open sea, he and his glorified dinghies would be quite literally blown out of the water.

As he walked his decks, Morgan would have passed among men from every corner of the Old World and the New: There were adventure-minded English youths like Roderick, French Huguenots who had fled religious persecution, English freethinkers and jailbirds, old hands from Cromwell's New Model Army still dressed in the legendary scarlet coats, now tattered and stained; there were Portuguese adventurers, escaped slaves, mulatto sons of Spanish fathers and black mothers; indentured servants who had jumped aboard trade ships and made their way to freedom; perhaps an odd Dutchman or two. In the Old World, they would have been in a jail cell or working as disgruntled serfs. On Henry Morgan's ship, they were one move away from being a captain or just filthy rich.

The pirates called their council. "Some were of the opinion 'twere convenient to assault the city of Havana under the obscurity of the night," Esquemeling writes. Havana was "one of the most renowned and strongest places of all the West Indies, . . . defended by three castles, very great and strong." But among the pirates were men who had been held prisoner in those castles, and they said that "nothing of consequence could be done, unless with fifteen hundred men." Morgan had less than half that. Other city names were tossed out and debated, until a consensus formed around the city of Puerto del Príncipe. One of the buccaneers knew it and gave two things to recommend it: The town was rich and, sitting forty-five miles inland from the Cuban coast, had never been raided by pirates. Buccaneers loved fresh, untouched cities, and here was one grown prosperous on the trade in animal hides. The motion was approved, and the pirates set out for the Gulf of Ana María.

But Morgan's illustrious career was almost deep-sixed before it even began in earnest. A Spanish prisoner who was being held by the pirates escaped from the ships and began swimming toward shore. The pirates, who didn't think the man could understand English, had let him listen in on their council, and as soon as he reached Puerto del Príncipe, he began to tell the terrified towns-people exactly what Henry Morgan had planned for them.

This was a problem that would plague Morgan's career and the career of many other marauders. It was nearly impossible to keep the element of surprise in an attack. If one approached a city by land, there were often settlers or Indians who would send a warning to the target settlement; if one approached by sea, fishermen and lookouts could often give the enemy at least a few days' warning, especially as ships were dependent on a good wind to make landfall and could sit becalmed for days, in full view of their opponents. And with so much money at stake, men regularly informed on the pirates for rewards and for special treatment. The pirates themselves would brag about upcoming expeditions, especially when drunk, and the Spaniards had spies everywhere. Loose lips did sink ships, and that included pirate ships.

The Spaniards immediately began to dump their plate into the local wells and dig holes for their money. The governor, who was a former soldier and knew his defensive strategy well, ordered "all the people of the town, both freedmen and slaves" to lie in ambush for the English, and he instructed that trees be cut down and laid in the buccaneers' path, to slow their approach; fortifications were also thrown up "and strengthened with some pieces of cannon." Eight hundred men were rounded up; Morgan, who had landed by now, marched on the town with 650.

Morgan immediately began to show what he'd learned in the Jamaican jungles. Finding the approaches to the town impenetrable, he took his men into the woods, where progress could be made only "with great difficulty," but which took the pirates safely past the ambushes on the trail. After a long, sweaty march, the pirates emerged onto a plain, la Savana, that lay before the city. The governor spotted the advancing ranks, now formed into a semicircle, and sent his cavalry to break them up. The pirates did not flinch: Their spirits roused by the sound of their drummers and by marching behind the flag of the Brethren, they began picking off the riders as they swept toward them. The assault was broken, and the skirmish on la Savana devolved into a classic, head-to-head, open-field battle in which marksmanship was all-important. The French muskets proved their worth: Soon the governor went down, and more and more Spaniards were dropping one after the other under the privateers' wickedly accurate shooting. Finally, "seeing that the Pirates were very dextrous at their arms," the Spanish relented and the men turned toward the wood line to try to escape. Morgan and his men did not let them get far; "the greatest part of them" died as they retreated. The battle had taken four hours. The Spaniards lost most of their men, the pirates only a few.

Within an hour Morgan was on the outskirts of the city, where the pirates found the people holed up in their houses, taking pot-shots at them. This was too much for Morgan; he'd won the city fair and square. He sent the following message to the town's men: *If you surrender not voluntarily, you shall soon see the town in a flame, and your wives and children torn in pieces before your faces.* The Spanish relented, and Morgan had all the prisoners locked up in several of the city's churches. After pillaging the empty homes, Morgan then sent his men out into the countryside, "bringing in day by day many goods and prisoners." There was wine, too, and the privateers guzzled it like water.

The admiral then turned to an old pirate standby: ransom. Four prisoners were sent into the adjacent woods to find the people who had fled and demand money for the imprisoned families. The four returned a few days later to tell Morgan they'd been unable to find anyone and asked that he give them fifteen days to complete the job. Morgan agreed. A few hours after the four messengers had left, some of the privateers returned from pillaging and reported they'd taken substantial booty and also captured a Negro who was in possession of letters. When Morgan read them, his eyes must have narrowed with fury. The missives were from the governor of Santiago, capital of the adjoining province. In them he told the prisoners to delay paying any ransom and to "put off the Pirates as well as they could with excuses and delays; expecting to be relieved by him within a short while, when he'd certainly come to their aid." Morgan had been double-crossed. As the men had swilled the local wines and fell over themselves collecting booty, an army was being organized to defeat them.

Morgan began barking out orders. He told his men to load the ships with all the treasure and demanded that the Spanish slaughter and salt five hundred head of cattle for his men, which they did along with the buccaneers in great haste. Finally the beef was loaded—after an unfortunate incident in which an English privateer stole the marrow bones from a cow being slaughtered by a Frenchman. As they walked to a dueling spot, the Englishman "drew his sword treacherously" and fatally wounded the other man in the back. The French were ready for war right there on the beach, but Morgan had the man arrested and promised his Gallic allies justice once they returned to Port Royal. The French grumbled but agreed.

The Spanish were impressed by the raid. The governor of the province that included Puerto del Príncipe wrote to the queen regent to express his shock and outrage at what the privateers had done. He reported that he'd charged his sergeant major and another officer with misconduct, because the rugged country and long distances should have enabled a much smaller force to destroy the buccaneer army. The privateers were less thrilled. They sailed off to the South Cays and counted up their booty, which came to a disappointing 50,000 pieces of eight (or $2.5 million in today's dollars). It sounds like a windfall, but when deductions were made for the king's share, for Morgan's and the captains' and the surgeon's and carpenter's take, for injuries, and with the remainder being split among 650 men, the seaman's share was hardly a small fortune. And besides, Port Royal, where many of them made their homes, was one of the most expensive cities on earth in which to live, as nearly everything except rum and food had to be imported from Europe. "The sum being known," reports Esquemeling, "it caused a general resentment and grief, to see such a small booty; which was not sufficient to pay their debts at Jamaica." Roderick was among the complainers. His share would barely pay his back rent, let alone allow him the bacchanal he'd been dreaming of for weeks. From a callow youth, Roderick had grown into a shrewd, toughened buccaneer, with hardly an ounce of fat on him. For the first time, he looked at his leader with a cold eye.

The mission could not stop now; another city would have to be hit. Morgan's reputation, his future as the admiral of the Brethren, was at stake. If he returned with such a small payday, he might be voted out of power. Already some elements of the force were withdrawing their confidence. The Frenchmen pulled out of the mission, even after Morgan used "all the persuasions" he could think of to convince them to stay. It was a shocking blow.

And Morgan must have known exactly what had gone wrong: He hadn't been cruel enough. Failing to torture the captives, as most pirates would have done, and allowing them plenty of time to raise their ransom, went against the proven methods of buccaneering. A follower of the gallant Mansfield, he'd played the gentleman, only to have the Spanish string him along, toy with him as if he were an amateur. His softness had cost him dearly. The French made this point clearer when they left Morgan to join one of the legitimate monsters of the pirate world, Francis L'Ollonais. In his report on the adventure, Morgan would say that the Gallic pirates "wholly refused to join in an action so full of danger," but danger was never the point. It was leadership. L'Ollonais represented the pirate code at its most extreme, but Morgan could not afford to ignore his methods. The privateers would sail with whoever found them the most gold, and L'Ollonais was a rising star who was making his boys rich. Morgan would have to meld his ideas with those of a ruthless killer if he were to avoid another embarrassment.

Born Jean David Nau, L'Ollonais got his name from the Sands of Ollane, the region in Brittany where he was raised. He came to the New World as an indentured servant and, after serving his time, arrived on Hispaniola as a free man. He joined some of the original *boucaniers* and then graduated to the Brethren at Tortuga. The pirates had not seen his like before; L'Ollonais was an innovator, as well as a complete and utter sociopath. His career gives an idea of what Morgan was competing against. The Frenchman began as a common pirate, boarding ships with the other men. "He behaved himself so courageously," Esquemeling tells us, "as to deserve the favour and esteem of the Governor of Tortuga." The governor recognized a good prospect and gave L'Ollonais his own ship "to the intent he might seek his own fortune." (One can be sure that the governor got his cut of any proceeds.) Word of the Frenchman's extreme cruelty immediately began to spread throughout the West Indies. "It was the custom of L'Ollonais that, having tormented any persons and they not confessing, he'd instantly cut them in pieces with his hangar [cutlass], and pull out their tongues," Esquemeling tells us, "desiring to do the same, if possible, to every Spaniard in the world." He delighted in putting men to the rack and in "woolding," or tying a stick around a victim's forehead and tightening with turns of a stick until the interviewee's eyeballs popped out of the sockets. But that was standard procedure, on both sides of the war between Spain and its enemies in the New World.

After outfitting his ship, L'Ollonais ran into bad luck when he was caught in a storm off Campeche; his ship was destroyed, and he and his men were forced to swim for their lives. When they made it to dry land, they were hunted through the forests by the Spanish, who killed many and wounded their captain. To survive, L'Ollonais "took several handfuls of sand and mingled them with the blood of his own wounds," then smeared the mixture all over his face and hands. Lying down among the slaughtered men, he played dead. When the Spaniards left, he disguised himself as a local and insolently marched into town; mingling with the Spanish, he overheard them calling to his ex-crewmen, now held prisoner, "What is become of your captain?" "He is dead," the men replied. "With which news the Spaniards were hugely gladdened, and made great demonstrations of joy, kindling bonfires and . . . giving thanks to God Almighty for their deliverance from such a cruel Pirate."

Returning to Tortuga, L'Ollonais scared up another ship and crew and set out to exact his revenge. The governor in Havana was informed by residents of a seaside town that L'Ollonais had risen from the dead and was again terrorizing them; he sent a small warship with ten cannon and fifty soldiers, ordering them not to return until they'd "totally destroyed those Pirates." (He even sent along a Negro executioner, who was told to hang every pirate except

L'Ollonais, who was to be brought to Havana for special atten-
tions.) L'Ollonais and his men stormed the ship on its arrival, boarding even in the face of barrages from its cannon. One by one the
captured crew members were brought up from the hold and were
beheaded. Finally it was the executioner's turn; the terrified man
begged L'Ollonais for his life. "This fellow implored mercy at his
hands very dolefully . . . and [swore] that, in case he should spare
him, he would tell him faithfully all that he should desire to know."
L'Ollonais must have laughed at that; as if he were not going to find
out everything he wanted anyway. He got the information he needed
and promptly lopped off the man's head. Only one man was spared,
and he was sent back to the governor's office in Havana with this
message:

> I shall never henceforward give quarter to any Spaniard whatsoever;
> and I have great hopes I shall execute on your own person the very
> same punishment I have done upon those you sent against me. Thus I
> have retaliated the kindness you designed to me and my companions.

Morgan would learn this: Pirates depended on their reputation
for cruelty. If townspeople knew ahead of time that you cut off people's heads for withholding information, they tended to talk a lot
more readily. Armies surrendered. Mayors bargained. Loot materialized. It was the difference between seeing the Hells Angels pulling
into your isolated town versus some strangers from the next county.
You might be willing to take your chances with the latter, especially
if you were guarding money built up over a lifetime of brutal hardship. But not with the Hells Angels—and not with the pirates. The
Angels' winged skull insignia sends the same message as did the pirate's flag: *You know who we are. Do as you're told.*

Some pirates cultivated a reckless image: The first description
that civilians throughout the Americas repeated over and over again
when retelling their encounters with the Brethren was "barbarous";
the second was "crazy." "I soon found that death was preferable to

being linked with such a vile crew of miscreants," wrote Philip Ashton, a young fisherman captured by pirates in 1722. The Spanish tended to torture captives according to a formula: There were probably in the advice ships crisscrossing the Atlantic booklets full of exact instructions for how to pull out a man's toenails for stealing a loaf of bread. The Inquisition's brutality was institutional. The pirates' was often just insane. One buccaneer, Raveneau de Lussan, recounted that captives were often ordered to throw dice for their lives; whoever lost, lost his head. Blackbeard took this management philosophy to a new level. The pirate commander was once drinking in his cabin with the pilot and another man. Without any provocation he drew his pistols underneath the table, cocked them, blew out the candle, crossed his hands, and fired the guns. One of the men was shot through the knee and lamed for life, while the other escaped shaken but unhurt. Blackbeard did not have any quarrel with either man, which naturally led one of them to ask him why he'd shot them. "He only answered by damning them, *that if he did not now and then kill one of them, they would forget who he was.*" [Emphasis in the original.]

This strategy also meant that the craziest often rose to the top of the trade. "He who goes the greatest length of wickedness," wrote Captain Johnson, the author of *A General History of the Robberies and Murders of the Most Notorious Pirates*, "is looked upon with a kind of Envy amongst them, as a Person of a more extraordinary Gallantry." One Captain Taylor was pointed out as being popular for all the wrong reasons, "a great Favourite amongst them for no other Reason than because he was a greater Brute than the rest." But other pirates were, after all, simply young men from coastal cities in England who had wanted a little adventure; they were not born lunatics but decent men who had sought out adventure and gold, not orgies of violence. A schism can sometime be detected in pirate narratives: Captain George Roberts was captured by pirates off the coast of the Cape Verde Islands in 1722; he was used to the rough ways of seamen, but the pirates' wanton cruelty appalled him. Roberts had the guts to try to challenge them and eventually gave a speech to the whole crew about God and conscience. When he finished, the men responded:

> Some of them said I should do well to preach a sermon and would make them a good chaplain. Others said, no, they wanted no Godliness to be preached there: That pirates had no God but their money, nor savior but their arms. Others said that I had said nothing but what was very good, true, and rational, and they wished that Godliness, or at least some humanity, were in more practice among them; which they believed would be more to their reputation and cause a greater esteem to be had for them, from both God and man.
>
> After this, a silence followed. . . .

The picture that emerges from many accounts is of new recruits lured by tales of riches and freedom, slowly being molded by peer pressure and constant alcohol intake until they succumbed to what might be called the culture of piracy and grew as savage as their mentors. John Fillmore, the great-grandfather of American president Millard Fillmore, was captured by pirates on a voyage from Massachusetts in 1723 and later wrote that anyone who practices a vice too long soon thinks it a virtue "and in such case conscience ceases to alarm the understanding."

L'Ollonais pursued cruelty to its extremity; he was violent not only for effect but because he enjoyed violence. One instance, when he was reported to have cut a man to pieces with his sword and then licked the blade clean, suggests a level of pathology not found in the ordinary pirate. Only in the wilds of the Americas could he have flourished as he did. And in the summer of 1667, he was tearing through the Spanish West Indies like a cyclone and setting a mark that Morgan would have to match. In Tortuga, L'Ollonais put out the call for men and soon had at least eight ships and over six hundred pirates under his command; he set out for the Spanish Main. Almost immediately the crew spotted a Spanish ship out of Puerto Rico bound for New Spain, packed to the decks with "one hundred and twenty thousand weight of cacao, forty thousand pieces of eight and the value of ten thousand more in jewels." L'Ollonais called off the rest of the fleet and took on the vessel alone with his ten-gun ship. Three hours later the prize was his. Another ship was caught off the Isle of Savona, and its holds revealed stacks of muskets, 12,000 pieces of eight, and, even better, "seven thousand weight of powder" for their guns. It was a smashing start.

L'Ollonais now set course for the city of Maracaibo, which lay on the huge inland lake beyond the Gulf of Venezuela. Maracaibo was a center for ranching and boasted huge plantations; its inhabitants had grown rich on hides, tobacco, and cacao-nuts. The Frenchman attacked the fort that guarded the city, and the Spaniards began to flee "in great confusion and disorder, crying: *The Pirates will presently be here with two thousand men.*" Maracaibo had been sacked by pirates before, and its people knew what lay in store for them. But they had not dealt with L'Ollonais. He hacked men to pieces as they stood before him and even threatened his own men: "Know ye withal," he told them, "that the first man who shall show any fear, or the least apprehension thereof, I will pistol him with my own hands."

The pirates fought ferociously, not only overcoming Maracaibo's fortress but also putting to death an army of 800 men sent by the governor of Mérida, a military man who had fought for King Philip IV in Flanders. Faced with an artillery of twenty pieces and a determined band of soldiers, L'Ollonais outmaneuvered the governor by pretending to retreat pell-mell. The Spanish were overjoyed and began pursuing the bandits, crying, *"They flee, they flee, let us follow them!"* As soon as the soldiers had outrun the range of their artillery, the pirates turned on them and began slashing the ranks to pieces. It was a military maneuver of some sophistication, which many pirate captains could not match. L'Ollonais broke the Spanish force, captured the pieces, and occupied the town, starving many of its residents to death. And, most pointedly to Morgan, who surely heard of his exploits, he ransomed the surviving townspeople for 10,000 pieces of eight and gave them only two days to collect it. When they failed to do so, his men began torching the houses. "The inhabitants, perceiving the Pirates to be in earnest, . . . promised the ransom should be readily paid." It was. When the pirates returned to Tortuga, the count of the assembled loot came to 260,000 pieces of eight ($13.2 million), a fabulous sum. L'Ollonais had squeezed Maracaibo for every last cob it possessed, faced down superior forces, and found his men food, drink, women, and gold. He quickly surpassed Morgan in the eyes of the Brethren. He "had got himself a very great esteem and repute at Tortuga by this last voyage," Esquemeling tells us. "And now he needed take no great care how to gather men to serve under his colours. . . . They judged it a matter of the greatest security imaginable to expose themselves in his company to the hugest dangers that might possibly occur."

✠   ✠   ✠

If Morgan took a lesson from L'Ollonais's use of cruelty in the Maracaibo campaign, he must have learned the cost of it from the Frenchman's next, and last, exploit. Having gathered 700 men, L'Ollonais set off for Nicaragua but ran into a becalmed sea; they were unable to make any distance and so put into the first port they found and immediately began terrorizing the local Indians, "whom they totally robbed and destroyed." They moved on to the port of Puerto Cavallo, where they took a Spanish ship and burned two huge storehouses to the ground, seemingly out of sheer willfulness. The local residents did not escape either: "Many inhabitants likewise they took prisoners, and committed upon them the most insolent and inhuman cruelties that ever heathens invented, putting them to the cruelest tortures they could imagine or devise." L'Ollonais topped it off with a final flourish. The pirates found themselves on the road to a prosperous town; from their torture of locals, they knew that soldiers were waiting ahead of them in an ambush. What they needed was an alternative route, but one after the other the Spanish told them there was no other way forward. L'Ollonais finally snapped. "[He] grew outrageously passionate; insomuch that he drew his cutlass, and with it cut open the breast of one of those poor Spaniards, and pulling out his heart with his sacrilegious hands, began to bite and gnaw it with his teeth, like a ravenous wolf, saying to the rest: I will serve you all alike, if you show me not another way."

The pirates pushed on, enduring wave after wave of Spanish ambushes. It must be said they fought with astounding bravery, regularly repelling superior numbers of soldiers hiding behind strong fortifications. After vicious fighting, the Spanish could finally take no more and put out the white flag. L'Ollonais granted them only one concession: They'd have two hours to assemble their things and run for the forests. Once the two hours had passed, the pirate captain ordered his men to chase the Spaniards into the forest and capture them. When it came to the king's subjects, the Frenchman gave no quarter.

But his luck now began to run out. The buccaneers heard rumors of a rich-cargoed Spanish ship due near the mouth of the Guatemala River and, after three months of waiting, finally found that it had arrived. A ferocious battle ensued, where the pirates attacked under the blazing roar of the ship's twenty-two guns, but when it was over, L'Ollonais found that the vessel held only "fifty bars of iron, a small parcel of paper, some earthen jars full of wine," and little else. Now, like Morgan, L'Ollonais faced defections from his ranks. He held a council to rally the men for an attack on Guatemala, but some of them quit the whole business, mostly those "new in those exercises of piracy . . . who had imagined at their setting forth from Tortuga that pieces of eight were gathered as easily as pears from a tree." The remaining pirates began to feel the pangs of hunger, as they'd run out of provisions and were forced to forage through the jungle every day. Finally they were reduced to killing monkeys, a notoriously tough business. Another pirate, Basil Ringrose, was on another voyage forced to hunt the macaques and found it unnerving. It would take fifteen or sixteen shots to kill three or four, "so nimbly would they escape our hands and aim, even after being desperately wounded." In addition, there was something disturbingly human about the monkeys' reaction when one of their troop had been shot. "The rest of the community will flock about him," Ringrose reported, "and lay their hands upon the wound, to hinder the blood from issuing forth. Others will gather moss that grows upon the trees, and thrust it into the wound and hereby stop the blood or chew and apply as poultice."

Things got steadily worse. L'Ollonais managed to beach his ship in the Las Pertas Islands, where it stuck fast. The Las Pertas were the last place you wanted to get stranded. The local Indians were reputed to be excellent hunters; it was said they could run "almost as fast as horses," were fantastic divers, and hunted their prey using wooden spears with sometimes a crocodile tooth attached to the end. Rumor also held that they were cannibals. So with one eye on the woods, the pirates were now forced to begin the work of breaking up the ship for its wood and nails and constructing a new, much smaller longboat. While the work was going on, two pirates—a Frenchman and a Spaniard—went into the jungle looking for food and were spotted by a group of local Indians. A furious chase ensued; the Frenchman escaped, the Spaniard did not. Several days later a squadron of pirates was sent into the jungle to find out what had happened to him. Near the spot where the Frenchman had last seen his compadre, they found the remains of a recent campfire and near it "the bones of the said Spaniard very well roasted." Farther out they found more evidence of the man's fate: "some pieces of flesh ill scraped off from the bones" and a hand with two fingers left on it.

The increasingly desperate journey illustrated how badly things could go wrong for pirates. Once they were outside of their ports, the pirates had no guaranteed food supplies, no access to repair facilities for their ships, no sure alliances with locals, no stockades where they could get a solid night's rest away from Indians, no way to call for reinforcements. The Spanish cities were distant from each other, but they were self-sufficient: An army had all the resources it needed to survive. L'Ollonais, the golden boy of the Brethren, was quickly learning a lesson that would haunt Morgan in the near future: One small setback could begin a cascading set of disasters. This meant that their leaders had to keep them moving forward constantly toward new sources of food and treasure, or they'd perish.

The new boat took six long months to build. When it was finished, L'Ollonais and a group of men selected by casting lots set out for Nicaragua, where they hoped to find some canoes, take them back to the Las Pertas, and carry the rest of the men back to Tortuga. But at the mouth of the Nicaragua River, the pirate's trip came to a final end. L'Ollonais was attacked by both Spaniards and Nicaragua's Darien Indians, who were one of the few tribes that the conquistadors were never able to defeat. The Frenchman, always lucky in battle, escaped and decided to try one last stab at fortune by heading for Cartagena, the great galleon port in present-day Colombia. But he did not get far. "God Almighty, the time of His Divine justice already being come," Esquemeling tells us, "had appointed the Indians of Darien to be the instruments and executioners thereof." They captured L'Ollonais and tore him to pieces while he was still alive, "throwing his body limb by limb into the fire, and his ashes into the air; to the intent no trace nor memory might remain of such an infamous, inhuman creature." The men left behind suffered an equally bad ending; they were rescued by another pirate in canoes and set off for Cartagena. But starvation soon haunted them again, and they were forced to eat their own shoes and the sheaths of their swords, to hunt for Indians to eat (they never found any); the majority of them starved to death or faded away from hunger and disease.

L'Ollonais was the expression of how the pirates had turned away from civilizing influences. He'd become a legitimate monster, a savage throwback tramping through the savage jungle. To survive, Morgan would have to blend the Frenchman's ruthlessness with subtler strategies. It was not going to be easy. For, in fact, every pirate, down to the fresh-faced youths like Roderick, had some of L'Ollonais in him; it was a prerequisite for the job.

7

Portobelo

Morgan, abandoned by the French in the South Cays, now showed why he would outshine L'Ollonais. He began by giving a speech. By all reports the thirty-three-year-old Morgan had the common touch and was able to motivate even the most hardened privateer; one of his peers wrote about his "generous and undesigning way of conversing." Seeing the doubt in his compatriots' eyes, he "infused such spirit into his men as were able to put every one of them instantly upon new designs," Esquemeling writes, "they being all persuaded by his reasons that the sole execution of his orders would be a certain means of obtaining great riches." Among the listeners was an anonymous pirate from Campeche who had rendezvoused with Morgan's tiny remaining fleet and was obviously judging whether to throw in his lot with them or go off hunting with someone else. Morgan, who "always communicated vigour with his words," won him over. Soon Morgan's fleet was back up to strength, boasting nine ships. A further mark of Morgan's renewed confidence is that he persuaded the pirates to sail without voting on a destination, a violation of the pirate code. Fresh off a defeat, he was reasserting control. Roderick and the other English privateers now formed the backbone of his army.

The privateers sailed to the coast of Costa Rica in July of 1668, and Morgan revealed the target: Portobelo. Some of the pirates protested instantly. The Panamanian city (originally known as Porto Bello) was a major stronghold; it boasted two large castles, the mammoth Santiago and San Felipe de Todo Fierro (the Iron Fort), one on each side of the harbor mouth, bristling with forty-four guns that would fix any enemy ship in a withering fire. (It was also said that the Italian who had laid out the city chose the spot because it stood on a peculiar type of coral that could withstand cannon blasts.) Should a pirate ship miraculously make it past the two castles, farther up the river toward the town there were layers of military redundancy: sentry posts, blockhouses, lookout positions manned by armed soldiers. Near the quay another huge fort was being built by the unfortunates who had been captured at Providence, slaving away during the day and chained in a prison at night. There were only two cities with stronger defenses in the entire Spanish Main: Havana and Cartagena. Even the great Sir Francis Drake had died outside Portobelo harbor, unable to penetrate its defenses.

Portobelo was a seasonal Fort Knox: It was the terminus for the tons of raw silver dug out of Potosí and made into pieces of eight at the king's mints. For most of the year, it was a tropical hellhole: hot, breezeless, full of "noisome vapours," a place where various diseases competed for supremacy and fresh victims, where the smell of the rotting, fetid mud that the low tide revealed would blast into a visitor's nostrils, never to be forgotten. To be posted to Portobelo was the Spanish noble's biggest dread; it boasted few of the amenities of bustling Cartagena or sophisticated Havana. It existed only for those four or five weeks when the Spanish treasure fleet appeared on the horizon and Portobelo went from backwater to boomtown in record time. Merchants from Peru, Colombia, and the far reaches of the Spanish Empire, including Madrid itself, would pour into the city, sending rents spiraling. The wealth of the king's dominions, which had been brought up the coast of South America and loaded onto mules at Panama, flooded into the town. The population exploded from 2,000 permanent residents to perhaps 10,000. Traders brought their best slaves. Farmers brought chickens (whose price would increase twelvefold). Two thousand mules were kept at the ready for transporting the king's treasure; long trains of the sturdy animals that had laced the hills above the town in the days before would suddenly appear in the streets, loaded with jewels and bullion from Peru and beyond. Thomas Gage, while a Dominican friar, had visited the town before a fair and counted two hundred mules entering the town square in one day and dumping their load of treasure there. "Silver wedges lay like heaps of stone in the street," he marveled; but with the town crawling with Spanish soldiers, no one dared touch a bar. Instead of coins, wedges of silver were traded for the rich spun cloth, the fine muskets, and the hundreds of other goods that arrived from Spain on the treasure ships. The assembled treasure during the fleet's visit could amount to 25 million pieces of eight, double the king of England's annual revenue.

Portobelo was the result, in many ways, of one man and one day in the summer of 1544. A young Inca named Diego Huallpa had spent a long morning tracking an elusive deer on the mountain called Potosí in the kingdom of Peru (now Bolivia). The lining of this throat began to parch as he ascended beyond the thirteen-thousand-foot mark, high even for an Inca who spent his life in thin air. But fresh meat was precious, and Huallpa pressed on, determined to claim his prey. As he reached for a shrub to steady himself on the slopes, the plant tore away, and in its thick, dangling roots was entwined something that flashed in the sun, distracting Huallpa. He brushed away the clots of dirt; the metal gleamed under his thumb. Silver, unmistakably.

The Spanish were soon knocking on his door, threatening Huallpa with the rack, one of their earliest imports to the Americas. He pointed them to the mountain. Even when their Indian workers began to dig out piles of silver from the spot where Huallpa led them to, the colonial administrators could not conceive of what they had found. In the next two centuries, Potosí would yield almost 2 billion ounces of high-grade silver ore, at a time when the metal was just as valuable as gold. The entire European economy, tamped down for decades because of a lack of precious metals to serve as currency, took on a new life when the first ships began arriving in Spain groaning under the weight of the mine's silver bars. The famed city of El Dorado, the city of the Golden Man, drove the conquistadors mad with its tales of unfathomable riches, but it was a myth. Potosí was real. To this day when a Spaniard wishes to talk of any crazily wealthy thing, he simply says, "It's a Potosí."

The men seeking the treasure rarely thought of the price paid for each ounce extracted. A Spanish visitor described the Inca workers who recovered the ore. He reported that they worked twelve hours a day, descending as far as seven hundred feet into the mine "where night is perpetual" and the air thick with fumes to gather the ore, and then climbing four or five backbreaking hours to rise again to the surface. If any of them slipped, they'd plunge to their deaths at the bottom of the pit. It was for the product of this misery that Morgan was coming to Portobelo.

To attempt the town, Morgan again had to rally his men, among whom numbered mulatto pirates along with blacks, Portuguese, Italian, French, and English. Many of them considered him crazy even to suggest Portobelo; it was beyond them. But Morgan made them see. "If our numbers are small," he cried, "our hearts are great, and the fewer we are, the better share we shall have in the spoils!" It was a wonderfully condensed battle cry tailored for pirates: It combined the David-versus-Goliath odds that they seemed to relish in certain moods with the brute economic reality that fewer men meant bigger shares. The pirates quickly signed on.

The Welshman had prepared well. An Indian informant from inside Portobelo had given him an accurate picture of the garrison's numbers and state of mind. The soldiers manning the various defenses hadn't been paid in over a year and a half, leading some of them simply to disappear from their posts and others to take up side jobs as tailors or grocers in the town itself, where they slept at night, leaving the castles seriously undermanned. The mammoth Santiago boasted only 75 or 80 men on a typical night, when there should have been 200 trained soldiers on guard. The castle forces were supposed to be backed up by civilian militias (one each for Spaniards, mulattoes, freed blacks, and slaves), but they, too, were depleted by sickness or other duties. Many of the Spaniards were in Panama, away from the miasma that was Portobelo; the loyal blacks were chasing maroons in the hills around the town, leaving fewer than a hundred men able to fight.

And then the pirates stumbled on unimpeachable witnesses: Half a dozen bone-thin and badly sunburned men approached the fleet in a canoe as it headed for Portobelo. It's not clear if they'd heard rumors of Morgan's approach or had simply happened on the fleet, but they knew the target city well; it turned out they were some of the long-lost English soldiers from the garrison who had been taken during the Spanish reconquest of Providence and shipped as slaves to Portobelo, where they'd suffered unspeakable torments. As he listened to the men tell of their inhuman treatment, Roderick looked at these half-dead wretches, knowing that the same fate awaited him if he was captured by the Spanish. His anger built to a fever pitch; not in years had he felt so English. He and the others swore they would see the Spaniards bleed for what they'd done to the captives. But two extra nuggets of information tantalized the coolheaded Morgan: The newly freed men reported that an expedition against Jamaica was being planned and that funds were being raised through a levy in the province of Panama. The rumors of war, it seemed, were true. The men also swore that one of their fellow captives was none other than Prince Maurice. Maurice was the king's nephew who had fought for him throughout the Civil War after a youth spent drinking and dueling in The Hague and elsewhere. He and his brother Rupert had been cruising the Caribbean in 1652 when they'd run into a ferocious storm and Maurice's ship had disappeared. "He was snatched away from us in obscurity," wrote one cavalier who had been on the voyage, "lest, beholding his loss would have prevented some from endeavouring their own safety; so much he lived beloved, and died bewailed." Rumors had flown ever since the sinking: Maurice was dead and at the bottom of the sea; he was alive and being held by the Spanish at Morro Castle in Puerto Rico. Now Morgan had a fix on him. To find Maurice would earn the eternal gratitude of the king, a useful thing considering that Morgan was set to attack Spain in a time of peace. "We thought it our duty to attempt that place," Morgan wrote in his report on the mission.

Portobelo sat at the southeastern end of a small bay. On the northern shore of the bay sat the fort called San Felipe and on the southern shore, farther in toward the city, sat Santiago, the Iron Fort. An approach through the narrow mouth of the bay was out of the question; the castles were undermanned, but it would take only a few decent gunners to blow the fleet to splinters. Instead Morgan devised a plan based on stealth. The fleet anchored at Boca del Toro, a quiet bay to the southeast of the town. There, according to Morgan's own narrative, 500 of the men transferred into twenty-three canoes that the ships had been towing or carrying. These were the same type of forty-foot, single-sail canoes that Morgan had used in his odyssey to Central America, and now the men bent low over their sides, dipping the paddles into the black water and speeding the boats along with the strong easterly current. The canoes were becoming a Morgan trademark; so was traveling by night. The buccaneers paddled through the darkness "to be ye more undiscryed" and found hiding places on the deserted shore by day, sweltering beneath the trees. They slid under the guns of San Lorenzo, the fort that guarded the river Chagres, and sped on. It was like a journey through the primeval world, uninhabited and tomb-quiet except for the night cries of parrots and the growls of jaguars.

For four nights the fleet of canoes remained undetected until it came upon a fishing boat manned by two blacks and a "zambo"; in other parts of the Americas, the term would come to mean someone who was three-quarters black and one-quarter white; here in the Spanish territories it meant a person who was half black and half

Indian. The pirates began to torture the blacks, what the Brethren called "questioning with the usual ceremonies." [Pirate argot tends to be drier, more English, than the "Avast!" and "Shiver me timbers" flung about by buccaneers in Hollywood films: Escaping from a tight situation was called a "soft farewell"; "a forced loan" was any theft from the Spanish; a pirate's corpse left out as a warning to others was described as "sun-dried," while poking captives with knives as they ran around a circle of laughing pirates was a "sweat." These intermingled with sailor lingo such as "belly-timber" (food), "fudled," (drunk), and "Davy Jones" (the devil's minion), who lived at the bottom of the sea, aka "Davy Jones's locker."] The Negroes refused to guide the pirates to Portobelo. Morgan had learned the lesson of Puerto del Príncipe—the cutlasses came out, and the pair was soon fed to the sharks. The zambo quickly agreed to cooperate.

Finally the men arrived at a position between the Isla de Naranja (Orange Island) and the shoreline, within sight of the castles of Portobelo. There were a total of four fortifications to overcome, beginning with a lightly manned blockhouse called La Ranchería, where sentries watched the coastline for unfamiliar ships on the southern shore of the bay that led to Portobelo. Two miles away, on the outskirts of the town, sat Santiago Castle. Then one reached the town center, with its merchant houses, churches, and slave quarters. Beyond the town proper, just off the shoreline in the shallow harbor itself, waited the still-uncompleted San Gerónimo fort, which the captured Englishmen had been working to finish. Across the harbor, on the northern tip of the bay, sat the final obstacle: San Felipe, guarding all entries and exits from the harbor.

The men guarding these forts were a cross-section of the Spanish populace. Some had joined the Spanish army as early as age ten, fetching wood and cleaning the boots of the regular soldiers, and worked their way up the ranks. The bulk of them would have been from the lower classes, while the officers were often wellborn. Both were seeking their fortune in the New World. They were more rooted than the privateers; many of them were married and had side jobs such as cobbler or grocer; they had houses in the town and children to care for. They were often not hugely experienced: A minority of them would have been in battle before, although some of the older ones might have seen action in Flanders or elsewhere on the Continent. And they came from a long and proud tradition that decreed that death was preferable to surrender or defeat. But in the New World, that tradition seemed distant and in some ways beside the point: The armies of Spain's traditional enemies were thousands of miles away. Not to mention that they often went for months on end without pay, which hardly endeared their king to them.

As it approached the prize, Morgan's lead vessel was spotted by a group of sharp-eyed Negro woodcutters, who reported the rogue ship to the mayor of Portobelo. Reluctantly, as he'd have to pay for the expedition himself, the mayor sent out a canoe to inquire just what the vessel was: merchant, slaver, pirate, or advice ship? The people in the town were not unduly concerned with the matter: One boat sailing up the river was not much of a threat. As the canoe set out, the fleet, under cover of night, was angling toward the shore where the zambo advised a landing. The men had been given their assignments; they'd checked their powder, cleaned their guns one last time, adjusted their pistols in their belts, made sure they'd tapers to light them, sharpened their cutlasses, and ate a last bit of turtle or *boucan* to fortify them. Now they grimly eyed the spot on shore and drove the canoes forward. There was nothing left to say; the battle was imminent.

In the middle of the night, Morgan's spotter detected movement ahead, a silver flash against black. It was a paddle splash from the mayor's canoe. The Spaniards must have noticed the fleet at the same time and instantly recognized that these were not Dutch traders or slavers but corsairs, because they turned and raced for home. The fleet could not hope to catch them; instead Morgan concentrated on getting his men ashore. An hour later the men heard the gravelly crunch of wood hitting a beach. They'd hit their target: Buenaventura, three miles from Portobelo. They'd skirt the shoreline and attack the city from the west. An Englishmen who had been one of the prisoners at Portobelo now took over as point man; he and three or four pirates were sent forward to take the sentry, "if possible, to kill him upon the place," so that he would not fire his musket and raise the alarm. The men did one better: They captured the man and brought him back to Morgan, his hands tied and, no doubt, his legs weak with terror. Morgan asked the sentry about the local defenses while the other pirates stood close, cutlasses unsheathed, eyeing him meaningfully. "After every question," Esquemeling tells us, "they made him a thousand menaces to kill him, in case he declared not the truth." To ensure that his information was accurate, the man was marched bound and gagged at the head of the column as they made their final approach along the treasure road, pounded to a hard patina by the mules carrying Potosí silver. Any volley from an ambush would kill him first.

The pirates reached the blockhouse on the outskirts of the city at La Ranchería and found it guarded by five men. The soldiers were told to surrender, "otherwise they should all be cut to pieces, without giving quarter to any one," but the men answered Morgan's shout with a quick barrage; two pirates sank to the ground, wounded. Screaming that they'd avenge the English captives, Roderick and the others swarmed over the blockhouse, put the men there to the blade, and soon had it under control. But the element of surprise was gone; the reports of the muskets could easily be heard in the city itself. Now Morgan shouted at his men to hurry as the town's startled residents struggled from their sleep. Groggy and confused, they asked each other what the shots could mean and then heard more, repeated insistently. When the citizens looked out to the harbor, they saw the mayor's canoe surging toward shore, the men in the boat firing their muskets and yelling, "To arms! To arms!" The canoe passed Santiago Castle, and, according to Spanish reports on the attack, the men cried to the soldiers there, "The enemy is marching over land!" The soldiers ran for their muskets, while families in town uncovered their silver plate and jewels from their hiding places and rushed to throw them down wells or bury them in their yards.

The attack was a test of the Spanish colonial military, and the first sign was actually good. The sergeant on duty at Santiago lowered the castle gate so that the part-time grocers and bartenders who slept in the town could make it back, a smart move for an undermanned fortress. But things went downhill from there: The sergeant went to report to the lord of the castle, or castellan, Juan de Somovilla Tejada, and found the man still asleep in his bed. The sergeant informed his superior that the infidels were inside the city, but the lord simply brushed him off, saying it was only the English escapees causing trouble. The sergeant insisted: This was a large body of men, not the six pathetic souls who had fled Santiago in rags. Survivors of a shipwreck, the yawning castellan replied. His subaltern must have bitten his lip as he informed his lord that as he spoke, hundreds of armed corsairs were racing across the beach toward the castle. At this the castellan rose from his bed.

Morgan's men had indeed arrived at the beach near the foot of the castle, gasping for breath, having double-timed it the two miles from the blockhouse. And here Morgan experienced a crisis of faith. Seeing the soaring stone walls of the fortress, which rose out of the sand like some medieval Spanish colossus, he lost his nerve. "Many faint and calm meditations came into his mind," Esquemeling wrote, in an account backed by Spanish sources. The Brethrens' prisoners reported an even more nerve-racking scene, with the admiral reaching for the throat of the Indian guide and screaming, "We cannot go that way! This is a trick to slaughter us all!" It was a rare break in composure for Morgan, who was, in the pirate vernacular "pistol-proof": calm under fire. His men soon laughed him out of his terror, and one of the former English prisoners told the captain that Santiago's defenses were far less formidable than they looked. Morgan nodded, took a deep breath, and gave the command. The pirates burst in two groups from their hiding place and went tearing toward the castle.

One group aimed at the base of the castle walls, while the other angled off and headed toward a hill that would give them a commanding view of the castle's rear. The men ran across the open space expecting at any moment to be atomized by a blast of grapeshot, but Santiago's constable of the artillery had mistakenly loaded the cannons with ball (a large cannonball designed to sink ships) and not partridge (small balls designed for killing men). The only cannonball that was fired at the men came nowhere near hitting them and instead kicked up a sheet of white spray as it slammed into the blue harbor waters. The main group of pirates, exhilarated at their survival, hugged the castle walls as they made their way past the fortress to the city streets, onto which they burst "firing off their guns at everything alive, whites, blacks, even dogs, in order to spread terror." They met only token resistance and took control of the town within minutes. Now that they had Portobelo by the throat, they had to slowly disarm it, like a handler defanging a snake. First in their sights was San Gerónimo, the partially finished, lightly manned fort that lay across an expanse of water. The castellan there replied to the demands for surrender by saying that the men "would fight unto death like good soldiers"; it was the response the king expected of his officers. But he was bluffing: Spain's decay was immediately evident at Gerónimo: The soldiers found only a single working cannon that could cover the direction from which Morgan's assault had to come, and there was only damp powder to charge it. The Englishmen hid behind some canoes as Morgan and his commanders tried to gauge the depth of the water, to see whether canoes would be needed and what approach would be best. In the middle of their deliberations, a few of the fort's former captives strolled by and began walking out into the water toward the walls of Gerónimo. The pirates watched as the captives failed to sink; the water, in fact, came up only to their knees. Laughing, the other pirates charged after them. Utterly exposed but by now scornful of the Spanish gunners, the men splashed their way across the gap. The castellan, seeing that his handful of men had no chance, surrendered; the first of the castles belonged to the pirates. Now the twin teeth at the mouth of the harbor, through which Morgan's ships had to pass to load the expected treasure, had to be neutralized.

In the city they found something to give them added motivation: the remaining prisoners from Providence. They were discovered chained in a dungeon, "eleven English in chains who had been there two years." But Prince Maurice was nowhere to be seen, only a clue that would continue the romantic myth of the man: "We were informed that a great man had been carried . . . six months before to Lima or Peru, who was formerly brought from Puerto Rico." Having freed the English hostages, the men set out for Santiago, which they'd simply run past on their way to the city. The smaller squadron of men had remained on the hill overlooking its walls, picking off any Spaniard who dared stick his head above the ramparts. The French muskets were earning their ridiculous prices: With the pirates "aiming with dexterity at the mouths of the guns," the Spaniards found they "were certain to lose one or two men every time they charged each gun anew." The long-term advantage lay with Morgan, but the defenders inside could postpone the inevitable defeat almost indefinitely: Scaling the fort's sheer walls under fire would be a nightmare. So Morgan, now fully committed to the ruthlessness his trade demanded, decided to use one of the most controversial stratagems of his career.

Namely, human shields. Morgan "ordered ten or twelve ladders to be made, . . . so broad that three or four men at once might ascend by them." He then had his men bring him a selection of the prisoners, chosen with care to appeal to Spanish sensibilities: the august (Portobelo's mayor), the religious (friars and nuns), and the wretched (several elderly men). Shaking, the prisoners were marched at the head of a column that passed through the city streets and then out onto the open road that led to the castle. Now the Spanish could see what was happening: Their leading citizens screamed at them for God's sake not to shoot, while the pirates—ladders, grenades, and cutlasses in hand—crouched behind them. It was a terrible dilemma for the men inside, but finally the gunners opened up, spraying the particularly lethal chain shot (two small balls of iron connected by an iron chain, designed for ripping apart the masts of enemy ships, which would rotate with a terrifying keen before beheading or de-limbing anyone it caught in its path) into the advancing crowd. Two friars fell wounded, and the chain shot found one English victim. The rest of the party pushed the human shields out of the way and began hacking at the wooden gate with their axes and lighting it with their torches.

At the other side of the fort, a separate scenario was unfolding. A squadron of privateers had taken advantage of the spectacle unfolding at the main gate to slip away and stage a rearguard action. They scaled the walls of the fort with ladders while the Spanish fought them off with everything they could find, including "great quantities of stones and earthen pots full of combustible matter." It took an extreme form of courage to climb a ladder into the barrel of a musket, but this was the privateer style: fast, unrelenting attacks that depended as much on psychological terror as they did on sharpshooting. "We must have put up a pretty stiff fight," wrote Raveneau de Lussan of another battle; "in a word, we must have fought like regular *filibustiers.*" The men swarmed over the ramparts and cut down the last of the defenders in their section of the castle, then raised the infamous red flag. Red stood for "no quarter"; every enemy met under it would be sacrificed. None of the various black banners later used by the pirates—ones adorned with skull and crossbones, skeletons, hourglasses, spears, and bleeding hearts—was as terrible in the sight of their enemies, as black meant quarter would be given to those who surrendered. The pirates assaulting the front gate of the castle soon breached it and joined up with their compatriots. Seventy-four of the Spanish defenders lay dead, including the castellan. Morgan in the entire operation lost eighteen and thirty-two wounded, one-eighth of the number who had staged the attack. Roderick had a deep gash from a Spanish sword on his thigh; he was carried screaming to where the doctor was treating the wounded. Hours later, after the more badly wounded had been treated, the doctor held a sword in a blazing fire and then walked over to Roderick. Three buccaneers held him down as the doctor positioned the sword flat over the wound, then pressed it into the flesh. Roderick fainted from the pain, but the wound was cauterized. He'd sleep until the next day.

On the horizon, San Felipe remained in Spanish hands, but the pirates felt, with justification, that they'd accomplished enough for one day. They got so drunk that "fifty courageous men . . . might easily have retaken the city." There was soon news of far more than fifty men who were intent on doing just that; the Spanish would not take the capture of one of the Main's jewels so lightly. In Panama, just seventy miles away, a horseman brought the news of the city's capture to the president of Panama, Don Agustín de Bracamonte, the rider arriving just one day after Morgan had begun his siege of Portobelo. Bracamonte instantly knew how the capture would be received in Madrid: It was as if Morgan had seized a state mint and was now cavorting in its vaults. When reacting to crisis, Spanish administrators believed devoutly in consensus, drawing as many important people into the process as possible, thereby sharing out the blame and reducing their chances of being summoned back to Madrid and prison. Calling a junta, or council of war, would be standard operating procedure. But young and new in his position, Bracamonte ordered that the city's militias be organized immediately to save Portobelo. Drummers walked the city streets calling the men to arms. "I swore to God," Bracamonte testified, "that I would leave on Friday morning and be at Portobelo on Saturday."

Back in Portobelo only the final castle, San Felipe, stood between Morgan and the city's riches, and on the second morning of the raid he set out to take it peacefully. Two pirates in a canoe rowed out to the castle to deliver the surrender terms, but apparently Spanish honor was not quite dead: The canoe was met with a barrage from the castle guns. Morgan must have sighed wearily. The Spanish were defending a lost cause. The fortress held only 49 soldiers, and they were in bad shape, sharing just four pounds of bread and some wine among them. Nevertheless, this handful of men stood in the way of clear passage for his ships through the harbor mouth, so

Morgan sent 200 men in eleven canoes to take Felipe. Two Spanish prisoners were acting as guides (at gunpoint), and one of them, Sergeant Juan de Mallveguí, had a plan: After landing on the shore near the castle, he led the pirates along a path that would bring them directly in range of the gunners above. Seeing what was about to happen, his compadre, Alonzo Prieto, asked him whether he'd lost his mind. They'd die along with the infidels. Mallveguí was undeterred. It was very possible, he told his friend, that God would save them for their good intentions and, if he didn't, it was better that they should both die and kill all the English than the castle be lost. Prieto blanched. "Oh, no, amigo," he told Mallveguí, "I have a wife and children and I do not want to die."

It was a conversation between old Spain and new Spain. In the old country, Mallveguí's plan would have been considered a thing of genius. Death was its own moral drama for the Spanish; to die well was superior to living well. Mallveguí's plan would bring a public martyrdom (witnesses were essential, as they were needed to spread the word of one's behavior) connected to nobility—in fact, to the king himself, as it was his castle they'd be dying for. The honor this glorious death would bring to Mallveguí would be incalculable. The Spanish thought differently about these things: In the fifteenth century, the poet Jorge Manrique wrote that there were actually three stages to earthly existence, not two; to the temporal life and the afterlife he added the afterglow of one's name, which was most important of all. This "chivalric religion" was strong in Spain and had been for centuries. A witness to the kingdom's battles against the Italians wrote, "These crazy Spaniards have more regard for a bit of honor than for a thousand lives." But honor mattered far less in the New World, which was more sensual and more attuned to the here and now. Prieto wanted to go home and eat a beefsteak with his wife. The king was far away, and one could not eat or make love to honor.

The debate ended with the sound of wood on skull. The English had among them ex-captives who knew the town's layout well, and one of them, having realized what was happening, cracked the butt of his musket against Mallveguí's head. The pirates changed course and soon began probing the castle's defenses, sending one group of men to set fire to the main gate, while others staged a series of charges on the fort. The Spanish repulsed the assaults at the cost of only five men, but with little food and no reinforcements on the horizon, their situation was grim. The castellan huddled with a lieutenant and gave him some awful news: "We shall have to surrender." The soldier was shocked to hear those words from the mouth of a fellow Spaniard. Surrendering San Felipe, and thus Portobelo, to the heathens would be a sharp loss to the Catholic cause. "We must fight to the last man," the lieutenant said in reply. But the castellan ignored him and soon had put his name to the terms of surrender. The other officers were appalled, and the pirates added insult to injury when they reneged on the generous terms of capitulation, which preserved a shred of honor for the king's troops by allowing them to leave the castle with their muskets at their sides and their flags flying high, and stripped the men of all but their swords. The Spanish stumbled out of the castle like slaves. The castellan soon suffered an attack of conscience and was granted his last wish: poison, which he gulped down. The pirates who had dishonored him were soon extracting every last piece of eight from the locals and the men and women who had fled into the hinterlands.

They also came across some information to tantalize Modyford back in Jamaica. "The Prince of Monte Circa," Morgan later reported, "had been there with orders from the King of Spain to raise 2,200 men against us out of the Province of Panama." This was added to the earlier intelligence that Morgan had gathered on the approach to the city: Seventy men "had been pressed to go against Jamaica," a levy had been exacted to raise funds, and "considerable forces were expected from Vera Cruz and Campeachy, with materials of war to rendezvous at the Havannah. . . ." Morgan had his smoking gun: The plot against Jamaica was real.

The acting governor of Panama was the town's last hope. But

the Spanish Main had the habit of entangling bright ambitions in its tentacles and slowly squeezing the life out of them; almost immediately Governor Bracamonte's bold moves were countermanded by ennui and distance. His 800 men rushed out of the city into the trails to Portobelo without adequate supplies of food or armament, and days were wasted as the necessary rations caught up with the army. In that time the jungle began to work on the men. Some fell victim to the usual fevers, but others experienced more exotic tortures, like *mazamorra,* the excruciatingly painful foot disease that would centuries later nearly cripple Che Guevera's army on the approach to Havana. As they got closer to the besieged city, refugees met them and gave them news: The castles had fallen, and the pirates were everywhere and strong. Bracamonte sent for urgent assistance to Cartagena and Havana, where the Armada de Barlovento, with orders to exterminate the pirates, was stationed. Messengers flitted through the trees and set out in canoes to race down the coast. But Morgan was smarter than he'd been in Puerto del Príncipe and was not going to wait for the collected armies of the empire to arrive. Bracamonte would have to face Morgan alone.

So began an exchange of letters, with Morgan's first:

> Señor, tomorrow we plan to burn this city to the ground and then set sail with all the guns and munitions from the castles. With us we will take all our prisoners . . . and we will show them the same kindness that the English prisoners had received in this place.

The reference to the men in the dungeon was ominous, but Morgan's insouciant tone (he signed himself "Henrrique") must have been even more daunting for the Spanish noble. The pirate also included eight conditions for the surrender, including the price for the return of the city unburned: 350,000 pesos ($17.8 million), a tremendous fortune. Morgan proposed a unilateral cease-fire so that the ransom could be brought to the city, and he demanded that the castles surrender all of their artillery.

Bracamonte responded with consummate disdain. "I take you to be a pirate," he wrote back, "and I reply that the vassals of the King of Spain do not make treaties with inferior persons." He expressed nothing but contempt for the people of Portobelo, who had allowed themselves to be overcome by corsairs. "And if you decide to decapitate the prisoners," he finished, "you will excuse me for not ordering you to do it." Many pirates would have been goaded by Bracamonte's taunt; one can only imagine L'Ollonais's bug-eyed response. But Morgan felt himself to be a highborn gentleman, fully the equal of this Spanish noble. His answer was pure acid:

> Although your letter does not deserve a response, since you call me a pirate, despite that I am writing you these lines to ask you to come quickly. We are waiting for you with great pleasure and we have gunpowder and bullets with which to receive you. If you do not come very soon, we will, with the favour of God and our arms, come and visit you in Panama. Now, it is our intention to garrison the castles and save them for the King of England, my master, who since he had a mind to seize them, has also a mind to keep them. And since I do not believe that you have sufficient men to fight with me tomorrow, I will order all the poor prisoners to be freed so that they may to go to help you. As to whether I will order them decapitated, I respond that I will not. I am not so bloody as to kill people in cold blood, as the Spanish are used to doing.

Morgan *hated* being called a pirate; in his mind, he was a soldier of the English king. He'd come to the New World to make his name and his fortune from weaker men, not to be called a criminal.

As the missives shot back and forth, the governor was receiving his own intelligence from those who had escaped the pirates. A pair of Spanish sailors told him that the French defection from the pirate fleet after Puerto del Príncipe, when they'd supposedly gone to join L'Ollonais, was a ruse: They'd actually agreed with Morgan that the English would attack Portobelo, which would cause the leaders of

Panama to raise a rescue force. When that army left Panama, the French would attack the defenseless city. It was a terrifying thought to men who had left their women, their children, and their fortunes back in Panama. Bracamonte finally attacked, but it was a half-hearted attempt. Squads of men were sent into Portobelo to retrieve captives (and some Catholic images the English were sure to desecrate if they got the chance) but they were not to try to take back the castles. There was only one pitched battle, which Morgan exaggerated hugely: "The 5th day arrived the President of Panama with 3,000 men," he reported, "whom [the pirates] beat off with considerable damage."

Another barrage of letters passed between the adversaries after the attack. Bracamonte wrote, "In case he departed not suddenly with all his forces from Porto Bello, he ought to expect no quarter for himself nor his companions, when he should take them, as he hoped soon to do." Morgan shot back, "He would not deliver the castles before he had received the contribution-money he'd demanded. Which in case it were not paid down, he would certainly burn the whole city, and then leave it; demolishing beforehand the castles, and killing the prisoners."

Both armies were wilting under the assault from the diseases that made Portobelo so notorious. With the rumors of a French attack on Panama, Bracamonte felt the pressure to settle; he called a junta. One Spanish commander spoke out: "We find ourselves today with just eight hundred men, inexperienced and poorly armed people who, man for man, are not the equal of their enemies." It had to be said. The soldier continued, "I consider it impossible for us to recover Portobelo and its castles," he said. "We would get smashed to pieces if we attacked, whichever way we went." Many of the other officers chimed in their agreement. Bracamonte had at least provided a paper trail showing that he was only bowing to his subalterns' advice. Finally he relented.

An intermediary was sent into the city under a white flag and found that Morgan, who was also seeing his men sicken and die, would not budge from his price: 350,000 pesos, payable immediately, or the city would go up in flames. The negotiations continued back and forth with, at one point, the Spanish cheekily offering to fulfill half their proposed ransom of 100,000 pesos by a bill of exchange, payable sometime in the future by the kingdom's Italian financiers, the equivalent of giving a kidnapper a personal check. Morgan declined the offer. At length the deal was struck: 100,000 in ready cash. The booty was raised by the rich merchants of Panama and delivered by mule train: gold coins, twenty-seven silver bars, chests of silver plate, and a backbreaking load of silver cobs. One suspects that the incredible wealth generated by the mines undercut Spanish courage. Why fight when you can pay the hoodlums off? There would always be more silver flowing out of Potosí.

The pirates loaded it onto their ships, along with their own looted treasure and their captured slaves, and bade farewell to the town that had made them wealthy. Morgan had certainly learned from L'Ollonais on this expedition, but he also made a point to report on the pirates' gallantry. He claimed that the lady prisoners chose to travel with the pirates rather than go to the governor's camp, finding the Brethren "more tender of their honours" than the Spaniards. It's a wonder Morgan did not have them begging to return to Jamaica as the pirates' wives.

The Spanish had actually gotten a bargain in the Portobelo negotiations, but Morgan had proved he could attack the empire's strongholds at will. Now his reputation would grow immeasurably. Even the president of Panama, after the deal had been struck, succumbed to an "extreme admiration" for Morgan's feat of arms, "considering that four hundred men had been able to take such a great city, with so many strong castles: especially seeing they had no pieces of cannon, nor other great guns. . . ." He sent a messenger to Morgan, asking the admiral to send a sample of the arms that the pirates had used to take Portobelo. If the story is true, Morgan must have shaken his head: It was not the weapons that had proved themselves; it was the men and their leader. He sent a pistol and a few bullets back, with a note saying that the president should keep the guns for a year, after which he'd come to Panama himself "and fetch them away." The president, seeing that the pistol was a common type, sent it back with a gold ring and a warning: If Morgan came to Panama, he wouldn't find the success he'd achieved at Portobelo.

The president would have been well advised not to dare Henry Morgan.

The pirates sailed toward Port Royal with numbers running in their heads. They'd left Portobelo in a rush, and there had been no chance to total up the various "loans" they'd extracted from the Spanish; now the loot had been whisked away and was stored under guard. Did it add up to 100,000 pieces of eight? Or 150,000? Was 300,000 completely out of the question? The worth of the swag they carried fluctuated with the price of silver and gems in Port Royal and the going rate for slaves, so all the way back to Jamaica the men gossiped like accountants. Morgan was known to be dissatisfied with the ransom money, but they'd rifled the fabled city of Portobelo, for God's sake.

When the ships arrived at their rendezvous point off Cuba, the treasure was piled up, inventoried, and priced. When the total was announced, it came out to 250,000 pieces of eight, plus an unspecified but sizable sum to be gained from the slaves and trade goods they'd seized. In today's money the Brethren had taken about $12.5 million in Portobelo. The average pirate received about 240 pieces of eight, or $12,000, plus any compensation for injuries he might have suffered or bravery he might have displayed. In a time when an average laborer in London earned the annual equivalent of $3,500, the ordinary pirate had collected a minimum of three-plus years' wages in the expedition, enough to set himself up in business or buy a good piece of land or a long stretch of unrestrained debauchery. Anyone who lost an arm earned the equivalent of ten years of a London workingman's salary. Most of the pirates, like Roderick, would choose to spend their money on pure pleasure, a decision that will lead to one of the great mysteries at the heart of the Brotherhood.

✤   ✤   ✤

In Spain the news of Portobelo's fall and the pirates' rich haul was bitter news in a bitter season. The kingdom was bowing under the lash of one misfortune after another. The issue of money was especially galling: The Crown had been cash-strapped since the reign of Philip IV. There were days when the royal larder was nearly empty and the queen would be offered a rancid, midget chicken that "stank like a dead dog." During one meal, Queen Mariana had requested a bit of pastry and was told the castle's pastry chef would send no more desserts until an overdue bill was paid. Mariana, the daughter of the unimaginably rich Hapsburgs, took a ring off her finger and told her servant to go out into the street and find her a pastry at any cost. Her fool, appalled, gave the man a coin and put the ring back on her finger. It would embarrass everyone to have such a story get out.

Morgan's haul was not a huge loss to the Crown's coffers; when the treasure ships arrived, they brought millions in pieces of eight and gems, so to lose a few hundred thousand to a Welsh corsair was not a crippling blow. Besides, the local merchants and traders would be expected to make up their own losses. Only the capture of a galleon or the treasure waiting for a galleon at one of the New World ports would show an immediate result, such as the kingdom defaulting on its loans or canceling a major offensive in its European wars. But the Portobelo raid was important, because it showed the world that the empire was vulnerable. It would spawn a thousand imitators, it would embolden Spain's enemies, and it would weaken the infrastructure that delivered the treasure.

The king's poverty was shocking, but more dangerous to the Crown were the plots whirling around the misshapen head of Carlos II. Morgan's victory found Spain at peace with her enemies for the first time in memory, but at war with herself. As poor as it was in ready money, the Spanish Crown was still a thing of tremendous possibilities. And Carlos's bastard brother Don Juan wanted it for

himself. In 1668, as Morgan sacked Portobelo, the battle was coming
to a head. France's Louis XIV was receiving a steady stream of reports about Carlos's weaknesses. "The doctors do not foretell a long
life," a French diplomat wrote to the king. "And this seems to be
taken for granted in all calculations here." Louis and the emperor
of Austria had secretly agreed to carve up the kingdom and its empire
between them as soon as Carlos should die. And Don Juan certainly
had his half brother's frailty in mind. He was the illegitimate son
of Philip IV and La Calderona, an actress who had initially attracted
Philip because of a piece of intriguing gossip: The Duque de Medina
de las Torres told the king that lover after lover had failed to de-
flower the young thespian because of a certain anatomical oddity
(most likely a thick hymen). The king, who always wanted what
he could not have, marched straight off to see her, only to meet the
same fate as the other swains. After corrective surgery the two became lovers. Don Juan was born in 1629 and grew up to be one of
his father's favorites of the rumored thirty-two bastards he sired.
Philip recognized him in a way he never did his other illegitimate
children, and the special treatment gave Don Juan the idea that
he was destined for the greatest things. This certainty led him to
overestimate his power. The incident of the painting was just one
example.

Since a bastard could never be king, Don Juan decided that he
must marry one of his half sisters, the legitimate daughter, Maria
Theresa, and thus solve the problem of an heir. Even by the inces-
tuous standards of the Hapsburgs, this was beyond the pale. But
Don Juan was not to be put off by niceties. He even sent an inquiry to the august theologians at Belgium's famous Catholic university, Louvain, to see if the pope could grant an exception to
divine law and allow the marriage. Nothing came of the idea; in
1665, with the monarchy resting on the slender reed of Carlos II,
Don Juan revived it, with his half sister Margarita now in the role
of his bride. He had decided to broach the idea when his father invited him for a talk to decide whether the favorite son would be

named inquisitor general or archbishop of Toledo, both powerful positions. Knowing he was dying, Philip had been looking for a place for his strong, quick-minded favorite; and he must have considered himself a generous parent to think of bestowing such prestigious titles on a bastard. Little did he know what Don Juan held in store for him.

Don Juan had come up with a novel way of presenting the idea to his father: He'd give him a painting, a very special painting he'd done specifically for this occasion. In the curious portrait, Saturn, the Roman god of the harvest, watches his son Jupiter (the king of all the gods) and his daughter Juno (the protector of marriage) frolicking like lovers. In mythology Jupiter and Juno were married; even if Jupiter cheated scandalously on his sibling-wife. To make his point even clearer, Don Juan had given his own face to Jupiter, while Philip's mournful visage sat atop Saturn's body, and Juno became Margarita. Don Juan must have thought the work of art would give the idea of the scandalous union some precedent, along with a subtle message: *You and I, Father, are like gods; we are above human laws.* The painting does not survive, but it must have been grotesque. You have to sympathize with Philip as he was presented with the painting. He was a sick, exhausted man and probably expected some loving tribute from a dutiful son. Instead he was handed this piece of pornography, which would have brought back to him the (now much regretted) sexual voraciousness of his youth. After comprehension set in, Philip turned away in disgust. The awkward gesture had gone terribly wrong, and the king never agreed to see Don Juan again.

One would have expected Don Juan's ambition to be checked by his father's reaction to the marriage idea, but he was beyond embarrassment. With Philip IV fresh in his mausoleum, he turned his sights on the new reigning power, Queen Regent Mariana; specifically, he targeted the queen's confessor, Father Nithard, a Jesuit who was casually hated by the Spanish man in the street for being Austrian and so close to power. Don Juan tried gambit after gambit to draw the dour Jesuit close to him, first supporting the priest's pet cause: the making of the Immaculate Conception into an article of faith. The belief in Mother Mary's chastity had not been recognized as official dogma by the church (and would not be until 1854), and now Don Juan declared himself a wholesale advocate of its adoption. It was ironic that the amorous Don Juan would choose virginity as his secret devotion, but he revealed to Nithard that indeed it was. Nithard took him up as an ally. Don Juan also met secretly with the confessor to ask him to intervene on his behalf: His carnal urges were so strong that he could no longer observe the vow of chastity he'd sworn when he'd been appointed to religious offices. As usual with Don Juan, he had the perfect resolution: He'd resign all his offices, marry the niece of the elderly king of Poland, and take the throne for Spain when the monarch died. It was a pipe dream, as were so many of Don Juan's schemes, but it was wrong to underestimate him: He was young, dark, virile, and unmistakably Spanish. The folk identified with him against the pale, foreign-born Mariana.

Don Juan's maneuvers—including a marriage to the Archduchess Claudia Felicidad when the Polish option turned sour—all came to nothing. Meanwhile Nithard's star was rising even higher. When Mariana named him as inquisitor general, the Spanish were outraged. Sensing an opening, Don Juan played all his cards and arranged the Jesuit's murder. Before it could be carried out, the plot was exposed, and Don Juan fled to Barcelona, where his supporters gathered around him into a rebel army intent on purging the foreign influence from the Spanish throne. Spain seemed ready to tear itself apart. It was not until the pope stepped in that negotiations began. Don Juan set one condition for his cooperation: the removal of Nithard. "If by Monday the fellow has not left by the Palace door for ever," he said, "I shall go with my men on Tuesday and throw him out of the window." Nithard left Spain for Rome; Mariana was weakened, and Don Juan went into exile. At the center of these swirling currents of hate and intrigue, Carlos II sat as a spectator.

When told that Nithard was gone, he cried out, "What evil there is in the world!"

Queen Mariana retained power, but she was ruling with a five-man junta, with members from the grandees (the highest level of Spanish aristocracy), the church, and the state bureaucracy, while a subservient body, the Council of State, directed foreign affairs (at Mariana's direction). It was not a structure that lent itself to action. So it was with Portobelo. The *junta de guerra* of the Council of the Indies, a subset of a subset of the Council of State, met to discuss the raid on February 17, 1669. At first the junta declared all-out war on the Brethren: The galleons and the Armada de Barlovento, along with any available ships that could be mustered to the cause, would be sent out to retake Portobelo and smash the pirate ring. Not only that, the junta decreed that should the fleet find that Portobelo was in Spanish hands, they were then to turn and attack the source of all the trouble in the West Indies: Jamaica itself. As long as the island remained in English hands, the region would not be safe for the workings of empire.

The watering down began immediately: The galleons could not be spared, as the Crown was too dependent on Potosí silver to divert the ships to other missions. The supply could not be interrupted even to protect the supply. A commitment was made to strengthen the New World's defenses, but the governors of the Main had heard that before. Like any addict, Spain thought only of short-term fixes. "We certainly do not wish to impede [the treasure ships] . . . ," the council decided. "If we did, the Royal Treasury would be starved of its returns in silver and the Kingdom would be starved of its commerce that the silver fertilizes." And so the boats would keep hauling treasure and not hunting pirates.

The reaction to Portobelo exposed a hypocrisy: Spain's rulers told themselves they'd conquered the New World for God. But when it came time to truly defend it, it was the treasure that they wanted from the territories. The souls of the settlers, the land itself— they had to be sacrificed so that the kingdom could survive another day. The soldiers and administrators in the New World had learned a harsh lesson: Their safety was to be forfeited for the larger good. It was as cogs on the conveyor belt that delivered the king's treasure that they mattered.

Spain protested the capture of Portobelo vehemently. Months after the raid, an English diplomat was still getting an earful, "many storms and loud outcries . . . not only from ye Minister but from ye common people, upon the assaults on the maineland and depredations at sea committed on them by our privateers." But the English were in no mood to apologize. It was Spain who had devised the policy of "no peace beyond the line," and if the Spaniards wanted to live by the sword, they could die by it, too. The English responded to the protests by reciting instances of Spanish violences against their own: this ship captured, this captain detained or tortured, this town burned to the ground. They also brought up the plans for the invasion of Jamaica that Morgan had uncovered. "It is almost certain that the Spanish had full intention to attempt this island but could not get men," Modyford, Morgan's protector and ally, told his superior back in London. "And they still hold the same minds." When the Crown's share of the Portobelo loot was brought to London, the Spanish ambassador immediately filed a claim in the High Court of Admiralty for its return to Madrid and was just as quickly denied. Behind this tough stance was the king's desire to negotiate a new treaty that would allow the English a free hand to trade with the Spanish colonies. For that he'd sell out Morgan and the privateers in a moment. But until he got it, Spain needed the English more than they needed Spain.

The queen regent did have one original idea: to steal a page from England's book. Mariana decided that Spain would authorize its own privateers to fight Morgan and his ilk. It was a natural solution, but a rather embarrassing one for a nation that had not thought in terms of empowering individuals to do its work since the days of the conquistadors. Nevertheless, the queen had no other good options and sent notice to her governors that the vassals of her son the king were to move against the English "with every sort of hostility" and expel the enemy from the territories they'd captured. From now on, Morgan would have to deal not only with the Armada de Barlovento and the garrisons of the Main's towns but with any Spanish adventurers who cared to challenge him. One in particular would take the queen's letter to heart.

8

Rich and Wicked

The town that greeted Morgan on his return from Portobelo had changed as well, or simply intensified its character. Far from being the Protestant beacon that Oliver Cromwell had envisioned, Port Royal was now known as the undisputed Western capital of sin. Priests sent to the country reported back on "the Torrent of Wickedness and Vice rushing through" its streets. The thousands of pounds' worth of illicit goods the privateers brought with them would only accelerate the process: Port Royal was now the biggest, wickedest, richest, and most populous city in English America.

From the water it looked very much like any other English port, with only an occasional architectural note reminding that one was in Jamaica and not Yarmouth. Brick buildings with gambrel roofs lined the shore, dwarfed by the huge storehouses, three and four stories high; in a region where dwellings were relatively small, these buildings were mountainous. They were nests of activity on a typical day, with slaves or indentured servants straining against ropes, hoisting into the air fat hogsheads of rum, great chests filled with iron goods or the newest fashions from London. Other workers leaned out of the large windows cut into the storehouse walls, snagged the rope, and began pulling the cargo inside. The windows consumed and disgorged everything the empire produced: sugar, tortoiseshell, cowhides, pimento, ginger and cinnamon. The West Indies supplied luxuries to the expanding European market, including dyes that satisfied the booming demand for color. There was fustic for yellow and brazilwood and heart of logwood for red, the latter felled by the cutters in the Bay of Honduras, men who lived hard lives in the swamps and on riversides, where poisonous worms spiraled into the bottoms of their feet. There was indigo for blue, a dye mentioned as far back as Herodotus; the demand was so strong that the boats from India could not keep up, and farmers cultivated the native West Indian plants, which the Indians used to dye their hair. The city was so rich because it was both a trading post for a burgeoning empire and a large fencing operation for one of the most successful networks of thieves in history. The fledgling sugar plantations also added revenue, but their heyday was in the future.

Port Royal was a rollicking town, where rum drinking was so common that it seemed to flow through the town via a municipal pipe system into the mouths of the thirsty. Morals were not highly prized: Centuries later the merchants' scales used to weigh the privateers' gold and emeralds were found to be illegally weighted (in the merchants' favor, of course). Compare this to the scene that greeted another set of Morgans who arrived in the New World two decades before Henry. In 1636 the twenty-year-old Miles Morgan, direct ancestor of the financier J. P. Morgan, arrived in colonial Boston, sixteen years after the *Mayflower* landed. Along with his two brothers, Miles wanted to make a new life for himself in America, but the scene that greeted the Welsh immigrant must have given him a cold chill: The corpses of adulterers twisted slowly in the New England breeze, hung on crudely built scaffolds; those accused of blasphemy were paraded through the streets to the whipping post, where their backs were reddened in the name of the Lord; settlers had the letter *D* (for drunkard) sewn on their jackets, while if Miles looked close he could see signs of mutilation—cropped or missing ears, for example—meted out to those who challenged or spoke out against John Winthrop, the founder of the Massachusetts Bay Colony. Boston was a gray place, grim and deadly serious, where the pillory was used to cleanse the conscience of new Americans. It was in many ways still caught up in the religious struggles of the Old World.

In the colonies, among religious men and civic leaders, Port Royal was often a byword for evil. One Bostonian told an employee whom he was sending to Jamaica as his business agent to "keep your New England principles, . . . hear God's Word publicly preached every Lord's Day [and] be a Law to your self." But among the common people and those interested in a sweet deal on goods that had, so to speak, fallen off the back of a ship, the pirates were folk heroes. The pirates of the Caribbean brought much-needed trade goods pillaged from Spanish ships and sold them all over the colonies. Morgan had little or nothing to do with the North American territories, but other pirates sailed there regularly to trade and find refuge from authorities that had placed a price on their heads. One buccaneer, nicknamed "Breha," was so popular in Boston that when a dutiful citizen told the governor that the man and his posse were in town, his enraged neighbors nearly lynched the rat.

But Boston still considered itself a city on a hill. Port Royal had no such illusions about itself. The town that Cromwell and Gage had dreamed of had never materialized. Instead it had become the first Wild West town, fabulously on the make.

For the brahmins there were balls for the king's birthday, masquerades, "strolling puppet players" on a swing through the island; there was family life as well, because many of the richest men brought out their families, dressed as if they were strolling along the Thames on Sundays. Below them swirled the life of the pirates and their ilk; few of them had families or long-term plans. There weren't many activities that did not revolve around drinking. At the Bear Garden, bearbaiting and bullfighting were popular; cockfights drew a crowd, as did gambling and shooting games (though the games got more dangerous as the night progressed). Drinking was the national pastime. "The Spaniards wondered much at the sickness of our people," wrote Modyford, "until they knew the strength of their drinks, but then wondered more that they were not all dead." The local rum was fermented from crushed sugarcane and was famously potent; its nickname, "Kill Devil," accurately described a liquor that could knock riders from their horses. For ordinary pirates like Roderick, the ties to England had been loosened, and the memories of their working-class lives back in London grew dimmer by the week. Religion couldn't hold them; neither could law. One young Spaniard, José Crespo, who had been captured by English pirates and jailed in Port Royal, was interviewed by the Spanish after his escape. He estimated that only 1,000 of Port Royal's residents were professional soldiers and sailors, with the 4,000 to 5,000 other citizens being "seamen of little prestige, most of them scoundrels." When asked if the men had religion, Crespo replied that he saw them go off to church on Thursday and Friday, but at noon they'd return home to get drunk "without any regard or respect for married women."

Besides rum there was one other thing that lured the pirate on a spree: the female sex. In Port Royal, for the most part, that meant whores. And there was no more famous whore, and none more representative of the type of grandiose scoundrel that called the city home, than Mary Carleton. To understand the kind of person that ended up in Port Royal and made it such a sink of vice in the eyes of the world, one must know Mary.

She'd been born the daughter of a fiddler and raised in the rural English district of Canterbury, and she arrived in London in 1663 on a river barge. She'd no intention of remaining a lowborn nobody, however; like Morgan, like Roderick and many of the buccaneers, she wanted more out of life than the common round and didn't care if mere legality stood in her way. Her route was impersonation: As she entered the first drinking house that would admit her, the Exchange Tavern, Mary suddenly became Maria von Wolway, a German princess down on her luck. The story she made up seemingly moment to moment was a heartbreaking one: With "teares standing in her eyes," Mary revealed that she was a noble orphan who had been forced into an engagement with an old count against her will. She'd come to London, in disguise as an ordinary woman, leaving estates and mounds of jewels behind in Germany. She quickly married a local who thought he was getting a catch. When her scam was uncovered, her husband called her an "Out-landish Canterbury Monster," and she was prosecuted for bigamy (it turned out she'd married before). Her trial at the Old Bailey became a Restoration drama of the first order. Spectators fought to get seats; reporters hung on her every word; the gentry argued pro or con at dinner parties. Samuel Pepys was decidedly pro-Mary; he even visited her in prison.

Carleton's real sin was rising above her station. Like the privateers she'd soon consort with, she was unsatisfied with the fate she'd been allotted and she did whatever she had to do to change it. Moralists were outraged that she'd pretended to be royalty, but Mary shot back that if she was not noble by birthright, she was a fast learner. During the trial she detailed her "intent care and elegancy of learning, to which I have by great labour and industry attained."

Mary was acquitted of her crimes and became a public personality, in the style of the times. She published her own pamphlets, in which she stuck to her story. She went onstage, of course, in a play written for her called *The German Princess* (Pepys panned it). But when she was caught in yet another marriage, Mary was shipped off to Port Royal, which was the last stop for many English criminals sentenced to exile. There she dropped the act and went into prostitution. Mary would not arrive until 1671, in the wake of Morgan's greatest triumph, but she embodied the wide-open days of the pirates there. She joined other professionals whose names basically gave their stories: Buttock-de-Clink Jenny, Salt-Beef Peg, and No-Conscience Nan.

To keep her image fresh in her public's mind, Mary sent back a letter from Port Royal. "I could not in reason expect much civility from the Commander of Seamen of the Ship," she told her old mates. "Yet contrary to all expectation I was treated like my self, I mean a Princess." On her arrival at the city, crowds swarmed around her, "especially the looser sort of persons," and competed to see who could pay her the bigger compliment. She was amazed to see the town packed with London underworld figures, "so many of my acquaintance," but quickly realized that this was the end of the line for her type. Mary joined other waterfront denizens in the business of swindling buccaneers, and she found plenty of business among Morgan's men. As she arrived, the pirates blew into town and went on a binge: "Such hath their success been in some late dangerous exploits," she reported, "that it hath blown their excesses to that height of expence, that they have almost delug'd this place in liquor." She called the pirates "Bully-Ruffins" and said the only danger she faced was either drowning in rum or being killed with the buccaneers' kindness.

It was a fantasy, of course. Mary would have worked hard for her pieces of eight in the taverns that lined the harbor street. She painted the pirates, tongue in cheek, as gentlemen rogues; but pirates stinking drunk on Kill Devil would not have been gentle customers. An old song that Mary most likely heard in her rounds was not far off in its description of the average pirate:

> *Him cheat him friend of him last guinea,*
> *Him kill both friar and priest — O dear!*
> *Him cut de t'roat of piccaninny*
> *Bloody, bloody buccaneer!*

Still, as the most famous whore in the West Indies, Mary would have commanded a high price, and she probably ended up with more of the pirates' money than they did. More likely than not, she met Morgan; certainly she met his men. "A stout frigate she was," wrote one of her chroniclers, "or else she never could have endured so many batteries and assaults. A woman of unexampled modesty, if she may be her own herald. But she was as common as a barber's chair: no sooner was one out, but another was in. Cunning crafty, subtle, and hot in the pursuit of her intended designs." She didn't lack for customers.

Mary was Port Royal personified. In the dusty towns of the Spanish New World, a person could hope to rise only one station in life, at most. The system discouraged risk taking and enterprise.

Mary, on the other hand, had vaulted from the very bottom of English society straight to celebrity by imagination and hard work. Her life simply would not have been possible in the Spanish system.

It was appropriate that Mary ended up in Henry Morgan's home. It was a frontier town full of the empire's discards given one last chance at realizing their fortune. "There have been few cities in the world," wrote one historian of the place, "where the thirst of wealth and pleasure had united more opulence and more corruption." In its shops every form of currency that flowed through the Spanish Empire could be found: pieces of eight, crude cobs, piastres, golden moidores, cross money, newly minted doubloons. In fact, the haul from Portobelo was so enormous that the piece of eight was declared legal tender in Jamaica. But if you traveled inland, another Jamaica presented itself that could make the port town seem almost giddily innocent. The tightly packed streets of Port Royal gave way to the sprawling plantations. Sugar would be to England what silver was to Spain: the reason for sustaining the New World empire. Various cash crops had been tried in the islands, but West Indian tobacco could never compete with the rich Virginia variety. Sugar was a difficult crop and required backbreaking work from an army of indentured servants and slaves to produce. The land had to be cleared, hoed, weeded, dewormed, degrubbed, planted, tended with care. Small planters desperate not to sink back down into servitude drove their servants pitilessly, beating them with cudgels or whacking them with sticks when they did not keep up, until the white men's backs blistered and ran with pus. The men slept in tiny shacks "rather like stoves than houses." They needed permits to travel around the island to meet a friend or a sweetheart, and for every two hours they were off the plantation, they had to donate an extra month of servitude. When they rebelled against the treatment, even minor offenders received harsh sentences from planters whose dreams and gossip were filled with scenes of uprising: When one John Wiborne published a book that spoke out against a member of the Barbadian elite, he was sentenced to have his ears nailed to the pillory; after they took him down from this minor crucifixion, he was whipped and branded. Disease killed between a third and a half of the bondsmen before they finished their term, and if they died, their bodies were tossed into unmarked holes. When these men finally earned their freedom, they found that there was little demand for unskilled laborers like themselves; often they had to sell themselves back into servitude just to eat.

The plantations became factories for rebels and pirates; servants who were sick to death of the hellish life sneaked away to the ships waiting in Port Royal's harbor. The pirates offered the only other outlet for men who were tired of being beaten. Port Royal was the way station: Indentured servants and slaves were trundled off the boats arriving in the harbor by day. By night, runaways from the interior would appear in the town, looking to join a pirate crew. The planters constantly complained that the privateers were a menace and drained off badly needed manpower from their fields. But the planters had no army. Little did the pirates know that their long-term enemies were not the Spanish but these planters and merchants who slapped their backs and bought their illicit goods at cut rates. As the plantations grew more and more profitable, as the global model of trade built on the currency minted from Potosí silver solidified and grew, the white gold produced by black slaves and poor "buckras," or white men, became more valuable than the latest haul of pirate booty.

The Brethren believed they were helping to kill off an oppressive system—the Spanish Empire—as they enriched themselves. But they were also helping to bring into being a different system that would become their worst enemy.

The privateers were the sole protection for Jamaica; the English Crown could not afford to send warships to Jamaica—or to any of their colonies, for that matter—and so the privateers became the navy, the intelligence service, and the infantry. Ever fearful of attack from the Spanish or French, the merchants and planters relied on Henry Morgan and his men for protection. The pirates "were very welcome guests at Jamaica," one Jamaica historian recounts; "the planters and men in power caressed Morgan, while the inferior sort contrived every sort of bait to drain his associates of their money."

And the pirates were willing; they sprayed pesos around the harbor as if the money were water. Portobelo stood out in Morgan's résumé for one reason: loot. And the privateers did their best to distribute it in the vice industries of their hometown. This is perhaps the greatest mystery the pirates have left us: why they spent their money the way they did. Men like our representative pirate, Roderick, endured incredible hardship to get their rewards: They were felled by malaria, beheaded by Indians, separated from loved ones, excommunicated from the church, hanged from gallows; they ate rats, dogs, grass, leather sheaths, or nothing at all; they had poisoned arrows shot at them, flaming pots of oil dumped on their heads, pikes thrust through their entrails, and were faced with "instruments made especially for cutting off the legs" of those attacking Spanish forts; they were stung by scorpions, bitten by poisonous snakes, or drowned (one out of seven ships that sailed out of harbors in the age of sail were never seen again); they hacked their way through godforsaken jungles and marched or paddled their way through crocodile-infested swamps and across half of the Spanish Main. Despite the happy-go-lucky image, pirates were hunted like vermin, and the memories of that fear often stayed with them for years. One pirate reported symptoms among his comrades similar to shell shock after they arrived home in France. "Some of our men whose spirits were so misguided," he wrote, "and whose minds had given way from the suffering they'd experienced to such an extent that they were always imagining Spaniards were coming, upon sighting from the deck of the boat some men on horseback riding along the seashore got out their arms ready to fire thinking they were enemies." They did all this in the hopes of getting a small fortune, and, once they did, an astonishing number of them immediately gambled and whored the money away within a matter of days. "Men who had been the owners of millions," wrote one observer, "were in a brief space totally ruined, and finding themselves destitute even of raiment and provisions, returned again to sea."

Poor men live by a different logic than those who have never starved; being rich means spending money on all those things one has been denied, not soberly stashing the money away for future needs. Woodes Rogers, another privateer turned pirate hunter, offered some corsairs plots of land if they'd give up the profession and build a home on it. He was hoping to make them into prosperous farmers, but many refused the offer or built only miserable shacks and planted just enough to get by. "For work they mortally hate it," wrote Rogers. "They thus live, poorly and indolently, seeming content, and pray for wrecks or pirates." But the pirates went beyond any Lotto winner or Bolivian miner who hits a rich vein: L'Ollonais's men were reported to have blown through 260,000 pieces of eight, or $13.5 million in today's dollars, in three short weeks after one of their expeditions, "having spent it all in things of little value, or at play either cards or dice." One buccaneer was said to have showered a whore with 500 pieces of eight, or about $25,000, just to watch her strip; others, according to a historian of Jamaica, went through 2,000 or 3,000 pieces of eight in a single night. The men practically threw the money away with contempt. And when they weren't spending, they were giving the stuff away. "Among themselves, and to each other, these Pirates are extremely liberal and free," Esquemeling wrote, in an observation that was backed by other chroniclers of the pirate life. "If any one of them has lost all his goods, which often happens in their manner of life, they freely give him, and have him partake of what they have."

Why, when they'd earned it at so high a cost? In fact, there were only a few options for the common pirate who came into money. With his hefty shares, Henry Morgan could (and did) buy large estates and stock them with slaves; other captains or even thrifty buccaneers sailed back to England and bought property. But on his share a common pirate would have to buy a smaller plot in Jamaica, purchase some cheap indentured servants, watch them closely, whip them when needed, and husband his money. In other words, become a kind of tight-fisted farmer with regular hours and work seven days a week. He might set up shop in town, but these were uneducated men used to a life of drinking and freedom. How could they go and buy a grocer's stall and nickel-and-dime their way to a living? It went against the whole joy of being a pirate. After years in the life, pirates had become accustomed to long periods of drunken tedium interrupted by binges of extreme violence and spending. If they had been meant to be shopkeepers or yeoman farmers, they would never have ended up on Henry Morgan's ship in the first place.

Now walking with a pronounced limp from the wound suffered at Portobelo, the twenty-seven-year-old Roderick dreamed of gushers of wine, of staining his newly grown beard with groaning platters of meat running with savory juices, of specific prostitutes and specific acts he wished to commit with them. The silver begged to be spent. Money attached him to the land; there was the danger he could buy a piece of property or do something equally respectable and leave the pirate life forever if he didn't get rid of it now. And there was no better town in the world to be sailing into on a pile of gold than hot Port Royal; Roderick had in his short time in the Brethren lost sight of anything besides the next score, the next woman, the next adventure. He dealt only in immediate gratifications; it was almost as if the pirate code had short-circuited his ability to think of a regular life outside it.

Treasure had transformed the Spanish Empire and heightened its flaws. It did the same thing to the pirates: From being ragamuffins scraping out a living on the edge of civilization, they had become the avatars of the New World. No one was freer than they were, but the easy money meant they never had to think beyond the next stake. However, forces were gathering that would end their reign, and there was a turncoat in their midst who would help bring their flashy ride to an end.

In the meantime Port Royal was their playground, and it was earning a reputation as the baddest place in the Americas. "This town is the Sodom of the New World," wrote one clergyman, "and since the majority of its population consists of pirates, cutthroats, whores and some of the vilest persons in the whole of the world, I felt my permanence there was of no use and I could better preach the Word of God elsewhere among a better sort of folk." He was as good as his word, leaving Jamaica on the same ship that had brought him. Every few years it seemed a preacher would come through town and, horrified at what he saw, would predict that God would destroy the city.

It was the biblical Sodom and its sister city Gomorrah to which the Jamaican port was compared. The two ancient towns had sat on a beautiful plain near the Jordan River. Although they became the byword for vice, Sodom and Gomorrah were accused of specific crimes: "She and her daughters were arrogant, overfed and unconcerned," the accusation goes in Ezekiel 16:49. "They did not help the poor and needy." To these charges were added sexual offenses (which means either homosexuality or rape, depending on which scholars you believe) and inhospitality. As with Port Royal, the towns had a bad reputation that even reached the ears of God. "The outcry . . . is so great and their sin so grievous," the Lord tells Abraham, that he was forced to investigate the rumors. Once he'd seen the sinful ways of the towns' rich inhabitants, he rained down burning sulfur on them and wiped Sodom and Gomorrah utterly off the face of the earth. The devastation was so complete that when the Allies decided to launch the most destructive aerial bombing campaign in history to that point, against the city of Hamburg in 1943, they named the raid Operation Gomorrah.

Every society must have its Sodom, the place that absorbs the evil expelled from more righteous communities. In the Bible it was Sodom. In the modern world, New York, Las Vegas, and other metropolises have played the role. In the late 1600s, in the New World, it was Port Royal.

The city's days were, it was believed, numbered in the hundreds, and at times it seemed as if the moment of judgment were at hand. The English had been on the island for a decade and a half, and by now they noticed that the notoriously tremor-ridden sands of Port

Royal were restless, especially during spells of hot weather. The earth would tremble under their feet when the heat came, and the longer the spells lasted, the more severe the tremor.

The earth was largely a mystery to the seventeenth-century mind. But the leading theory centered on caves: Many "natural philosophers" (there was no such thing as a "scientist" in the late 1600s) believed that the earth was honeycombed with caves and caverns, in which tremendous gales swept back and forth, looking for a place to escape from the brimstone-filled underworld. In 1692 the astrologer Edmund Halley would expand the cavern idea to a much more intriguing theory, proposing that the planet consisted of four separate spheres: Inside the outer crust were three smaller planets, the size of Mars, Venus, and Mercury, respectively, each placed inside the other like Russian *matryoshka* dolls and each spinning at its own rate on its own eccentric axis.

The theory of tectonic plates was, of course, centuries away. That model would not have calmed Port Royalists, for in fact the city lay in a major tectonic region laced with faults and active volcanoes. The Caribbean Plate that Jamaica sits on dates back tens of millions of years, to when molten rock from the earth's mantle surged up into the waters of a nameless sea. For millennia it has been grinding, slipping, and bucking against three other plates, the North American, the South American, and the Cocos. The border with the North American Plate lies just off the northern coast of Jamaica; that huge mass is pushing west, while the Caribbean moves east. The resulting fault is a treacherous "strike-slip" zone, prone to low tremors and shattering earthquakes.

All that the Jamaican citizen knew was that something odd was happening beneath his city.

9

An Amateur English Theatrical

After a few weeks in port, most of the pirates had exhausted their credit in the taverns and with the street-walkers. Roderick, now sporting a beard, a new gold ear-ring, and a scar of unknown origin across his cheek, was nearly broke. He'd been forced to sell his pistols to pay off his debts and had slept rough on the beach for a few nights. He and other bucca-neers came to Morgan, practically demanding another mission. There was a certain logic to the careers of pirate captains: Their ex-peditions tended to become progressively more ambitious after each success. Like any businessman, a privateer needed richer and richer targets to sustain the momentum of his own growing reputation. And there was something in the pirate code that disdained conserva-tive business plans. Morgan now had in mind an even more danger-ous target: Cartagena. It was the biggest port in Spain's vast empire; here was collected the treasure from all of Peru. If in modern-day terms Portobelo was Fort Knox, Cartagena was New York, the center of trade and culture. But it was also a fortress. After Drake and his English and French peers had ransacked the city in the late 1500s, the Spanish Crown had begun a massive building program that studded the lagoons that led to the city with castles and forts, which were now manned by 400 soldiers and fifty cannon. The story was told that one of the kings of Spain looked out his westward-facing window one day and remarked that he expected to see the battlements of Cartagena visible across the ocean, as he'd spent so many fortunes building them.

It was an audacious target for Morgan. If he took Cartagena, Morgan would prove he was the strongest force in the New World, bar none. And become filthy rich in the process.

Like L'Ollonais in the wake of his great raids, Morgan and his captains had little trouble raising men. "There flocked to them great numbers of other pirates," writes Esquemeling, "both French and English, by reason of the name of Captain Morgan was now rendered famous in all the neighbouring countries, for the great enterprizes he had performed." Roderick was now considered a veteran privateer, and he signed up for the next expedition without a second thought. He admired Morgan, the way he'd walk into one of the taverns and buy a round of drinks for everyone in the place and then match any of them rumbullion for rumbullion. He didn't put on airs. He was one of them, but he wasn't, too—he could speak eloquently, as if from a book, and he snapped out commands with the assurance they'd be obeyed immediately. Roderick had never been invited to the admiral's estate, but he'd listened to him tell stories of the English Civil War at a tavern and had caught the great man's eye and nodded. It was a moment he relived again and again. Despite his poor background, Roderick had pressed into him an unthinking respect for the gentry, and Morgan had a touch of the gentleman about him. Roderick, despite his newfound self-regard, respected it. That is, so long as Morgan produced.

As the admiral gathered in his fleet at Cow Island, off Hispaniola, the English government showed its appreciation in the form of the *Oxford*, a twelve-year-old, seventy-two-foot frigate armed with twenty-six guns and 125 men that had been sent over "for the defence of his Majesty's plantation of Jamaica, and suppressing the insolence of privateers upon that coast." It was the Crown's first

material gesture of support for the Brethren. Morgan was enchanted with the vessel; it immediately became the most powerful
pirate ship in the Caribbean, and he made it his flagship. The *Oxford*
was exactly the kind of floating arsenal needed to give him a fighting
chance at Cartagena.

There was some dissension between the English and French pirates in the fleet, which the appearance of the *Oxford* only heightened. As soon as the frigate arrived at Cow Island, its captain
arrested the crew of the French ship *Le Cerf Volant*, who had been accused of robbery and piracy by a Virginian captain. (The fine line
between privateering with a commission and piracy without one was
murky—the famous privateer William Dampier found that some
French "commissions" carried by so-called privateers were actually
hunting licenses.) The French were hauled back to Port Royal,
where the captain was sentenced to death and the boat renamed
Satisfaction, at which point both it and the *Oxford* returned to Cow
Island, ready for duty. The French captain's harsh sentence was
later commuted, but the incident rankled in the Gallic camp.

With the fleet now at twelve ships and 900 men, Morgan was
ready to begin. On the first day of 1669, he sent a message to the
other ships' captains that the next day they'd hold their war council
aboard the *Oxford*. The morning came, and the captains boarded the
spacious vessel and began their deliberations. Names flew back and
forth, but the bulk of the ship that lay under their feet practically demanded they try Cartagena, and finally Morgan's wish was approved. Now the punch bowl was replenished and the party began
in earnest, one whose atmosphere was heightened by the glow
of certain riches that lay just over the horizon. "They began on
board the great ship to feast one another for joy of their new voyage
and happy council," Esquemeling writes, describing a scene echoed
in other privateer narratives. "They drank many healths and dis-
charged many guns, as the common sign of mirth among seamen
used to be." They fired guns under the table, another buccaneer tradition. They toasted 1669; they toasted Cartagena; they toasted the

king; they toasted the whores back in Port Royal. They drank themselves insensible.

As the mellow Caribbean dusk descended, candles were brought out. The ship echoed with laughter and shouts in different languages; since pirates were fond of music, it's likely the sound of a fiddle or a guitar went floating over the water toward the dark woods of Hispaniola. On deck the spidery white rigging would suddenly be illuminated with a flash of a pistol shot as the pirates fired away at the stars. The smell of burnt powder drifted down into the ship's cabin, where the gregarious Morgan was playing host and telling his guests to sit down to a lavish (by pirate standards) dinner. It was going to be a long night, and they needed to fortify themselves, as this would be their last unhurried meal before the rigors of the approach to Cartagena. The flashes of pistol shots continued; the singing never stopped. And then a huge white flash followed by a shocking concussion blinded the captains, and they were lifted into the air and then down into the sea, with splinters of the *Oxford* showering upon their heads. The living surfaced and floated on the black water for a moment, pieces of burning sail drifting down, their eardrums shattered or ringing with the echo of the massive boom. Limbs of the men they had been sitting next to a moment ago bobbed on the waves.

The ship's magazines had exploded, touched off by an errant spark, "the negligence of the gunner" or (some said) the French, still nursing their grievance. The latter seems unlikely, as the saboteurs would have gone up with the ship. But the magnificent *Oxford* was gone, along with 200 of its men. Only ten buccaneers had survived the blast. Miraculously, Morgan and the other captains who had been sitting on his side of the cabin table had all come away shaken but alive. One by one they were picked out of the water by the other ships in the fleet. (Roderick had been lying drunk on the deck of a smaller ship and had shot bolt upright when the *Oxford* went off, then rushed to join in the rescue.) The pirates spent little time mourning. When Morgan dispatched boats to search for the bodies of the dead, it was "not out of any design of affording them Christian burial, but only to obtain the spoil of their clothes and other attire." If the dead were wearing gold rings, their bloated fingers were snipped off with a cutlass and the jewelry collected, while the bodies were left "exposed to the voracity of the monsters of the sea."

The Spanish rejoiced at the news of the *Oxford*'s demise, especially the citizens of Cartagena. They credited their patron saint, Nuestra Señora de Popa, with the deliverance; she dwelled in the convent that looked over the city from a high hill that can be seen well out to sea. For decades to come, any Cartagena schoolboy could tell you that the morning after the explosion the saint was seen returning over the water from the direction of Hispaniola, her clothes wet and torn, her face lined with exhaustion from the work she'd done against the diabolical Morgan.

The disaster forced a change in the privateers' plans; Cartagena was no longer a realistic target without the *Oxford* and the extra men. Morgan sent out a call for more ships and buccaneers and set up a rendezvous for a month in the future. Meanwhile he sought out supplies, even landing on Santo Domingo in Hispaniola to hunt for some of its famous cows. The Spanish, who knew that Morgan was resupplying on the island, set a trap for fifty of his men by assembling a great herd to draw the privateers in as the Spanish watched from a hiding place. At a signal, the soldiers attacked. "They set upon them with all fury imaginable," Esquemeling tells us. "Crying, *Mata, mata!* that is, *Kill, kill.*" The privateers ran for their lives.

The *Oxford* accident hadn't damaged the admiral's reputation; in fact, his miraculous escape probably burnished his name as an invincible leader among the buccaneers. "While Morgan was safe," the historian Leslie writes, "they thought success sure." Morgan was less sanguine; a "huge impatience" was gnawing at him. Too many things could go wrong on a pirate expedition, as the *Oxford* disaster proved, as the lesson of L'Ollonais reinforced. After resupplying the ships, he set out for the rendezvous, Saona Island. When Morgan arrived weeks later, the news was not good. Saona lay at the southeast end of Hispaniola toward Puerto Rico, directly north across the North Sea

(now known as the Caribbean Sea) of the Gulf of Venezuela, meaning that the privateers, once assembled, could swoop straight down
into the heart of the Spanish Main. But it was also windward of Port
Royal and the other major pirate haunts, which meant that the ships
had to tack and beat against the trade winds to get there. It was a
rugged haul, especially in the small, open ships that offered little protection from the whipping spray; three of the ships gave up, claiming
that their vessels could not handle the pounding. "Sails chafed and
stitching rotted in the alternate bright sun and heavy rain," writes
Morgan biographer Dudley Pope, "hull planking spewed caulking,
rigging stretched, chafed and parted, men became worn out, unable
to remember a time when they were not crashing to windward, their
ships rolling violently and pitching as though every wave was a cliff
edge over which they were falling." The Spanish seemed to be stalk-
ing Morgan: Another mission to Hispaniola for supplies returned
empty-handed after encountering a strong contingent of soldiers,
"now so vigilant and in such good posture of defence" that it was not
worth the risk of battle. Morgan's very success was making him
a target.

The Welshman finally decided he'd have to set out with the assets at hand: 500 men in eight ships. Morgan had been thinking of
ransacking Venezuela's eastern shores, "having hitherto resolved to
cruize upon the coasts of Caracas, and plunder all the towns and vil-
lages he could meet," but the ships had taken a beating already, and
there was little appetite for a long slog to windward. He began talking with a French captain who had served with L'Ollonais in his
glory days, when the Gallic terror had pillaged the city of Maracaibo
for 260,000 pesos. This man knew the approach to the city, its "entries, passages, forces and means," and he convinced Morgan that
the fleet was perfect for the mission. And besides, it had been two
years since L'Ollonais's raid.

The cities of the Spanish New World were amazingly resilient.
The elite tended to diversify their holdings: They might have interests in agriculture, in hides or textiles, in silver recovery, in real estate and other concerns. The buccaneers could devastate one aspect

of their wealth, but they rarely stayed around long enough to damage everything. And the cheap labor and innate riches of the treasure territories meant that there was always another mule train of silver on the way. In the meantime governors would write Madrid reporting the raid and asking for engineers to be sent out and new forts and castles to be built, but there was a limit to what could be done. Cities often had to be located where they were to accommodate the treasure fleets or other business of the empire, and if they were moved, the buccaneers would find the new locations anyway (as was the case with a future Morgan target, Panama). Combining far-flung towns didn't fit the needs of the king, and that was paramount—one needed his permission to relocate. Buccaneers knew that the coffers of their favorite towns replenished quickly, and they tended to let cities lie fallow until jewelry boxes and hidden reserves could be filled again. The French had pillaged Maracaibo a full two years earlier. It was ready.

The fleet set off, dropping due south with the trade winds to port. They sighted the island of Ruba (now Aruba) and stopped for supplies: wood from the island's forests and sheep and goats from the local Indians. Two days later the ships set off for the Gulf of Venezuela; they were on war footing now and sailed only at night. By morning they'd entered the vast gulf, a large bay on top connected to the inland lake named Laguna de Maracaibo by a narrow channel, the whole formation from above looking like a figure eight, with the gulf on top and the lake below. The gulf is a notorious ship eater; its shallow waters hide sandbars, and its featureless coast makes navigation difficult, especially for the inexperienced. Luckily, the French captain knew the waters well and guided the fleet to an anchorage just off the three islands lying across the twelve-foot-deep channel that led to the bay. There they spent the night. The next morning the navigators would have to slalom between two of the islands, San Carlos and Zapara, without wrecking. It would be a pretty piece of sailing.

But by first light Morgan knew he had bigger problems. After

L'Ollonais's raid the Spanish had built a new fort on the eastern shores of San Carlos, and as the sun rose, Morgan realized he'd have to pass under the fortress's eleven guns before he could reach the bay. Now the loss of the *Oxford* made itself felt; Morgan's flagship was the fourteen-gun frigate *Lilly*. He could have used the extra dozen cannon of his former vessel, but there was nothing else except to run the channel and take their chances. The Spanish had chosen the castle's location brilliantly, but as usual they'd failed to provide enough money to staff it. Inside, there were just nine men, no doubt astonished by the sudden appearance of the long-dreaded privateers in their peaceful cay. But they knew their duty and began furiously loading and firing the eleven guns as Morgan sailed up to the beach and offloaded his men in the teeth of the barrage, while his gunners provided covering fire. "The dispute continued very hot on both sides," says Esquemeling, whose account is seconded by Spanish reports of a vigorous resistance, "being managed with huge courage and valour from morning till dark night." The pirates hit the beach with Spanish ball kicking up spray as they landed and sought the only cover they could find: a ridge of sand. The buccaneers were targets in a firing gallery until they could get within musket range. The afternoon breeze kicked up in the middle of their assault, and its keen raised itself notch by notch until it was a full-blown squall, making communicating and loading the privateers' guns much more difficult, as the Spanish poured ball and shot down on the shapes below. Morgan waited until dusk to give his approach the cover of darkness and, as soon as the sun had set, burst for the fortress walls. Strangely, the Spanish held their fire. Pistol cocked, Roderick hugged the stone wall as the pirates approached. Finally they found a gate. Morgan signaled his men, reared back, and kicked the gate with all his force. It swung open; after the stealth of their approach, it had been unlocked. The Spanish could do their sums as well as anyone; none of them wanted to spend a night being carved up by the likes of L'Ollonais. They'd fired one last volley, jumped into a boat, and headed for town to raise the alarm. When Morgan's men entered the fort, they found it echoing with the sound of surf on the beach.

Roderick and his mates hallooed into the dark and slapped one another's backs in delight: Maracaibo now lay open to them. But Morgan was warier; suspicious of a fort left so invitingly empty, he began to search it room by room. Soon he smelled something acrid and quickly went running toward the source. In the fortress magazine, he found what he was looking for: a lit fuse laid into a trail of powder that led straight to the barrels of gunpowder. He stamped it out, with only an inch and a few minutes to spare. Morgan's touch had returned; he'd saved almost half his men's lives. He then ordered the cannon spiked, which involved driving a piece of sharpened metal into the touchhole, rendering it unusable, and buried in the sand, so that any reinforcements could not use them to blast Morgan's ships on their way home. The fort yielded up huge quantities of powder, always a favorite piece of pirate booty on the way to a fight, and a stash of military hardware: muskets, flints, ramrods. It was like the moment in a gangster film when the bad guys raid the precinct armory and start handing out the guns: Whatever Maracaibo had in store for the pirates, they'd be armed to the teeth.

The supplies were divvied up and transported to the ships, which had been brought to anchor near the San Carlos beach. The next morning the ships set sail for their target, but twenty miles from Maracaibo their way was soon blocked by a shallow bank of deadly quicksand that the ships could not pass. Maracaibo's natural defenses were proving more formidable than her human ones. Morgan's second trademark was forced into play: canoes. They were lowered into the water, and the men dropped down onto their benches and pulled out their paddles. The Brethren rowed into a stiff wind and soon found the shore at the foot of the fort named de la Barra. Yesterday's script was repeated: a beach landing, a cautious approach, an empty fort. The locals had escaped into the woods.

It was savages like L'Ollonais who made such running-in-panic-before-the-barbarians possible. Indeed the Spaniards told awful

tales about the pirates to their children and even came to believe the
stories themselves. It was said the privateers were strange creatures
"formed like monkeys" or "mad dogs" who could flit soundlessly
through a jungle and then appear in a village like sorcerers, where
they'd help themselves to a meal of townspeople. "This caused them
to conceive a keen horrore and aversion for us," recalled the gallant
French pirate Raveneau de Lussan. He gave as an example one incident when he was escorting a Spanish woman who kept glancing
nervously at him as they walked. Finally she could stand it in no
longer. "Sir," she cried, "for the love of God, do not eat me!"

The Maracaiboans had not waited around to see if the pirates
really did want to eat them. On hearing of Morgan's approach, the
captain of the city's defenses had sent drummers to muster the men
to defend it and rang the war bell summoning volunteers. The bell
tolled again and again, echoing out over a town that seemed suddenly deserted and silent. Only a handful of citizens showed up. "It
was discovered that no more than ten or twelve men had come to
help him," a Spanish report on the invasion said. "The witness who
was present heard the captain curse some people for having left him
alone." The captain tried again, this time hanging two banners that
told the town's four hundred families that "there will be the penalty
of death for traitors of the Realm of Spain." Still, when Morgan arrived, Maracaibo was a ghost town. Roderick led a squad of men
who searched every corner of the eastern section of the town, looking for people who "might offend them unawares," but the wind
whistled through empty doorways and swung doors left ajar. The
men chose houses for themselves and chose the church as their
headquarters, where they committed "many insolent actions." This
probably referred to the English habit of desecrating captured
churches, much to the horror of their French allies. Roderick and
some mates entered one Spanish church and raced up to the altar,
slashing at the crucifixes with their sabers, knocking the heads off
statues of saints, and bending their own heads in mock prayer before
upending the altar. It was hilarious, but Roderick called a halt to it
when he was nearly holed by a bullet meant for an image of some

Spanish saint hanging on the wall. The buccaneers then marched out into the countryside in the next few days and brought back thirty prisoners, who were questioned for information on the missing citizens and their valuables.

Much of what precedes this is recounted in Morgan's brief report on the mission, in Spanish testimony on the raid, and in Esquemeling's narrative, giving a reliable picture of the events. But for the dark passages that follow, Esquemeling is the only source, and one should draw a bright line around the descriptions to come and regard them as only a possible version of what happened. What the surgeon relates was not out of character for pirate missions, but whether they happened on Morgan's watch at Maracaibo is not definitely known.

According to *The Buccaneers of America*, the rack was used on some prisoners, while "others had burning matches placed betwixt their fingers, which were thus burnt alive." The pirates lived in an age when torture was commonplace, almost expected. The rack and woolding were standard punishments during the Spanish Inquisition; the New Model Army in which so many of Morgan's original raiders had been trained (and whose red coats many of them still wore, "for the terrible name thereof") had committed hideous savageries while conquering Ireland; and armies and bandits alike thought nothing of lopping off their enemies' heads and sending them to the other side. It was a message that was sure to be understood. The Spanish gave as good as they got: When in 1604 they intercepted English ships in West Indian waters, they "cut off the heads, feet, noses and ears of the crews and smeared them with honey and tied them to trees to be tortured by flies and other insects." If the pirates were distinguished in anything, it was their inventiveness. Chinese pirates were known to nail prisoners to their wooden decks and beat them with rattans; a certain English pirate, Captain Low, ordered that a Portuguese captain's lips be cut off and broiled as the man watched. Low had, in his defense, been provoked—the captain had kept a bag filled with Portuguese gold coins hanging from a rope outside his cabin window; when the pirates appeared, he severed the rope and let the bag drop into the ocean—an incredibly stupid thing to do. Low made another sailor eat his own ears "with pepper and salt." The Irish mutineer and pirate Philip Roche initiated a massacre of his French mates that coated the entire deck with gore; the pirates were "all over as wet with the Blood that had been spilt, as if they had been dipp'd in Water, or stood in a Shower of Rain, nor did they regard it any more." What in Esquemeling's account is perhaps more amazing than the pirates' cruelty is the behavior of the tortured. Many of them resisted giving up information about their silver plate until they'd been mutilated beyond recognition.

This becomes clear in the next city that came under Morgan's care: Gibraltar (not to be confused with the island in the Mediterranean). After pillaging the countryside for thirty miles around, taking captives and raking in piles of silver and cobs, Morgan decided to follow L'Ollonais's path and take the city that sat at the far end of the bay. Morgan sent a group of prisoners ahead, to impress upon their neighbors that the city should surrender at once. Instead, when the pirates sailed up to Gibraltar's fort, they were met "with continual shooting of great cannon-bullets." After Maracaibo the men had expected an easy victory, but now they encouraged each other with this thought: "We must make one meal upon bitter things, before we come to taste the sweetness of the sugar this place affords." Morgan reversed course, anchored beyond the range of the guns, and waited until morning. Then he ordered the assault. But one night of thinking about how little pirates liked to be trifled with was enough for the townspeople. By morning, when Morgan began his assault, the people were gone, "carrying with them all their goods and riches." A bad reputation was as good as bullets to a pirate, and by now Morgan's had spread far and wide. As Esquemeling put it, in a description seconded by the Spaniards' own reports of encounters with Morgan, "the fears which the Spaniards had conceived . . . were so great, that only hearing the leaves on the trees to stir, they often fancied them to be pirates."

The only person left in town was a "poor man born a fool," a mentally handicapped Spaniard. He was questioned closely by the pirates, but to everything he answered, "I know nothing, I know nothing." The buccaneers put him to the rack and demanded to know where the residents had fled to with their valuables. Finally the man broke and cried out, "Do not torture me anymore, but come with me and I will show you my goods and my riches!" Esquemeling reports that the pirates believed that the man was a rich citizen who was faking idiocy so he'd be left alone, though it seems like a daft idea. The pirates left no one alone who might have a morsel of information. What happens next is one of the few passages in the many pirate narratives that could be described as poignant:

> Hereupon they went with him; and he conducted them to a poor and miserable cottage, wherein he had a few earthen dishes, and other things of little or no value; and amongst these, three pieces of eight which he'd concealed with some other trumpery underground. After this, they asked him his name; and he readily made answer: *My name is Don Sebastian Sanchez, and I am brother to the governor of Maracaibo.* This foolish answer, it must be conceived, these men, though never so inhuman, took for a certain truth. For no sooner had they heard it, but they put him again upon the rack, lifting him up on high with cords, and tying huge weights to his face and neck. . . .

It got worse. The pirates took burning palm leaves and scorched the man's face with them. He lasted only thirty minutes before dying; the pirates cut the cords and dragged him out to the forest and left him there, unburied.

Roderick headed into the bush with his mates and soon came on an Indian; they offered him a "mountain of gold" if he'd give them information on his former masters. Morgan's men regularly sought out informers to point them toward the richest men in the area; once they caught these people, the price of freedom was often calibrated to how much the pirates estimated the rich man would be able to pay or raise from his neighbors and family via desperate letters sent out into the bush. (At least some townspeople always managed to escape the privateers' raids, as their targets usually received some advance word of the attack.) Those who wouldn't or couldn't pay would often be tortured and forced to march along with the privateers as they made their way back toward their ships. If no ransom materialized, and the prisoners were considered valuable enough to warrant the effort, they'd be carted on board the fleet. In these cases a last-chance fire sale would be had where Morgan would give the captives one final opportunity to pay a sharply reduced price for their liberty just before sailing for Port Royal. Morgan would always rather have cash in hand than a prisoner. If they paid, they might be sent home on a rowboat or dropped off on shore. If they called his bluff, they might be freed or they might be put to death by the annoyed pirates and their bodies tossed to the sharks—a common enough practice among Morgan's fellow buccaneers. There was no set price for any one captive and no hard and fast policy governing captives' treatment. Occasionally whole towns and their captured citizens were ransomed en masse, and if the pirates were hungry, food (especially beef) could become an acceptable substitute for money. There was no policy, that is, except that every last piece of eight should be wrung from every last prisoner.

The man led them to the hiding place of a group of Spaniards, and the usual ceremonies began, with a twist. According to Esquemeling, the pirates demanded that the slave kill some of the Spaniards as an initiation rite, "to the intent that by this perpetrated crime he might never be able to leave their wicked company." The slave agreed, murdering one Spaniard after another and committing other, unnamed "insolent actions." Meanwhile the other pirates tortured the captives, with a Portuguese getting special attention. The slave marked him as a rich man, and Roderick worked him over with gusto, forcing his hands behind his back, tying cords to them, and lifting his arms straight up until they rotated over his head, "breaking both his arms behind his shoulders." (It was a torture method still in use up to the Vietnam War, when it was inflicted on American POWs.) The man still would not talk, so the furious Roderick tied his thumbs and big toes to stakes and stretched him out, "the whole weight of his body being pendent in the air upon those cords." He then took a stick and thrashed the cords until the man's body was whipped back and forth, up and down. Nothing. Swearing that he'd kill the Spaniard, Roderick found a heavy stone and carried it to the man's side and placed it on his belly, but the man held out. Roderick turned away, but another pirate took a torch from their campfire and began burning the man's face, beard, and hair. The Spaniard said not a word. Finally he was starved for five days before agreeing to pay a ransom of 500 pieces of eight, or $25,000 in current dollars.

The pirates were underwhelmed. "Old fellow," Roderick told him, "instead of five hundred you must say five hundred thousand pieces of eight; otherwise you shall here end your life." Still the prisoner held out. The Portuguese man claimed he was just a poor tavern owner who could raise no more; a "thousand protestations" flowed out of him, until the pirates must have been sick of his voice. At last he agreed to 1,000 pesos for his release; he raised the sum in a few days, paid up, and then walked free, "although so horribly maimed in his body, that 'tis scarce to be believed he could survive many weeks later."

None of this is outside of the norms of battlefield behavior. But what Esquemeling reports next did go past the norms: crucifixions, men and women "lacerated in the most tender parts of their bodies," the deaths of female prisoners and children from neglect and starvation. There is little in the record outside of Esquemeling's account to suggest that Morgan was a monster capable of such things, and one should take the report with a grain of salt; the writer may well have been embellishing at the prodding of his publishers. If Esquemeling made it up, one has to say he had the makings of a novelist in him. The innocent fool chattering away to the pirates about his famous relatives, ensuring his own death, and the Portuguese miser who endured a Golgotha just to save 500 pesos—they are beautiful touches. The latter portrait was truer of the New World: Here it was money that brought respect, not honor. Men defended their gold the way they once had the names Jesus Christ and Santiago.

How Morgan felt about the cruelty that went along with most privateering expeditions, he never said. But later in life he did show that he could sympathize with the unfortunate. When entreating his superiors in London over some English prisoners in Spanish jails, he pleaded, "They are all great objects of compassion, so I hope you will not be unmindful of them." And in the same letter he agonized about granting sanctuary to a religious refugee. "I do not know if I have done right herein," he confessed. "Sure I am that [I] wished to follow the dictates of humanity as well as those of law and reason." But a Spaniard who was resisting probably got very little sympathy from Morgan the buccaneer: Everyone understood the rules of engagement, and those who fought opened themselves up to every kind of treatment. For his part, Roderick had been raised to fear God, and the brutality he witnessed sometimes shocked him. But he'd found in himself a capacity to join in. He'd realized that the price for the life he enjoyed was that he could never question the methods of the Brethren. Anyone who shied away from woolding a captive was instantly suspect and risked marooning or worse. He expected the same if he were captured by Spanish musketeers. The pirates were like the Indian captive: They all initiated one another into torture. Any lingering doubts, any images of the burned merchant's face with the skin hanging off, were eradicated by Roderick's increasing intake of rum.

The buccaneers raked over Gibraltar for weeks and then left with their boats groaning under the weight of silks, slaves, and loot. The pirates were delighted and ready to begin the orgiastic spending of what they'd earned. But Morgan, one can be sure, had a clock ticking in the back of his mind. They'd spent a great deal of time gathering their prizes, and anytime the Brethren landed on the Spanish Main, riders galloped off to the centers of power to ask for help. Perhaps troops were on the way from Panama or Cartagena. As it happened, the situation was much worse. Waiting for the men of Port Royal was the dreaded Armada de Barlovento.

The fact that the armada had been dispatched to the Americas spoke volumes about how worried the queen regent was about Morgan; its arrival on the Main was a direct result of the shock of Portobelo. The fleet of five ships and its commander, Don Alonzo de Campos y Espinosa, had been sailing up and down the coasts of Cuba and Campeche, hoping to catch the pirates as they lurked in the cays and off the islands. The return on the significant investment that the armada represented had been slim: one small ship nabbed in the North Sea. No wonder the queen, after only six months or so of the armada's fruitless patrols, ordered the two most formidable ships in the fleet back to Spain. The dozen ships that had been initially approved for the protection of the Main were now down to three, but all of them outclassed anything Morgan had in his motley little navy. Alonzo commanded the *Magdalena*, a forty-eight-gun galleon, and was supported by the *San Luis*, which boasted thirty-eight guns, and the *Nuestra Señora de la Soledad*, a fifty-ton vessel that had last seen service as a French trade ship and carried ten guns. As historian Peter Earle has pointed out, the *Soledad* would have been an afterthought in the European navies, but it was still the equal of Morgan's flagship.

Alonzo had mile upon mile of open sea to patrol; to increase his chances of running into Morgan, he depended on seafront-tavern rumors and a web of informers. Pirates were inveterate gossips, and it was well known in West Indies ports that Morgan had assembled his fleet at Cow Island and that the Spanish Main was to be his next target; that could mean that Panama, Cartagena, Maracaibo, or a host of other towns were now in his sights. Any pirate fleet would likely sail east before attempting to sweep down onto the Main, so the admiral decided to head to Puerto Rico and surprise them en route. But it was a long shot, and when the fleet arrived in San Juan, the governor reported they hadn't spotted the pirate's flag. They were nine days too late: As Alonzo scoured the port for news of the buccaneers, Morgan was already in Maracaibo, deep into pillaging. Alonzo raced west to Santo Domingo, where he arrived on May 25, and finally got a hot lead: The president there reported that Morgan's men had arrived in their port and attempted to push their way into the city and were only held off by the island's infantry. A French prisoner chimed in that he'd been rounded up during one of the pirates' cattle hunts on Hispaniola and the pirates had revealed they were victualing for a raid on the Main. This was confirmed by a Dutch trader; pirates had been buying meat and talking about a specific town: Maracaibo. The admiral pointed his ships south and went racing after Morgan.

When they reached the Gulf of Venezuela, a mestizo who was acting as "corporal of the Indians" confirmed the admiral's hunch. Morgan was at Gibraltar. It was incredible news: His enemy was now within his reach, trapped like a dog, without the possibility of escape. How the words must have sung in Alonzo's ears! Morgan's ships could overawe a town because of the men on them: ferocious soldiers who regularly churned through Spanish armies like a meat grinder. But on water Morgan's outfit was vulnerable: His undersize ships were mere water taxis meant to shuttle the rogues from one sacking to the next. They were no warships. Now Alonzo would be the instrument of royal, indeed of divine, retribution. Henry Morgan was going to surrender or die. Or, since we are talking about the Spanish system, he was going to surrender and then die.

Alonzo was not going to miss his chance; his career, not to mention the fortunes of his king and nation, now depended on stopping Morgan. The admiral sprang into action, arranging for pilots to steer his ships through the hazardous gulf, shooting letters to the general governor of Venezuela, the governor of Mérida, and other strongholds asking for men and vessels; one of his messengers drowned in the undertow on the beach at Maracaibo, but other couriers went racing inland spreading the alarm. Alonzo approached the fort at Maracaibo carefully, expecting Morgan at least to have left a skeleton crew manning it, but there was none. Morgan had gotten cocky, or greedy, or both; he probably judged that he'd need every man to take the towns of the interior lake. Alonzo immediately began to put the fort back into fighting shape, unearthing the buried cannon and restoring six of them to working order, restocking the garrison with forty soldiers and supplying it with food and ammunition. The fort would in effect act as a fourth ship barring the exit of any ship from the lagoon; the admiral's vessels were arrayed across the channel so that no other vessel could pass without coming under direct fire from at least one of them. They acted as the cork in a bottle, and Morgan was caught inside. Alonzo gingerly steered his ships into position, struggling against strong gales ("the fury of the northern winds," he called them) that were threatening to smash his armada on the nearby reefs. "I was invaded by a total indecision," he confessed, "since serving His Majesty and the Glory of Spain, I had to prevent the enemy's entry while being totally responsible for whatever happened to my vessels." He tossed ballast into the water to lighten his ships and managed to avoid disaster. He was so confident of victory that, when seventy militiamen from Maracaibo arrived to bolster the blockade, he sent them to the fort, along with twenty-four of his own musketeers. He had more than enough men to stop the corsairs.

Morgan's fleet had been weighed down with the fruits of his success; the pirates had gathered in slaves and captives as well as stray vessels he'd commandeered in Gibraltar and along the coast. To lighten the load, he released all the prisoners who had paid their ransom and kept four citizens of the town as collateral for the monies still owed him; the freed Spanish requested that Morgan hand over the slave who had informed on them, but knowing they'd "burn him alive," Morgan quickly refused. His own affairs in order, he headed toward Maracaibo with "as much haste as he could to set things in order for his departure." Four days later the fleet arrived back in town and quickly learned from the sole resident, a sick old man, that three ships were waiting for them and, "moreover, that the castle at the entry thereof was again put into a good posture of defence, being well provided with great guns and men and all sorts of ammunition."

Morgan was startled, and he sent his fastest boat to confirm the facts, which it did quickly: three ships, ninety-four guns between them. The lagoon they were trapped in was enormous: eighty-six miles long and sixty miles wide at some points. But at the top the lagoon narrowed, and it was blocked by several islands and shoals. The only navigable channel, through which Morgan's fleet would have to pass, was approximately eight hundred yards wide. And the Spanish ships were arrayed in a line across it.

The news caused a "general consternation" among the pirates, and Morgan himself was said to "despond in his mind and be destitute of all manner of hopes." Even an escape by land was impossible. Not only would the pirates have to throw away most of their hard-won booty, but once they'd disembarked, Don Alonzo could land his men and hunt the Brethren in the woods. And in the event they evaded the raids, they'd be confronted with the fact that the Maracaibo lowlands were surrounded by mountains on three sides. The route to the Caribbean was blocked by the northeastern extension of the Andes range, with jagged peaks rising to 14,500 feet. The image of salt-sea pirates, their beards rimed with ice, scaling sheer mountain cliffs did not present itself favorably to Morgan; his men would probably rather face loaded cannon than pick their way across fields of snowdrift. Plus, they would have no ships on which to return to Jamaica, and no certainty of hijacking any. The land route was out, and the water route was bristling with Spanish steel. It was by far the bleakest situation Morgan had faced as a commander.

If he did really sink into a depression, he soon recovered. His first move was to send Don Alonzo a letter, not of surrender but one "demanding of him a considerable tribute, or ransom, for not putting the city of Maracaibo to the flame." It was typical of Morgan, who always bargained from a position of strength, even when that position was imaginary. The real purpose was to feel out the admiral, to see if Morgan was dealing with a time-server who didn't want any trouble or with a real Spanish soldier of the old school. Don Alonzo's reply ended speculation on that front. He wrote Morgan that he'd come to avenge the crimes against His Majesty and retake the castle "which you took from a parcel of cowards." He swore he'd pursue Morgan to the ends of the earth to carry out his sworn duty. Don Alonzo's tone was actually quite respectful; Morgan's stock had obviously risen since Bracamonte had tossed the epithet "pirate" at Portobelo. And the admiral extended to the Welshman a generous offer: Leave your booty and slaves and return to Jamaica and you will be allowed to pass "without trouble or molestation." Don Alonzo was a gentleman, and it is hard to imagine him setting up the same kind of double-cross with which the Englishmen at Providence had been suckered; but it's equally hard to imagine him letting this high-profile enemy of Spain skate away without so much as a slap on the wrist. The offer of free passage was a direct contradiction of Don Alonzo's orders to exterminate the pirates of the Caribbean. The letter spelled out what would happen if Morgan declined the offer: Don Alonzo would "cause you utterly to perish, by putting every man to the sword." He warned Morgan not to refuse the offer, because he had with him soldiers "who desire nothing more ardently than to revenge on you and your people all the cruelties and base in-famous actions you have committed upon the Spanish nation in America."

Morgan studied the letter and called his men together in Mara-caibo's marketplace; he read the offer, translated it into French, and then asked the only question that mattered: would the pirates rather "surrender all they'd purchased, to obtain their liberty," or fight? This scene is repeated again and again in the history of pirates: An offer is made by the authorities to surrender and give up the loot or die. To the pirates' credit, one can find few instances of a vote for laying down arms. Pirates usually chose likely death over captivity. The Brethren kept with tradition and roared back their answer: They would fight.

But how? A patented buccaneer head-on charge would be suici-dal. These were not frightened townspeople with children hanging around their knees; these were well-trained, well-equipped Spanish musketeers from the mainland, answerable to the Crown, with an

overwhelming superiority in firepower, led by a capable commander. No ghost stories about monkey-faced buccaneers were going to
cause them to turn and run. Morgan consulted with his men; the
best idea would win.

Before he revealed his strategy, Morgan sent another letter, saying he'd agree to give up half of the slaves, leave Maracaibo intact,
and free the four prisoners he still held. No mention was made of the
treasure they'd stolen; that, the pirates would keep. Don Alonzo answered brusquely; he'd tried treating Morgan like a gentleman, but
these thugs were so impertinent. Ignoring the counteroffer, he informed Morgan he had two days to surrender or face annihilation.
Morgan's last message was cheerful, telling Don Alonzo that since
he was so near, the English would come to him and introduce him to
the "hazard of battle." He also mentioned that he expected no mercy
from his enemies.

Now the townspeople of Maracaibo, those close enough to the
pirate ships, heard the feverish hammering from the direction of the
harbor, as if a small fort were being built. But they didn't see any of
the expected slaves or prisoners escaping to the jungle, as was typical when pirates let down their guard or were otherwise occupied.
Not a soul arrived to tell them what was happening in the town.

⚜   ⚜   ⚜

At the neck of the lagoon, Don Alonzo waited. A stream of informers stole toward his flagship and gave the admiral a series of reports:
The pirates were working on a captured trading vessel; new gun
ports were being added; shipwrights were working furiously in the
ship's hold. Clearly Morgan had transferred his flag to this ship,
which was bigger than his own and could give him more brawn to go
up against the *Magdalena*. Don Alonzo drilled his men, watched the
horizon carefully, and put in place a series of defensive measures:
Long poles were extended from the sides of his ships to prevent the
pirates from getting too close (for boarding or other nefarious activities); barrels of water were placed on deck for fighting fires.

The stalemate lasted for a week. Then, just before dark on April 30,

Alonzo looked toward the lagoon, and there, suddenly, was the out-
line of ships against the horizon: Morgan's fleet, now thirteen in
number with the captured vessels, had sailed twenty miles up the lagoon and taken a position within view of the Spaniards, but out of
firing range. Aboard the *Magdalena*, Don Alonzo studied the enemy
ships in his spyglass. The big Cuban trader the pirates had reportedly
been working on was flying Morgan's flag; that was comforting—at
least the admiral's spies were accurate. And when, two days later, the
pirate fleet raised anchor and came sailing straight at Don Alonzo, it
was in the lead, flanked by the old flagship *Satisfaction* and another
frigate. Don Alonzo watched them approach; as soon as they were
within range, he gave the order to fire. His ship's forty-eight guns
roared with a thunderous volley; ball tore into the sail of the oncoming ships. Morgan's ships responded as best they could, but their
barrages were decibels lower in volume.

To his astonishment, Don Alonzo saw that the buccaneers' ships
did not peel away as they drew closer. They were going to attempt a
frontal assault, as if his man-of-war were a pathetic merchant sloop
fleeing for its very life. Nothing could be more to his advantage, except a sustained artillery battle on the open sea. The pirates would
not go for that; their ships were being blasted apart by his gunners,
who inched down the mouths of their guns as the buccaneer fleet
closed on them, until they were pointed almost level, firing across
the gap of blue sea at the three fast-closing ships trailed by the
slower boats. The admiral could see the outlines of pirates on deck in
the morning haze, some of them wearing the soft *montera* hat, like
bullfighters, their cutlasses poised by their sides. They were unmov-
ing against the dawn sky. Don Alonzo had just a moment to admire
their steadfastness in the face of barrages of shot aimed straight at
their faces—*at least these infidels die like men*—before the ship plowed
into the *Magdalena* with a crash of snapping, buckling wood, and
grappling hooks came spinning through the air and snagged his
sails. His men, their anticipation keyed to a point, didn't wait for the
attack but leaped over the sides onto the enemy's deck.

And in that moment, realization. The decks were empty, except for wooden cutouts cunningly shaped by Morgan's carpenters to resemble men with cutlasses. The Spanish musketeers looked around in bewilderment before the word unfolded in their minds and came tumbling out of their mouths: *brûlot.* It was a fireship, a floating trap designed to set the enemy aflame. They could smell the sweet odor of tar over palm leaves as the deck around them lit up like a Roman candle and a concussion blew them up into the rigging. Don Alonzo shouted orders as pieces of burning wood and cordage came tumbling through the air into his ship. A seventeenth-century warship was a conflagration waiting to happen: Apart from the magazines of gunpowder filling the hold, its seams were caulked with tar, its ropes were covered with a layer of fat, and its sails were made of flammable canvas. The flames engulfed the tackling and rope, swept over the decks, bellowed by a strong wind at their back, burning men alive as they fled; fire ran and shot up the masts. Men dived into the water and swam for the islands, while Don Alonzo tried futilely to get the fires put out and tossed planks of wood to drowning men. "The flames built up rapidly and violently . . . ," Don Alonzo wrote in his report on the confrontation. "So that in a brief moment everything was ablaze."

The *Magdalena* was soon fully engulfed, "the forepart sinking into the sea, whereby she perished." Disaster tumbled into disaster: Her sister ship, the *Soledad*, wheeled away from the burning vessel but had a malfunction in its rigging and was soon unnavigable; as it dawdled pilotless across the water, the buccaneers chased it down and prepared to board. The terrified crew jumped into the water, and the Brethren swarmed up the *Soledad*'s sides, corrected the rigging jam, and soon had a fine Spanish ship as plunder. The Spanish swimmers were cut down, as "they would neither ask nor admit of any quarter, choosing rather to lose their lives than receive them from the hands of their persecutors." The sergeant major of the *Soledad* was one of the survivors, hauling himself "naked and wet" to the fort. The last Spanish ship, the *San Luis*, was luckier, making it to the fort, where its crew unloaded its provisions and armaments and then burned the ship down to the waterline, so that Morgan could not have it. Poor Don Alonzo survived the debacle and transferred to a longboat and headed for shore, pursued by Roderick and other pirates, paddling furiously in their swift canoes. He ended up running for his life from the men he expected to take back to the Main as "sun-dried" specimens for his queen.

The Brethren had prepared the Cuban decoy beautifully, cutting new gun ports into her side and, in place of the real cannon that should have jutted out of them, inserting logs filled with gunpowder and readied with fuses. Then they'd scoured Maracaibo for every highly flammable material available to them — pitch, tar, brimstone, palm leaves — and built their combustible doll men out of them. The carpenters whom the spies heard hammering away in the hold were not installing fortifications to the structure but removing them, so that when the ship blew, the explosion would not be dampened by excess timbers. They'd adorned the ship with banners and fitted it out like a flagship; in the history of naval warfare, fireships had usually been made of old and decrepit junks, not fine specimens such as the Cuban prize. Luck had been with Morgan in the following wind that blew out of the top of the lagoon into the narrow channel, giving the ship the necessary propulsion to ram it into the *Magdalena*. A skeleton crew of twelve men had steered it home and jumped into canoes just before the moment of impact. The costuming, the set design, the use of the murky glow of dawn to light the scene — the whole thing resembled nothing more than an amateur English theatrical.

Morgan's reputation for command had been well established before Maracaibo, but after this stunning reversal of fortune, he became *the* buccaneer commander. There was no way he should have been able to outmaneuver Don Alonzo: Morgan was a brilliant soldier throughout his career, but a subpar sailor. He regularly lost ships to reefs or, in the case of the *Oxford*, carelessness. The pirates usually used terror and marksmanship to win battles, but Morgan had won this naval confrontation by wit. "The Pirates were extremely gladdened at this signal victory," Esquemeling tells us. "Obtained in so short a time and with so great [an] inequality of forces; whereby they conceived greater pride in their minds than they had before."

If Don Alonzo had considered Spain's history, he'd have prepared more diligently. Indeed, the greatest disaster ever to strike his nation's navies, the loss of the Spanish Armada in 1588, turned on a fireship attack designed by the English commander and future privateer Francis Drake. The mighty Armada was thought to be invincible, but when it anchored off Calais before the planned invasion of England, the Spanish were spooked by the sudden appearance, at midnight on August 7, of a fleet of burning ships, their sails towers of flame, rushing at them out of the darkness. The Spanish were terrified that these were the dreaded "hell-burners" or "explosion-machines" (vessels loaded with gunpowder, housed in hulls closed in with brick, that would explode with tremendous force when the fire reached it); they cut their cables and scattered to the wind, canceling their D-Day and opening up the Armada to attacks by the nimble English navy, which hounded them onto the Dutch coast and sent them back to Spain as abject failures. Morgan had, in miniature, recreated the famous attack with equally devastating results. (In fact, included in Esquemeling's book was a rather fine rendering of the attack, titled *The Spanish Armada Destroyed by Captaine Morgan.*) Like Drake, he'd even volunteered his flagship for the conflagration.

What Morgan did not realize until days later was that Don Alonzo had been warned about the fireship. Although the pirates kept a strict guard on all their prisoners, a "certain negro" had made it to the *Magdalena* days before the attack and told the admiral, "Sir, be pleased to have great care of yourself, for the English have prepared a fireship with desire to burn your fleet." The Spanish noble had scoffed at the idea. "How can that be?" he thundered at the spy. "Have they, peradventure, wit enough to build a fireship? Or what instruments have they to do it withal?" Don Alonzo was a Spaniard to the bone: He simply could not imagine that he could be out-thought by scum like the Brethren. But the collective wisdom of the pirates had defeated the noble.

Don Juan carried with him the kingdom's certainty of its own rightness and superiority. When dealing with the privateers, who molded their thinking to the situation at hand, certainty could be a fatal flaw.

Morgan quickly divided up his men: Some dived to the wreck of the *Magdalena* and brought up silver cobs worth 20,000 pesos, some of them melted into gobs of pure bullion; another 20,000 in silver re-mained in the black hulk but could not be reached. Other men landed on the beach and began probing the fort's defenses, shooting at the musketeers lining the tops of the armaments. The castle, now packed full with Spanish soldiers as well as a resupplied garrison from Maracaibo, blasted back at the evening attack the buccaneers at-tempted. The pirates were seriously outgunned, having only muskets and "a few fire-balls" (crude grenades) to contend with the cannon above their heads. Men dropped under the barrage, blood gushing into the sand and turning it black in the dusky gloom. "We refused them the whole afternoon," reported the fort's castellan, "causing [them] great harm . . . and the deaths of many people, injured and burned." The Brethren lost thirty men, with many more wounded, before they realized they had no chance of storming the castle. But eventually it would have to be taken: The fort's artillery would shred the pirate fleet as it tried to sail through the narrow channel if the guns were not silenced.

There was now a three-way standoff between the pirates, Don Alonzo, and the residents of Maracaibo. The first wanted to leave but could not; the second wanted Morgan's head, and the last simply wanted the whole mess ended as soon as possible. Morgan inter-viewed the pilot of one of the vice admiral's ships, who had been captured in the fireship raid, and got the background on Don Alonzo's mission. He now learned, if he'd not already known, that he was the target of this mission; the pilot told him that it was the "loss and ruin of Porto Bello, and many others" that spurred the Crown to action and that the Spanish force was intent on "destroying as many of [the English pirates] as possible." The news put into doubt Don Alonzo's offer of free passage. The pilot spoke of the bitterness the Spanish people felt at Morgan's raids: "Of all which damages and hostilities committed here by the English," he told the Welshman, "very dismal lamentations have oftentimes penetrated the ears both of the Catholic King and Council, to whom belongs the care and preservation of this New World." The pilot also divulged the battle orders given by Don Alonzo to his men, and they were tough: "Having given a very good supper to his people," the man said, "he persuaded them neither to take nor give any quarter to the English that should fall into their hands."

Time was against Morgan. As the pilot spoke, there were frigates full of musketeers cresting the waves of the North Sea on a rescue mission to Maracaibo. Morgan had jiggled a main strand of the spiderweb that was the Spanish Empire; the news had radiated along the trade routes, and soldiers would soon be on the way from Panama to check on the disturbance. Morgan had been fortunate with Don Alonzo, but he could not afford to linger to try his luck again. There was, however, one weak link in the system: the Maracaiboans. They wanted him gone. Morgan sent Don Alonzo an offer to leave the town unmolested in return for safe passage out, but he could have no expectation that it would be accepted. He offered the good citizens a deal: the return of their prisoners and no torching of the city in return for 30,000 pieces of eight and 500 beeves. The Spanish paid up: after, that is, getting Morgan down to 20,000 pesos, or $1 million in modern terms; they were merchants, after all, and used to haggling.

Finally the citizens collected the funds and paid off the Welshman with huge relief. But then Morgan tweaked the conditions of the deal. He would leave the town alone, but now he told the citizens to go to Don Alonzo and get him to let the privateers sail off. He did not want the castle's guns blazing away at him as he ran the channel;

his ships would be sitting ducks. To motivate the messengers, Morgan announced that he'd keep the remaining townspeople captive until the vice admiral gave in.

The captives must have cursed him under their breath. But they elected representatives and sent them "beseeching and supplicating" Don Alonzo to let Morgan go; if he didn't, "the sword and the gallows" awaited them. Don Alonzo, humiliated first by Morgan and now by his own countrymen, reacted with disgust: "If you had been as loyal to your King in hindering the entry of these Pirates," he told them, "as I shall do their going out, you had never caused these troubles, neither to yourselves, nor to our whole nation; which has suffered so much through your pusillanimity. In a word, I shall never grant your request; but shall endeavour to maintain that respect which is due to my King, according to my duty." Old Spain thundered at the colonists. But Don Alonzo's real audience for the note, which was no doubt copied in triplicate, was back in Madrid, awaiting word of Morgan's demise. He was building a legal case for the disaster that was unfolding.

The deal was off. Morgan, who had bought time to think, now began perfecting a secret plan; this one was his alone. The first thing he did was to tally up and divide the loot from the mission; if he was going to lose a ship in the breakout, he didn't want it to be the one carrying all the silver. When this was done, the sum came to 250,000 pieces of eight ($12.5 million), not to mention the "huge quantity of merchandise and slaves." It was his richest haul yet, bigger than Portobelo (250,000 pesos in total, without the value of the goods and slaves), bigger even than L'Ollonais's near-legendary strike in this very same town two years earlier. He'd surpassed L'Ollonais in every way. Now all he had to do was get the treasure home.

Having drained every last bit of information from the pilot (and treating him splendidly in return), the buccaneer commander now knew much more about Don Alonzo than his opponent did about him. It could be said of Morgan the same thing that was said about Cromwell, who had created his career: that "he read men as others read books." Morgan studied the way the Spaniard had arrayed his forces and his arms, and he concluded that Don Alonzo expected an attack by land. It was the obvious choice. Morgan's men were past masters when it came to storming castles, while at sea they were amateurs. He saw that Don Alonzo was digging trenches and fortifying his landward positions. The muzzles of the guns were pointed away from the sea. Don Alonzo was not a complicated tactician: What you saw was what you got. Morgan decided to play to the man's certainties.

In plain sight of the castle's lookouts, canoes were unloaded from Morgan's ships, and men could soon be seen climbing down into them. The boats then rowed toward the shoreline. Once there they were concealed behind trees as they presumably unloaded the buccaneers and headed back to the main ships empty except for two or three oarsmen. This went on all afternoon, and Don Alonzo drew the obvious conclusion: Morgan was unloading his men for a land assault.

He was doing nothing of the sort. The canoes *were* full of men as they left the ships, but when they reached the shore, the men simply lay down on the bottom of the craft and returned to the ships, Roderick and the others lying with their backs in the brackish water that sloshed at the bottom of the rowboats, wondering if this childish trick could really work. When the small boats returned to the ships, Roderick and the others climbed up the ropes on the side hidden from Don Alonzo's watchful eyes, then made their way over to the side facing the Spanish and repeated the process. Don Alonzo again underestimated the imagination of his enemy, convinced that the men he was facing were simple and crude. The battlements of the castle that looked out over the water were left practically deserted as Don Alonzo massed his men for a midnight raid.

Night came, and with it an ebbing tide. With his men hidden out of sight, Morgan softly pulled his anchors up and let the currents slowly take them through the channel. When they were even with the castle, the ships sprang to life: Sails suddenly blossomed white against the moonlight on vessel after vessel. The canvas billowed in the night breeze, and the ships picked up speed. With what must have been a sick feeling of dread, Don Alonzo saw what was happening and wheeled his cannon to the seaside ports. They blasted away at the departing ships, but Morgan was now just out of range and fired back not in self-defense but with a derisive salute. The Spaniards could not reach him, and Don Alonzo could do nothing but watch his hopes sail with the buccaneers; the Crown would not take lightly his being outwitted twice.

Don Alonzo was arrested and put in chains, then transported back to Spain on the silver galleons. "I shall not find a person in the Kingdom of Spain that will testify in my favor," he complained in his initial report on the battle, and he was indeed found guilty of having acted rashly. But the war tribunal of the Council of the Indies voided the conviction and freed the star-crossed admiral. He'd at least *attempted* to fight Morgan, and his initiative was clear in the testimony. To condemn his rigid, top-down style and admit that he'd been bested by the very flexiblility and ingenuity that found little place in the Spanish system would be to implicate the entire system of governance in the far-flung kingdoms.

Why, it might be asked here, does it seem that the Spanish *never* won these showdowns with the pirates? In fact, it is a misconception: The Spanish did regularly defeat pirates in battle throughout the history of their New World possessions, and the historical records are littered with tales of buccaneers who ended their days on the enemy's beach or in his prisons. Just not Morgan. The Spanish had many handicaps: distance that made it nearly impossible to coordinate a common defense of distant cities or relieve besieged towns in time to do any good; rivalries between provincial governors; stifling bureaucracy that handicapped provincial leaders' ability to respond quickly to threats; bad, outdated weapons; restrictions on privately importing new, up-to-date weapons; a lack of money to maintain armaments; dependence on amateur militias to face off against hugely experienced buccaneers; the fact that flight and not fight often presented the most appealing option to soldiers and townspeople faced with a buccaneer army; the myth of the all-conquering Morgan; the fact that the buccaneers did not occupy their territories, thus giving the Spanish a chance to return to their normal lives soon after the invasion; and Morgan's strategic brilliance and his ability to leverage huge numbers of pirates against weak fortifications.

As for Morgan, he offloaded the prisoners on the way back to Jamaica, keeping only those unfortunates from Gibraltar who had still not paid their ransom. He sailed for Port Royal, having exposed the core weaknesses of the Spanish system. Happy and rich as Croesus, Morgan was ascending even higher in the firmament of outlaws. His New World dreams were coming true: He was on his way to becoming a wealthy, landed aristocrat. With every victory a little more space opened up between him and the Rodericks of the world.

10

Black Clouds to the East

When it comes to rating the enemies of the buccaneers, disease has to be mentioned first. It carried off more pirates than did enemy bullets. Then the Spanish. And then weather. Morgan had been lucky in his expeditions to avoid shipwrecking storms. But when one sails the Caribbean year after year, one eventually gets hit. And now, on the return trip from the magical victory at Maracaibo, it was Morgan's turn.

Esquemeling is light on detail, but the ships clearly hit a tropical storm, if not a hurricane, while fairly close to the shoreline. "They were surprised by a great tempest," he writes, "which forced them to cast anchor in the depth of five or six fathom water," or thirty to thirty-six feet. The boats, many of them undecked, could not ride out the tempest and were forced to pull up their anchors and face into the waves. It was not just drowning that concerned them: "If on either side they should have been cast on shore," says the surgeon, "either to fall into the hands of the Spaniards or of the Indians, they would certainly have obtained no mercy."

A storm in the age of sail was a terrifying event. The wind could tear the rigging to shreds. "What especially astonished us," wrote Raveneau de Lussan, who barely survived a "tornado" at sea, "was the fact that our yards, sheets, braces and other rigging were cut off as clean as if hatchets had been used." The mainmast could come down if the sails were not lowered quickly. The rats that lived in the holds would sometimes emerge during violent gales, seemingly maddened by the storm, and attack passengers, especially the sick and injured. And the men worked in terrible conditions: If the storm hit at night, they'd be tossed out on a slippery deck unable even to see the man next to them. Ropes caught in the blocks, spars snapped and flew off into the blackness, and flying tackle could brain an unsuspecting crewman.

The ocean a buccaneer sailed into was not the mapped, GPS'ed body of water we know today. Once they left the harbor, even the most forward-thinking buccaneers entered a world of superstition and hearsay. There were a thousand legends of the sea that mariners still adhered to, and many of them concerned storms. It was a world in which the elements were subject to the whims of witches and warlocks who "at their pleasure send hail, rain tempest, thunder and lightning" to sink their enemy's vessels. Roderick believed that witches could disturb the air by digging a hole in the ground, filling it with water, and then stirring the water lightly with a finger, or by boiling hogs' bristles in a pot; his father had told him the evil wretches could call up a hurricane by tossing a little sea sand into the air. This led to a ban on women aboard. As late as 1808, the English admiral Cuthbert Collingwood wrote that "I never knew a woman brought to sea in a ship that some mischief did not befall the vessel." One Mrs. Hicks and her daughter went to trial for witchcraft in 1716, and the prosecution claimed they'd created storms by swirling their bare feet in a pot and stirring up soapsuds into a foam. Or storms could be caused by a black dragon that emerged from the clouds and plunged its head into the sea, drinking up the water and any unlucky ship that happened into its way. The dragon might be a waterspout, but the danger was just as real; the only way to avoid it was to shout at the monster or to hold a knife with a black handle, read the Gospel of St. John, and then slice the knife across the waterspout (as Columbus's crew did once, successfully).

It was not just raging seas that concerned seamen. Above a sailor's head was another world, the cloud sea that sat atop the white cirrus vapor. It was believed that vessels sailed on this ocean in the sky. Roderick told the story of the sailor from Bristol who, when navigating this sea, dropped his knife overboard; the knife fell through the clouds and impaled itself in the wooden table in his home. As there was a world above, there was also a subterranean civilization of which mariners could catch only glimpses. Sailors swore that in clear water they sometimes saw buildings, church steeples, whole cities underneath the sea, and even heard the tolling of the cathedral bells on lonely nights when no ship or lighthouse was in view. In the huge troughs that followed powerful waves, sailors claimed to have seen the peaked roofs and winding stairs of the houses of the giants that lived below. Even the more familiar waters of the North Sea were subject to visions: St. Elmo's fire, the electrical phenomenon that seems to touch sails and ropes with a white flame, was believed to be a sign that St. Elmo, patron saint of sailors, was protecting the ship against tempests. "On these occasions, the sailors first recite hymns and litanies," wrote a French author in the eighteenth century, "and when, as if often happens, the light still remains, they salute it by a whistling sound." When the light disappeared, sailors would call "Lucky journey" after it. Certainly, on that voyage home, Morgan's men would have searched the black horizon for some sign of the saving light.

The buccaneers made it through the tempest, only to face another one when they arrived home. If the privateers had a champion in London, it was George Monck, the Duke of Albemarle, who had once depended on Henry Morgan's uncle Thomas as his second-in-command. This unabashed imperialist led the anti-Spanish faction in Charles II's circle, and to him Jamaica was an outpost of the empire, an empire that should be expanded and fortified wherever and whenever possible. Monck had begun his career as a Royalist but switched sides twice, first to Cromwell, when his star was on the rise, and then to Charles II, whom he'd almost single-handedly brought to power, something Charles never forgot. Winston Churchill described him with sincere if cynical admiration as the ultimate soldier's soldier, the kind who "waited about doing their duty on a short view from day to day until there is no doubt whether the tide is on the ebb or the flow; and who then, with the appearance of great propriety and complete self-abnegation, with steady, sterling qualities of conduct if not of heart, move slowly, cautiously, forward." That sentence, which imitates Monck's sluggish and deliberate style, doesn't make him seem a romantic figure, but the privateers and their supporters were romantics only to novelists. To men in power, they were a heavy lever with which to prod and dislodge the Spanish. And so Monck argued their case with vehemence.

But Portobelo and now Maracaibo had been turning points. "We interpret what these nations have done, and are still doing, as insults," read a report to the queen of Spain from the Council of War of the Indies. "It can be said that there isn't a port or a coast in the Indies that they have not tried to invade or have indeed invaded." The councilors went on to say that it was clear the English did not respect any treaties and that they'd taken advantage of the "passivity of Her Majesty's subjects," something the council was determined to change. The Spanish, in their fury, considered every option, even the crackpot schemes of an Irish slave trader named Sir Richard White who came up with a host of options for getting to Morgan: paying off the governors of Jamaica and Barbados to rein in the privateers; seeding Cartagena, Havana, and other cities with 1,500 Flemish or Milanese mercenaries who would rise up and "help in the confrontations" when the Brethren attacked; and even penetrating the enemy's cities himself and spying on their fortifications. White was clearly something of a con artist: He demanded 7 million pesos ($357 million) and "a frigate to Cádiz" to arrange the truce, along with the right to continue trading in slaves on the Main (which was illegal for a non-Spaniard), the guarantee that the queen would pay all his expenses and additional, unspecified "voluntary donations" from the viceroys of Peru and New Spain. For this he tantalized the queen with his personal access to the governors of the English colonies and the rather hazy intelligence that the pirates "are not united, have no government and are not able to feed themselves well." White's high intrigue came to nothing, but the Spanish anger did not abate, and others in the English leadership nodded sympathetically at their complaints. The privateers *were* a menace. The secretary of state, Lord Arlington, was the leader of those who wanted closer relations with Spain and an end to the pirates' reign. (He'd spent several years in Madrid and was so identified with its causes that his code name in the French ambassador's dispatches was "the Spaniard.") The news of Portobelo had infuriated him; the queen regent was insisting on reparations and that Modyford be sacked. Arlington replied with the threadbare party line: The attacks were simply in response to Spanish provocations, and the only way to end them was by a treaty that recognized English interests in the region; only then would the king's subjects treat the queen's subjects "with love and respect." In the streets of London, however, Morgan was a hero, a Protestant avenger in a time when English military victories were rarer and rarer (the Dutch having recently humiliated the navy not once but twice). London had been consumed by the Great Fire of 1666, and plague had struck high and low; it seemed that one *annus horribilis* followed another. It would be difficult for the king to chastise the hero of Portobelo, especially as suspicions of Charles's Catholic affinities lingered among the common people. Hemmed in by circumstances, Arlington fobbed off the Spanish demands while sending Modyford cryptic, icy notes. Arlington's hopes lay with William Godolphin, the emissary working in Madrid to get a treaty signed. But Morgan's escapades were making his job impossible. "This way of warring is neither honourable nor profitable to His Majesty," Arlington wrote Modyford, "[and] he is endeavouring to put an end to it."

So when Morgan returned from Maracaibo on May 16, 1669, some things were the same as always: A significant percentage of the

town's populace was going wild at the dockside, their shouts interrupted by the throaty salutes of cannon. The tavern owners were
pulling the barrels of Madeira from their basements and buying
every drop of rum they could get their hands on; the whores' prices
were rising by the minute, as 450 nouveau riche buccaneers would
soon need servicing; the merchants readied their scales for the gobs
of melted silver the pirates would soon be bringing in and slamming
down on their counters with their filthy hands. In short, Port Royal
was humming. But there was one face that was missing in the rev-
elry: Modyford's. When Morgan scanned the line of dignitaries
waiting to grasp his hand and realized the governor was not there,
he instantly knew that something in London had changed. Morgan
hurried to Spanish Town to get the news. As he sat glumly over a
glass of punch, he learned that Modyford's son had sent a letter on
the last ship to arrive from England, painting a depressing picture of
the privateers' fortunes. Monck was dying of dropsy (he'd pass
away on January 3, 1670, surrounded by his veteran comrades,
"like a Roman general . . . with all his officers about him"). The government was leaning toward calling Portobelo a rogue action. The
Spanish demands were getting a hearing.

Morgan must have winced. He'd just returned from sacking Maracaibo and blowing up the queen regent's Armada de Barlovento.
What, he surely wondered, would Lord Arlington say to that?

Just over a month later, as bleary-eyed corsairs spent the last of
their credit, Modyford announced the new era. Port Royal's leaders —
including Morgan — marched into the marketplace on June 24 as a
drummer called the crowds to attention. Rumors had swept through
the town of a coming change, and now it was made official. A proclamation was read, praising Morgan for destroying the enemy fleet
and making null and void any commissions he'd issued. "From now
on," the crier proclaimed, "[we] prohibit any acts of hostility against
the vassals of His Catholic Majesty by whatsoever person or persons." And just like that it was over. The glorious tear of the Port
Royal pirates had run its course. The crowd dispersed, some of them

surely bewildered by what they'd just heard. The Spanish were now their "good neighbours and friends"? It was as if Modyford had announced that Jamaica had been declared an arctic region and rum was to be outlawed.

Still, Modyford had been a friend to the buccaneers, and he was now telling them to cease and desist. Lord Arlington had even asked him, on behalf of the king, how to "best dispose of this very valuable body of privateers, and whether it were not practicable to oblige them to betake themselves to planting, merchandizing, or service in his Majesty's men-of-war." The question of what to do with the Brethren once the Crown no longer had use for them was a tricky one. The old fears of a pirate army's terrorizing Jamaica resurfaced. Modyford must have shaken his head at the question: It was as if the king were asking if he couldn't find a few nice jobs for the drunken murderers they'd used to protect the empire and of whom they now wanted to dispose. Lord Arlington did not have to meet the pirates on High Street on his way to church. Some of these men would as soon cut off your face as say hello.

Modyford came up with a novel solution. On June 25, 1669, he sent the Conde de Molina, the Spanish ambassador to England, a letter. The fact that he was the governor of an upstart colony, completely illegal in Spanish eyes, addressing the representative of a world-straddling empire did not seem to cross his mind in writing this amazing document. "I know and perhaps you are not altogether ignorant of your weakness in these parts," he wrote, "the thinness of your inhabitants, want of hearts, armes and knowledge in warre, the open opposition of some and doubtfull obedience or of other of the Indians." Modyford warned the ambassador that, in the event of a permanent peace between England and Spain, the French corsairs would simply take up where Morgan had left off—unless the Spanish agreed to his proposal: namely, *that they hire the Brethren as a mercenary army to protect the Main.* "What we could have donn, the French will doe, unless these men may by your intercession be brought to serve your Master." If the queen regent refused, Modyford predicted that the Port Royal privateers would join their Gallic counterparts or sail without commissions, taking any job they could rather than starve. Modyford was apparently serious, but the letter fairly seethes with the Jamaicans' deep disdain for the Spaniard. Lord Arlington admonished Modyford: The proposal, he wrote, "will scarce be believed a practicall one." The Spanish recognized it as a barely disguised insult and never responded. Modyford did come up with more practical ideas later on: that the ex-privateers join the dangerous and lucrative logwood trade, which was thriving. He predicted that two-thirds of the Jamaican pirates could be employed this way and that the English could soon dominate the market, providing handsome tax revenues to the king. He did advise Arlington not to try to get tough with the privateers: "Other more violent ways will but make them in despair or revenge join with foreign nations or set up for themselves." It was the old fear of the merchants: the buccaneers' turning their guns on them.

All these possibilities hinged on Spain's making a real peace in the West Indies, which Arlington thought likely but Modyford said he "could but faintly hope for." Modyford felt that he knew the Spanish. In his letter to Modina was a frank assessment of Spanish strength and a cynical evaluation of their aims. Arlington was willfully deluded: Spain would never open its golden lands to other nations. The Spaniards would fight until they were bled dry.

Modyford could not know how right he was.

❖   ❖   ❖

Every move that the European powers made in the West Indies was blurred by time lags. Councils and kings would receive the news of events that had occurred months ago; they in turn often procrastinated and debated for months and then sent a slow ship with their new responses to last year's incidents. By the time their letters reached Caribbean ports, they were outdated by fresh developments, lapped by time. Such was the case now. While England and Jamaica believed themselves to be settling into a long, if troubled, peace,

Spain was pounding the drums of war. Before Modyford called in the privateers, the furious queen regent, believing that the English would do nothing to discipline their private warriors, had sent her missives to the governors of the New World, ordering them to "execute all the hostilities which are permitted by war, by taking possession of ships, islands, places and ports." She also authorized commissions for Spanish privateers. The orders arrived in Cartagena in late October 1670. Modyford had withdrawn the privateers' commissions in June, unaware that Spain had begun a war on Jamaica. Spain still considered the English there to be outlaws and trespassers, and no formal declaration of war was therefore necessary.

But back in Jamaica life was sweet. The admiral of the Brethren was sinking back into the life of a gentleman corsair. At just thirty-five, Morgan had a reputation that was secure, his name "now . . . famous through all those islands." He was rich and need not ever go out buccaneering again, if he chose not to. For his services to the Crown, the king had granted him in 1669 a large estate in the Jamaican parish of Clarendon: 836 acres, "bounding northwest and north on Waste Hilly Woodland & Easterly and Southerly on the river Minoe." The English were pushing farther and farther into the primeval interior, but there was still plenty of land for men who "singed the beard" of the Spanish king: In those days estates were cleared to the distance of a musket shot. For this generous gift, the king asked only one thing: loyalty. "The said Henry Morgan his heirs and assigns," the grant read, "shall upon any Insurrection mutiny or foreign invasion which may happen in my said Island of Jamaica during his or their residence there be ready to serve us." It was a formality: Morgan considered himself a patriot, and any attack on Jamaica would be an attack on his home. All he lacked was a son to pass the land down to: his wife, Elizabeth, had not been able to bear him a child. It was the only blemish on Morgan's charmed life. But Elizabeth had two brothers and two sisters, and their marriages produced the children whom Morgan so fervently wished for himself. With Elizabeth the eldest of the daughters and Henry as one of the most famous men in the West Indies, they became the leaders of the Morgan family in Jamaica. The admiral grew especially close to his nephew Thomas, whom he'd name as one of the trustees of his will. He spent his days as his fellow planters did: riding over his plantation and watching over his crops, discussing with his neighbors over punch in the evenings the latest prices for sugar, the rumors of slave insurrections, and the intentions of the Spanish. It was a peaceful, luxurious life, and although Morgan had for years been a legendary drinker, none of his enemies ever accused him of cheating on Elizabeth. It seems to have been a happy marriage. He was founding his line, just as he'd hoped to when he sailed for the islands. The fact that his life aims now diverged so drastically from men like Roderick's was the sign of a larger break that would soon turn ominous.

✠ ✠ ✠

Slowly, in the early weeks and months of 1670, cracks began to appear in the peace with Spain, cracks that threatened to end Morgan's idyll. It began with a gesture from Modyford: He released a number of Spanish prisoners who had been sitting in Port Royal's jail and he sent them to Cuba with a letter to the governor there "signyfying peace between the two nations." It was all in the spirit of the new relationship between the English and Spanish colonies; the deeply skeptical Modyford was at last extending the hand of friendship. The ex-prisoners and the neighborly note were sent in the *Mary and Jane*, commanded by a popular and veteran Dutch buccaneer named Bernard Claesen Speirdyke—Captain Bart to his mates. The ship was received cautiously, with the Spanish conducting no fewer than three searches of it before letting down their guard. All was found in order, the letter was delivered, the prisoners walked off the boat to freedom, and Captain Bart began pulling up some articles straight from London and Paris he happened to have in the ship's hold. If privateering was doomed, trade would have to take its place, and Captain Bart opened the action with gusto. The bartering was intense, and everything sold. Captain Bart sailed off toward Jamaica as the harbinger of a new status quo.

As he was passing out of the port of Bayamo, a ship appeared with the English colors flapping on her topsail. Captain Bart changed course and sent two men in a dinghy to exchange the latest gossip. But as soon as the men were aboard, the ship began acting strangely, veering toward the *Mary and Jane.* The customary call came floating across the water: "Where are you bound from?" Captain Bart replied, "Jamaica." The answer was unexpected. "Defend yourself, dog!" cried the ship's captain. "I come as a punishment for heretics!" To Captain Bart's shock and dismay, this was followed by a barrage of cannon fire. The English colors were a ruse: The ship was *San Pedro y la Fama,* commanded by one Manuel Rivero Pardal, a Portuguese corsair who had decided to take up the queen of Spain on her call for avengers.

If it hadn't been for this hero (to the Spanish), this mad fool (to the English), Morgan's story might have been very different. Rivero's ardor was the spark that would light a hundred fires on the Spanish Main and draw the Brethren into their greatest confrontation with their archnemesis. As Morgan perfectly represents the English personality of the era—with his wit, his enterprise, his ruthlessness, and his consuming desire for landed riches—so Rivero is the inheritor of everything Spain had been for a century or more. But he'd arrived too late: The Spanish were in retreat from the pirates, and the empire was under siege. This flamboyant and outrageously egotistical man wished to revive the nation's fighting spirit; what better way than to kill the English dogs who made his countrymen fly madly into the woods every time they appeared?

The attack on the *Mary and Jane* was his first strike in what Rivero hoped would be a rising of Spain to its former glory in the West Indies. To commemorate his taking up the standard, he'd written a poem; and he is such a key character in the final chapter of Morgan's exploits—and such an odd, manic figure—that it is worth quoting it. Appropriately enough, Rivero begins by invoking the pagan muse of tragedy:

> *Sacred Melpomene, I beseech thee*
> *Who in lugubrious moments grant fate.*

I invoke you reverently,
You, in your castalian choir,
One of the nine deities,
So that graciously you may assist me
In the endeavor that I intend.
Diligently I search
Ad honorem, so that I attain
Happy victories.

Rivero was no poet, but he did have the gift of self-promotion. In the poem he tells Melpomene of his recent exploits, attacking the island of Grand Cayman, where "with my great valor I opened fire and destroyed everything around." (In fact, he'd burned some fishermen's huts and taken four children hostage, an adventure that he believed would make "all the villains . . . tremble / Just upon hearing my name.") The captain resupplied at Trinidad, sailed to Cuba in search of more adventure, and there heard about a "thief" lurking in Spanish waters: Captain Bart. What happened next shattered the peace between England and Spain in the West Indies.

The two ships wheeled for position and began a duel at sea. The *Mary and Jane* was outgunned, six cannon to Rivero's fourteen, and sixteen men to the Spaniard's ninety-six. Captain Bart put up a spirited fight, surviving a night of broadsides and killing three of Rivero's men. They were apparently the first casualties under his command, and he wrote about it in an unusual way. "Though it was God's will," he wrote, "I felt it deeply." The deaths fueled his anger, and anger fueled his vanity:

I swear that with my arm and strength,
I will capture these villains and that
I will have them all at my feet.

The next morning the battle resumed. After four hours Bart was dead (Rivero, typically, claimed to have killed him personally), along with four of his men; the ship was burning, and surrender was inevitable; the English gave in. Rivero was grieved to find out they had only lost five men, but still he strutted like a peacock and announced to the Jamaicans that he had a commission from the queen regent good for five years throughout the whole of the West Indies. He also mentioned that it was a direct result of the attack on Portobelo. The ripples from Morgan's raid were now traveling back across the Atlantic and roiling the North Sea.

Nine of the captives were allowed to return to Port Royal. Rivero apparently wanted fame more than he did ransom for the seamen. Now it was the Spaniards' turn to welcome a conquering hero into one of their harbors: When Rivero sailed into Cartagena on March 24 with the *Mary and Jane* as booty, he was hailed as a savior. The town threw a riotous party in his name, and the governor granted him the privilege of hoisting the royal standard on his mainmast. The Spanish had for one of the few times in their recent history deviated from their military strategy and stolen a page from the English playbook. Rivero's success seemed to point a new way for defeating the infidels at their own game. Others joined the cause. "This great event has encouraged other inhabitants," wrote the governor of Cartagena, "who are preparing two other vessels with which we will punish the boldness and the damages inflicted by these Pirates."

For the Portuguese captain, it was nothing less than what he expected: The tragic muse, the mother of the sirens who call sailors to their deaths, had answered his call. Fired by his victory, toward the end of his poem he vowed to protect the empire against an unnamed villain who we must assume is Henry Morgan:

> *I am the defender against this monster*
> *I have been confirmed Captain of these coasts.*
> *By Saint Peter, I was the first.*
> *My name alone is enough*
> *To make the sea*
> *And all these barbarians*
> *Tremble.*

Modyford was stunned. The loss of the *Mary and Jane* was in-significant in itself: The Spanish were constantly attacking Ja-maican vessels and stealing their men away. But the news of a five-year letter of reprisal was worrying; the Spanish would never grant just one. It had to signal a wholesale change in policy. Rivero was only the spear point of a new offensive. Indeed, the Council of War of the Indies in Madrid had declared on April 9, 1669, that Ja-maica must be retaken, "since it is the source of all the problems." The councilors had decided that the objective was so important that it was worth putting at risk the "main cities of the Windward Islands and Mexico" and even leaving the coast of Spain unprotected. Modyford knew none of this, but he could sense that something was afoot. He consulted with Morgan, and they decided that they'd have to find physical evidence of this new policy to send back to England. That would checkmate any attempt Arlington would make to ex-plain the attack as an understandable retaliation. They didn't have to wait long. Two vessels out of Port Royal were headed for Campeche on a logwood run; their crew, just as Modyford had predicted, was peppered with former buccaneers who had turned to this hon-est trade when commissions were rescinded. As they cruised off the Yucatán Peninsula, they came under attack from the *San Nicolás de Tolentino,* a Spanish ship apparently in league with Rivero. To the Spaniards the much smaller boats seemed like easy prey, but the ex-Brethren reverted to their old form and soon overwhelmed the enemy crew. On board they found the smoking gun, the queen regent's letter authorizing commissions against Jamaica. When the logwood boats returned to Port Royal and the document was handed to Modyford, he learned that Spain had been at war with him for almost a year. Without informing Arlington or the English throne, the queen had instructed her ministers "to execute all hostil-ities which are permitted in war, by taking possession of all the ships, islands, places and ports" of the English infidel. It was not just a letter of reprisal against the pirates; it was a directive to retake Jamaica.

Now one report tripped in on the heels of another. A privateer arrived in Port Royal having just interviewed one Edward Browne, an English turncoat who had gone native, converted to Catholicism, and moved to Cartagena; when the privateer captured the boat he'd been sailing on, Browne told him that a declaration of war against Jamaica had been broadcast in the streets there. News floated in that the same proclamation had been cried out in Portobelo, with the added specification that no quarter was to be given. The governor of the Dutch colony of Curaçao wrote to Modyford urgently, telling him he held in his hands a copy of the queen's letter, suggesting that the order was being distributed widely. Then another English ship, the *Amity*, was captured by Spanish corsairs near Granada. Facts begot rumors: A new armada was on the way from Spain, an invasion was planned. Suddenly the whole North Sea seemed alive with enemy activity.

On June 11 came another escalation. Rivero appeared, not off the coast of the Main but right on the northern Jamaican shoreline, accompanied by a converted French prize, *La Gallardina*. Again disguised under English colors, again insulting his victims before the attack began (this time he called them "doggs and rogues"), he tried to run down a trader's vessel, which managed to land on the beach before Rivero could board it. The Spanish landed right behind and chased the men on foot into the interior, exchanging musket fire. But the Spanish had little chance in the thick jungle and soon gave up, taking the trader's sloop as a consolation prize. Modyford barely had time to digest the news of this probe before he learned that Rivero had brazenly returned to the north shore, landed thirty men, and burned houses of the plantation owners who lived there on the very fringe of the English empire. The war was drawing closer to Port Royal.

Rivero left a message behind, calling out Morgan to war by name:

I, Captain Manuel Rivero Pardal to ye chief of ye squadron of privateers in Jamaica. I am he who this year have done that which follows. I went on shore at Caimonos and burnt twenty houses and fought with

Captain Ary and took from him a ketch laden with provisions and a canoe. I am he who took Captain Baines [Bernard] and did carry the prize to Cartagena, and am now arrived at this coast and have burnt it.

And I am come to seek Admiral Morgan, with two ships of war of twenty guns, and having seen this, I crave he would come out upon the coast and seek me, that he might see the valour of the Spaniards. And because I had no time I did not come to the mouth of Port Royal to speak by word of mouth in the name of my King, whom God preserve. Dated 5th of July 1670.

Rivero's delusions of grandeur can bring only one figure to mind: Don Quixote. Cervantes could have been writing about the Portuguese adventurer as well as his hero: "He was seized with the strangest whim that ever entered the brain of a madman. . . . It was highly expedient and necessary, not only for his own honor, but also for the good of the public, that he should profess knight-errantry, and ride through the world in arms, and seek adventures . . . , redressing all manner of grievances, and courting all occasions of exposing himself to such dangers, as in the event would entitle him to everlasting renown." Rivero, at least, tilted at more than windmills and sailors' shacks. He'd taken the war to the English. He was attacking at will; he was exploiting the isolation of the Jamaican settlers; he was clearly as daring and independent as any of the privateers, not waiting for orders from Madrid. It was as if they were facing a Spanish double of Henry Morgan.

The Jamaicans were in a fever. One resident of Port Royal sat down to write this report on June 28: "The Spaniards have landed to leeward, burnt many houses, taken prisoners, and marched off," he recounted. "They last appeared off Wealthy Wood, but finding armed men on the shore, stood off to sea. . . . We talk of nothing here but burning Santiago de Cuba, being the first places that granted out commissions against us." The English had feasted on Spanish settlements for so long that it had seemed the natural order of things; and in fact the Spanish attacks paled beside the exploits of Morgan and other privateers. Now the hunters felt what it was like to be the hunted. Men watched the horizon in trepidation, hoarded their powder, met with the neighbors, and exchanged the latest rumors in low voices. There was only one solution, of course. The same letter writer revealed that all the privateers had been called in from other ports and assured they would not be arrested for fighting the Spanish.

It was an unsettled time. The Jamaicans were convinced that their colony was in danger from invaders. Preachers continued to predict that Port Royal was angering God into retribution. Seventeenth-century experts would have told Port Royalists to watch for signs that could predict the cataclysm suggested by the tremors that shook their town regularly: They should watch for the raging of the sea when there were no winds to cause it; a sulfurous smell "from the petulant Exhalations long inclosed within the Earth" (one author noted that landmasses with fewer "pores" were at a higher risk of tremors); any smoke, flame, and ashes shooting out of the ground; a sudden cold or calm breeze of air or a thin streak of "cold vapor"; noise coming from underground, especially "terrible groanings and thunderings"; and the forsaking of trees by birds, who then sat trembling on the ground. But the possibility of an earthquake concerned the people less than did an invasion by their archenemy.

Modyford yearned for word from London in this crucial time, but the ships that arrived from there carried no letters from Arlington. As in so many situations in the past, he was being left to his own devices. He called an assembly meeting for June 29, and there the planters and merchants stated that the queen regent clearly had decided "to make open Warr against the Subjects of our Sovereign Lord the King in these Parts." If they did nothing, the assembly expected that an invasion would soon follow. The result would be an exodus: The plantations would be abandoned, their cattle and slaves run to the jungle, and the settlers forced to start over again or disappear from the West Indies.

Feeling themselves under threat, the assembly was in no mood to tie Admiral Morgan's hands. Diplomatic language was tossed aside;

the Jamaicans wished there to be no misunderstanding in what they wanted. If the Spanish surrendered, he was to act with mercy. But if they did not, Morgan was given a mandate for utter destruction:

> If . . . the Spaniards and Slaves are deaf to your Proposalls you are then with all expedition to destroy and burn all Habitations and leave it as a Wilderness putting the Men Slaves to the Sword and making the Women Slaves Prisoners to bee brought hither and so sold for the account of your fleet and Army.

There were other powers thrown in: He could free any slaves who switched to the English side. He could impose martial law. He'd even be able to give commissions to any allied ships he encountered at sea. Modyford hedged his bets at the end of the instructions, in case a copy of a peace treaty arrived on the next ship from London. Morgan was told to "exceed [the Spanish] in civility and humanity, endeavouring to make all people sensible of his moderation and good nature and his . . . loathness to spill the blood of man." Morgan must have chuckled over that last part. But the document was a deadly serious statement. It was a declaration out of the *Iliad*. Its message? Total war.

The quickness with which the English responded underscores how they repeatedly gained the advantage over their Spanish enemies. The locals made the decision to attack without waiting for London's approval, placed the mission in the hands of one man, gave him every power to fulfill his objective, and then stood back and let Morgan shape the expedition. And on the crucial issue of money, which hamstrung Spanish governors again and again, the English didn't need to raise a penny. The privateers would be paid in swag. The privateers and their backers had, by necessity, grown to regard themselves as masters of their own fate. Their enemies had never been granted the same privilege.

Drummers marched through the streets of Jamaican cities calling for volunteers to man Morgan's ships, promising that all debts of those who sailed would be forgiven. Word came from Bermuda that the men there were eager to join, furious after a series of Spanish attacks on local ships. Morgan notified the Brethren at Tortuga that a major action was under way and that Île-à-Vache off the southern coast of Hispaniola would be the rendezvous point. "He wrote diverse letters to all the ancient and expert pirates there inhabiting . . . ," Esquemeling remembered, "and to the planters and hunters of Hispaniola giving them to understand his intentions, and desiring their appearance at said place. . . ." Other sources confirmed that everyone wanted in. John Morris signed up for the expedition in his ship the *Dolphin*. Lawrence Prince pledged to bring his fifty-ton *Pearl*, which he'd bought from Commodore Mings years before, after the old admiral had captured it from the Spanish. The *Pearl* had recently added six more guns to its original four, and Prince signed on sixty men to man the ship. Morgan sent urgent word for his flagship, the *Satisfaction*, to return from its patrolling of Spanish waters, but no one knew exactly where she was. With its twenty-two cannon, the *Satisfaction* was a floating battery, and he needed her for the challenge ahead.

The twenty-nine-year-old Roderick had never risen to the status of captain, mostly because of his disdain for networking among the Brethren and his lack of capital to buy a boat. But he swore his allegiance once again to Morgan, and he was one of many. One captain of a merchant ship, ordered by the ship's nervous owner to sail to Campeche for a load of logwood, thus putting himself out of reach of the war mobilization, secretly recruited some of the Port's renowned buccaneers, loaded extra cannon into his hold, and went rogue. He quickly came across and overpowered a fast, eight-gun Spanish ship, renamed her the *Thomas*, and sailed both vessels to Morgan's rendezvous. He was not alone. The buccaneers and hunters of Tortuga and Hispaniola "flocked to the place assigned in huge numbers, with ships, canoes and boats." Some of the Hispaniola contingent could find no vessels, so they trekked across the island, battling the Spanish as they went, until they arrived at the shore looking out on Île-à-Vache. In calling out these cow skinners, Morgan was harking back to the very roots of West Indian piracy. As they emerged out of the woods, their leather stained black with blood, their hair filthy and matted, their faces splashed with mud but with muskets polished, they must have appeared like shades from the Caribbean past. The legendary sharpshooting *boucaniers*, the men who lived as free as wild animals, the fathers of them all. Morgan was summoning ghosts.

Taboos were broken. Among the recruits was, reportedly, one "small, old and ugly, woman . . . who was publicly said to be a sorceress." The Spaniards reported that the buccaneers were disregarding the dire superstition against women on ships, let alone witches, and letting the Englishwoman aboard "to predict and warn them, telling them what they should do." There were even rumors (soon to be proved false) that Prince Rupert was sailing from England with twenty-five men-of-war and 5,000 crack troops. "No doubt this noble fleet would in a short time overrun and conquer all these Indies," wrote Richard Browne, surgeon general on Morgan's fleet, "but without Admiral Morgan and his old privateers things cannot go as successful as expected." For Morgan knew every creek, every Spanish tactic, and, even outnumbered and outgunned, the king could be assured that the Brethren "will either win . . . manfully or die courageously." Browne and others began to speak of the coming mission as the first step in taking the whole Caribbean for England.

As pirates, fortune seekers, and disreputables streamed toward Île-à-Vache from every corner of the Caribbean, Morgan finally traced the *Satisfaction* to the Cayman Islands and ordered it back to Port Royal. Modyford sent one last letter to London, hoping to cover for what was shaping up to be a scorched-earth campaign. Modyford as always found a way to depict this battle as the last resort of courageous underdogs. It might be "a fond, rash action for a petty Governor without money to make and entertaine war with the richest, and not long since the powerfullest, Prince of Europe," he wrote, but his hand had been forced. Jamaica was under attack, and his solution was to fight now to prevent a complete takeover, all at no cost to the English government. Arlington was also notified, and Modyford even asked that his superior send frigates in case of an attack launched on Jamaica from Spain itself. He must have known the chances of being reinforced from London were slim to none.

On August 1, Morgan received his official commission. The privateers would not be paid but would depend on "the old pleasing account of No purchase, No pay," meaning that their only compensation for the raid would be the booty they recovered. The rest was open-ended; Morgan could attack where and when he chose. The fleet was coming together: The local merchants were lending money at a furious pace to privateers in need of sail, rigging, and powder. The *Satisfaction* was now ready to serve as Morgan's flagship, while other substantial vessels and veteran captains lined up behind it: the frigate *Lilly,* commanded by Richard Norman, and the six-gun *Fortune,* commanded by Richard Dobson, along with the seventy-ton *Mayflower* with Joseph Bradley at the helm. Morgan's old comrades from past battles played a large part in the new mission; clearly he valued loyalty and would later rail against the backstabbers and gossipers whom he saw around him. "The remoteness of this place gives so much opportunity to the tongue and hand of malice," he wrote, "that the greatest innocence cannot be protected without much care and watchfulness." He kept his early allies close throughout his life, but it would become clear that he trusted very few men.

Morgan sailed on August 24, but soon after he was back at Port Royal: a letter had arrived from Arlington. Dated June 12, it dashed cold water on the Jamaicans' war fever. Rivero's attack "is not at all to be wondered at after such hostilities as your men have acted upon their territories." The king was seeking to put an end to privateering once and for all. A breakthrough in Madrid is "daily expected"; the English negotiator, William Godolphin, was working feverishly to finish the treaty. The main obstacle, as Arlington saw it, was the Spanish resentment over what the privateers had done. All in all, there was not much in the letter except a rehashing of Arlington's old complaints, but there was one key sentence that changed everything. "His Majesty's pleasure," Arlington wrote, "is, that in what state soever the privateers are at the receipt of this letter he keep them so till we have a final answer from Spain." This gave Arlington room to maneuver in any eventuality, and he cannily included a final injunction to Modyford: All attacks on land were strictly forbidden.

But Modyford had spotted the out: The fleet had been at sea when the letter arrived, and Modyford would not bring them in. Morgan could drive his fleet straight through that loophole, and there was nothing Arlington could say about it. The governor mouthed some words to Morgan about acting "with all moderation possible in carrying on this war," and Morgan promised to follow orders, except, that is, if necessity required him to land on Spanish territory for supplies or if he learned that the Spanish were laying up ammunition and provisions for an attack on Jamaica. With a little playacting, Arlington's language had been unspooled. Modyford assured Arlington that "those rugged fellows [had] submitted to a stricter discipline than they could ever yet be brought to," but something closer to the opposite was true: The attacks on Captain Bart and on Jamaica had made this mission personal for the buccaneers. Modyford wrote Arlington and insisted that the Spanish were still "borne up with false measures of their strength" and that Godolphin's mission was in vain. Knowing that he'd just unleashed the largest pirate army in the history of the West Indies, Modyford spoke with macabre wit of what awaited the enemy gathered in their towns and cities, unaware of the storm gathering over the horizon. "A little more suffering will inform them of their condition," he told Arlington. "And force them to capitulations more suitable to the sociableness of man's nature."

Morgan finally sailed for Île-à-Vache. But first he headed northwest to Cuba and scouted for any activity in the South Cays. John Morris stayed to monitor the area while Morgan headed to Santiago, the focal point of Jamaican anger. His first move was in keeping with his mandate: Destroy any invasion force. But there was no Rivero, no ships of any kind. Having done this basic reconnaissance, Morgan headed for Tortuga; in the West Indies, hurricane season runs from about June through the end of November, and Morgan was now in the heart of it. A storm struck, whipping spray into the pirates' faces as they rushed to bring down the sails, with the wind howling in the rigging. When the gales had died down, Morgan reassembled his little navy, and all arrived safely in Tortuga, where he recruited some French buccaneers to his cause.

Arriving at the Île-à-Vache on September 12, he found a handful of small vessels waiting for him with impatient buccaneers who had answered his call. Morgan knew that more were on the way, so he decided to build up the enormous stocks of food it would take to feed his pirate army. Sharpshooters were sent into the woods of Hispaniola to hunt, and they "killed there a huge number of beasts, and salted them." Another large contingent of 400 men in five vessels was sent to the Spanish Main to roust up beef and maize. The rest of the men fell to repairing the damage done to the sails and rigging during the open-sea gale; more work was required after October 7, when "so violent a storm" hit the fleet that "all the vessels except the Admiral's were driven on shore." Three ships were lost, and the fleet was getting increasingly crowded with the droves of men who arrived daily in dinghies, in canoes, or on foot. Morgan wrote to Modyford complaining that he had more men than ships to carry them; the response to his call-up had been unusually strong.

As the men at Île-à-Vache sweated in the broiling sun over ropes and planking, the 400 men under Morgan's vice admiral Collier took five weeks to cover the 450 miles to their target, the grain port of Río de la Hacha, west of the Gulf of Venezuela. Once they arrived, they were becalmed and couldn't make the harbor. The pirates fumed. The townspeople watched the limp-sailed ships, hid their goods, and made their decisions about whether to resist; Río de la Hacha had once been the center of a dazzling pearl fishery and had been visited by corsairs before, so the residents knew the drill. Finally, on February 24, Collier managed to catch enough of a breeze to land his men two miles from the town, where they disembarked at seven in the morning with such discipline and speed that the Spanish thought they must be soldiers from the king's armies in England. The Spanish "were scared stiff at their first sight of the enemy and did not want to fight." Some begged the English not to kill them, some ran deep into the woods, and others hid beneath baskets.

Río de la Hacha was a backwater, and Collier expected an easy time of it. The town's sole fort held four guns and a typically depleted garrison; the only difference this time was some unexpected visitors: a group of forty Spaniards who had attacked Jamaica with Rivero in their ship *La Gallardina*. The men probably suspected that burning houses and leaving posted threats had not endeared them to Morgan's men, and so when Collier sent a trumpeter to demand that they lay down their arms, they replied with brio: "No, we cannot surrender because this is a castle belonging to the King. We will only surrender through force of arms." That last bit indicated that the men felt a need to put up at least some resistance, for the sake of their necks if not their reputations. The Spanish fired their cannon, but casualties were light, and after blasting away at the heathen for a period of twenty-four hours, the Spaniards gave up the fight. Some of the soldiers were found hiding under mattresses, and Collier had two of them executed, one of them for refusing to produce some receipts for valuables; time was as good as treasure on the Main, and the men of *La Gallardina* had wasted his. "These men come once again from England . . . ," reported the governor of Santa Marta rather breathlessly, "and . . . the fifty vessels that compose their armada will come directly here to reunite." Roderick fell in with one of the squads that now roamed the town and the countryside freely, torturing, gathering up plate, and collecting prisoners. Collier was not as skilled an inquisitor as Morgan, and although his men "in cold blood did a thousand cursed things, "the buccaneers failed to uncover 200,000 pesos ($10 million) hidden within the fort. Finally the locals, wishing to "rid themselves as soon as possible of that inhuman sort of people," paid a ransom of maize and beef. Collier's threat to behead those who did not contribute hastened their efforts, and soon the squadron was sailing back to join Morgan. They'd been away for a long five weeks, and every kind of nightmare scenario had been running in Morgan's head: They'd been captured by the Spanish and given up his secrets; they had happened upon a galleon and decided to skip out on him with their winnings. When he saw all the ships returning, along with the eighty-ton *Gallardina,* a wave of "infinite joy" washed over the admiral. He needed the ships, the maize, and the information from Collier's terrified prisoners.

More good news arrived when John Morris sailed into the bay: The irrepressible Manuel Rivero Pardal was dead. Morris had come upon Rivero by sheer accident. After patrolling the coast of Cuba for intelligence about Spanish ship movements and war plans, he'd come up empty. When a storm whipped up, he put his ship in to a sheltered cove on Cuba's eastern shore. At dusk another vessel came gliding into the bay: the *San Pedro y la Fama,* also looking for a place to ride out the storm. On seeing the English ship, Rivero was delighted: He had fourteen guns to the *Dolphin*'s ten, and his crew was primed for battle, "having taken on eighty musketeers and good stores of ammunition, grenadoes and stinkpots." For Rivero it would be another notch in his belt, but this time he was facing hardened buccaneers, not frightened farmers in the Jamaican wilderness. But at the first shot, his men began abandoning their posts and diving into the water. Their appalled commander tried to rally them, but as he shouted at them to man their guns, a single bullet pierced his throat and he fell.

A bitter moment for Rivero. The spars swayed above him against the blue sky as blood pumped out of his wound and across the deck. The sound of English barrages splintering the side of the *Fama* alternated with the screams of his soldiers, desperate to escape the privateers who were advancing on them, killing them in the water. If only his musketeers would die like men. Rivero had come to the West Indies to restore Spanish courage; he believed himself divinely ordained to do so. But his men had broken at the first report of a musket. The vision of the buccaneers as unconquerable demigods had triumphed over Rivero's vision of a new Spanish fighter.

It's a pity that Rivero didn't last longer, for with his death Morgan had lost his most spirited enemy. So many of his opponents did not die like men: Rivero had. Who knows what further brilliance the Welshman would have been forced to display had Rivero managed to infuse the Spanish with his outrageous gallantry? The English mocked the Portuguese commander; "that vapouring captain," the surgeon Richard Browne called him, "that so much annoyed Jamaica in burning houses and robbing the people and sent that insolent challenge to Admiral Morgan." Modyford sent the commissions from the queen regent that Rivero had been carrying on his vessel back to his superior in London, "whereby his Lordship will find him a person of great value amongst them." He also sent the original canvas copy of Rivero's bold challenge to Morgan, from which, Modyford said, one could guess at Rivero's vanity. The cowardice of his men colored the English judgment of their commander. But Rivero had died like a conquistador, a rare event on the Spanish Main. At least one group of musketeers would soon follow his example.

❖　　　❖　　　❖

Other ships streamed in, fresh from their own adventures, but more men came than ships to carry them. The men were packed aboard even the tiniest boats until they were practically hanging off the sides: The French sloop *Le Cerf* had forty buccaneers crammed into every available space. Some vessels were so ill-suited for naval battle that they didn't even have a cannon on board, such as the appropriately named *Virgin Queen*. Some impatient captains couldn't restrain themselves from freelancing: Three privateer captains "went up the river of Nicaragua" and stormed a fort that had been built to stop French corsairs from penetrating to the cities farther inland. The Spaniards riddled the ships with shot, killing sixteen and wounding eighteen, but the buccaneers persevered and stormed the castle. When they interviewed the castellan at cutlass point, he admitted that four hours earlier he'd sent a canoe to warn the city of Granada, site of Morgan's first triumph. The buccaneers put their strongest paddlers in a canoe and sent them rocketing up the river after them. It took the double-manned vessel three days to catch the messengers, but they did it, and stopped the alarm from spreading. The rogue buccaneers entered the sleepy town as conquerors. Not everyone had Morgan's luck, however: His men extorted just over £7 in silver per man, "which is nothing to what they had five years hence." Modyford gave them a slap on the wrist when they returned to Port Royal and sent them to Île-à-Vache to bulk up Morgan's forces.

As Morgan's army grew, the Spanish began to experience what Jamaica had suffered through months earlier: reports of war accumulating ominously one after the other. Letters arrived in Santa Marta from the terrified residents of Río de la Hacha, describing pitiless buccaneers gathering matériel for battle. Much of the intelligence was astonishingly up to date: fifty ships, 2,000 privateers, with Cartagena or Panama as the target. Other pieces of gossip were less so: The king had sent soldiers from the mainland, went one rumor, while another attested that the Duke of York was behind the entire operation. But all of the gossip pointed toward a mighty fleet on the waves. "Hardly a letter was written which did not report some news of an imminent threat," wrote historian Peter Earle. Perhaps the most frightening piece of news came from Curaçao: A trader had just pulled into the harbor after having sailed along the coast of Hispaniola, home of the *boucaniers*. Usually when merchant ships arrived offshore, the blood-spattered wild men would appear from out of the forest to trade their cured meats for the necessities of life. But now few emerged. The woods had been swept clean; the buccaneers had gone to Morgan.

The governor of Cartagena received the reports that pointed toward his city as the most likely destination for Morgan's men and began to ramp up his response: Farmers in coastal areas were ordered to draw their herds away from any possible landing areas, cutting off the buccaneers from a food source, and citizens in the outlying areas were put on alert to rush to the city's aid in the event of an attack. Finally the governor called a junta, and military capabilities were enhanced. The city's defenses were, truth be told, lacking: Equipment was outdated or broken, soldiers had not received their wages for over two years, and the victualing of the garrisons had been neglected. The governor ordered a general call-up: All able-bodied men who could handle a firearm, "whether they were foreigners or citizens," was ordered to stand ready to man the city's fifty cannon.

As Morgan's endeavor sucked men and matériel into its vortex, the Spanish waited.

✠   ✠   ✠

With Rivero out of the way and his vessels reaching capacity, Morgan spent the days before sailing as a combination quartermaster and port inspector. He toured every ship and made sure it was "well equipped and clean." He divided up the maize and beef that had been brought in among the ships. He checked out the forecastles on the larger ships where the men had slung their hammocks and stored their sea chests, his nose flaring at the combined smell of burning sulfur (used to fumigate the vessels), damp canvas, tar, and decaying wood that was the fragrance of the wooden ship. He assigned his underlings double rank: On sea they'd be captains, on land they'd be majors and colonels. Realizing that the fleet was now too large for one commander to direct effectively, he split it in two and put Collier in charge of the second squadron. The little navy was formidable at the top—Morgan's flagship was a twenty-two-gun floating fortress that would have been a significant warship even in Europe, and it was followed by the French standout *St. Catherine* with fourteen guns and 110 men. But the size and quality of the ships dropped away drastically, and indeed the more remarkable vessels were the tiniest ones, some too small to host even a single cannon; Morgan fielded five of these fishing smacks. They were essentially troop transports designed to get the buccaneers onto land, where they were at home. The names of the ships were a clue to the mind-set of the men who commanded them. Captains of Morgan's generation in the West Indies tended to see themselves as gentleman adventurers, not rebels, and their ships were often given names such as *Satisfaction*, *Endeavour*, and *Prosperous*, as if they were nothing more than gleaming yachts that carried aging moguls from Portsmouth to Aruba every year. As later generations became more outlaws than patriots, the names got racier: Blackbeard sailed *Queen Anne's Revenge*, and vessels prowled the oceans with names like *Avenger* and the *Jolly Roger* (named, of course, after the skull-and-crossbones flag). Morgan, however, would sail with his outlaw army under a respectable name.

After inspecting his fleet, Morgan took it on a kind of shake-down cruise to Cape Tiburon on the southwestern coast of Haiti, accurately described by an eighteenth-century French traveler as a "narrow chain of mountains strewn in the middle of the sea" whose peaks give the scene a "magnificent, audacious character." It was an appropriate setting for the mission that was to be launched from the blue waters surrounding Tiburon as the fleet of thirty-eight ships sailed in from points west. On December 2 the fleet was finally ready. Morgan invited the captains of each ship, thirty-six in all, for the council of war. As they stepped on board, along with their glass of rum punch they were each handed a fresh commission, made out in their names authorizing them "to act all manner of hostility against the Spanish nation . . . as if they were open and declared enemies of the King of England. . . ." Roderick and the other common pirates celebrated their imminent wealth by shooting off their guns and singing sea chanteys deep into the night.

Aboard Morgan's flagship the admiral proposed the articles under which the buccaneers would sail. He'd take 1 percent of every piece of plate, every emerald or pearl, every peso, and every slave. The captains would get eight shares (eight times the portion allotted to the ordinary crew member), with the surgeon getting a fee of 200 pesos ($10,000 in modern currency), the carpenter 100 ($5,000), in addition to their common salaries. Then Morgan listed compensation for injuries, at rates "much higher" than on previous voyages. Men who lost both legs would get a whopping 1,500 pesos ($75,000); one leg, "whether the right or the left," 600 ($30,000). A hand, 600. An eye, 100 ($5,000). There were also generous terms for the especially brave: "Unto him that in any battle should signalize himself" by being the first to enter a fort or rip down the Spanish flag and raise the English, 50 pesos. Grenadiers would rake in 5 pesos for every bomb they lobbed into an enemy position. Men fight harder when they know they will have guaranteed months of rum should they lose a limb. The generous terms gave the mission a special status; Morgan would expect them to earn every peso.

The contract showed the brilliance of the Brethren's system as opposed to the Spanish. It rewarded greater risk with greater rewards. It gave individual men every reason to excel. The pirates understood what motivated their men. The Spanish, still drifting on the fumes of the Crusades, did not.

Now came the real matter of the evening: Where would they strike? There were only four contenders: Santiago, Panama, Cartagena, and Vera Cruz. Santiago was the name on Jamaican lips; people there believed it was the seat of the anti-English warmongering. But it had tactical disadvantages: The Cuban city was defended by a fortress that overlooked the only approach to the city. Morgan had survived a potential shooting gallery at Maracaibo, and no one was lucky enough to do that twice. Besides, it was not known as a rich target, so the city was dropped. If the mission was for booty alone, Vera Cruz would have been a natural choice: It received all the silver from Mexico and stored it up for the galleons' arrival. But Morgan had two objectives: to acquire a pile of treasure and strike a smashing blow to the empire. Vera Cruz could answer the first requirement, but not the second. There were no reports of its citizens arming for war against Jamaica, and so raiding it would not have the right political cover. Vera Cruz was out. Cartagena was a real power center on the Main, but its defenses were awesome (at least in the minds of the privateers): twice as many soldiers in its garrison as Panama and Portobelo combined, underground tunnels, fifty cannon, a large population of 6,000 free men and slaves to draw on for reinforcements. The city would come to be called La Heróica, and the mysterious explosion of the *Oxford* gave it a hexed quality. Cartagena would be difficult. So the buccaneers cast their eyes toward the oldest city in the Western Hemisphere.

Panama City was the brains and guts of a rich portion of the New

World; from here the levers of the sprawling province of Panama were pulled; bankers and administrators resided in its splendid wooden houses, riders rode out from its streets to direct the movements of mayors, soldiers, Indian workers. To take Panama would be to show Spain unable to protect its most valuable assets in the colonies. And besides, it was very, very rich; it had been said to rival Venice at its height. And once the terrible isthmus was overcome, the city lay open to invaders. The vote was taken, and the result was unanimous: Panama or death. As the serious drinking began, Morgan, who was important enough now to have his own secretary, had him draw up the Brethren's intentions into formal language. The proclamation read that the buccaneers had gathered "to prevent the invasions of the Spaniards" and had resolved to take Panama, because commissions against the English had been issued from that city. As the word spread throughout the fleet, the buccaneers—never ones to underplay their own abilities—still must have regarded their decision with a touch of awe. This was not just another escapade; there was no greater city in the Western Hemisphere than the one they'd just committed to destroy. It was as if the barbarians had laid plans to take Rome itself.

The plan immediately presented one problem: No one in the vast army that Morgan had assembled had ever been to Panama. Morgan never went into an attack blind, and so he decided to attack Providence, that old shuttlecock between England and Spain, on the way to his target. This is where the Spanish Empire housed its criminals, among which there were sure to be "many banditti and outlaws belonging to Panama." They would be his guide. And retaking Providence, which had been taken from the Spanish by the Jamaicans and then reconquered, would give him a bauble to dangle in front of the king, a tiny nugget of the empire reclaimed. Morgan probably assumed he'd need many successes to distract Charles II from what he intended to do in Panama.

On December 18, 1670, the great buccaneer fleet sailed.

❈   ❈   ❈

The Spanish knew the trajectory of pirates' careers as well as men like Morgan did. The only step up from places like Portobelo and Maracaibo would be Panama, Cartagena, or possibly Havana. Of these three, Panama was probably the most vulnerable, and the kingdom's energetic president Don Juan Pérez de Guzmán was furiously working to protect it from the coming storm. This was the same Don Juan who had recaptured Old Providence from the English and sent their leaders to the dungeons. He'd just emerged from the shade of a prison cell himself at the castle of Callao in Lima, where a power struggle with the viceroy had landed him. He returned to Panama in the spring of 1669 and immediately set to improving its defenses.

Panama sat on the other side of the isthmus from the North Sea and the hunting grounds of the privateers. Its best hope for protection lay in the fact that the journey to reach it was a nightmare: Mountains, deep rivers, swamps thick with fever mist, warlike maroons, sudden violent rains, and carnivorous animals waited for anyone brave enough to attempt it. It was an ancient route; Sir Francis Drake had walked it, and Indians before him. And it would claim victims for centuries after Morgan attempted it. When the California gold rush struck in 1849, men from the East Coast swarmed down to the town of Colón and then tramped through the black muck to Panama City, where boats waited to take them to California. Snakes, yellow fever, and dysentery made it a memorable trip; one commander of a surveying mission reported seeing mosquitoes so thickly bunched that they snuffed out lighted candles with their burned corpses. "For no consideration take this route," wrote one miner to a friend back home. "I have nothing to say on the other ones, but do not take this one." In 1852, when a U.S. Army regiment and the soldiers' families were assigned to new posts in California, they followed the same route, which now was now traversed via railroad, boat, and mule train, a much easier journey than in Morgan's time. Even when he disembarked at the starting-off point, modern-day Colón, the regiment's quartermaster was unimpressed. "I wondered how any person could live many months [there]," wrote the young Ulysses S. Grant, "and wondered still more why anyone tried." The Americans were no match for the cholera and tainted water, and Grant watched men grow delirious and die by the hour. He later wrote about the expedition that cost him dozens of men, women, and children. His judgment of the place? "The horrors of this road in the rainy season are beyond description."

Don Juan knew enough not to underestimate Henry Morgan, however, and he began to build up the fortifications on the trail. He begged the Crown for men to stock the garrisons at Portobelo and Chagres, the two main entry points to the isthmus. The authorities in Madrid relented, but when the treasure fleet finally arrived at Portobelo with his troops, Don Juan encountered some difficulties in claiming his men: A large portion of the soldiers had been assigned to other posts, had absconded, or had died from yellow fever or malaria. So many had died, in fact, that the captain of the treasure fleet snapped up the remainder meant for the defense of Panama and brought them back with him to guard the silver. A demoralized Don Juan was left to round up any stragglers he could find and press-gang them into service. It was a typical frustration for a Spanish leader facing the pirates: a top-down solution to his problems that was frittered away by distance and lieutenants eager to safeguard their own careers. "I myself am ready to die in the Kingdom's defence," the president of Panama wrote, "but that will not stop the enemy making war." Don Juan was the canary in the silver mine, but Madrid was deaf to his message.

Spain did not want its New World settlers to act and think on their own, or to become too dependent on one another. That would jeopardize the flow of treasure; it would disrupt the autocratic system that had made the nation a world power. Spanish towns were connected more tightly to Spain than they were to one another. Governors competed with one another for scarce resources instead of pooling them. The vast distances multiplied the problem. By tying the colonies so closely to the motherland, Spain weakened them. The pirates preyed on these isolated outposts again and again.

The president mobilized every resource he could: At San

Lorenzo Castle at the mouth of the Chagres, new cannon stations were mounted on the riverside, while letters went back to Spain with more warnings and requests for able-bodied men to stock the garrison. Don Juan had called in a military engineer, and he outlined the suggested improvements to Santiago Castle at Portobelo in a letter to the queen. "It was resolved to build two high redoubts with their motes [sic] and stockades on top of the hills that serve as obstacles," he reported. San Felipe received new stockades and raised parapets. San Gerónimo, which had been only partially finished when Morgan attacked Portobelo, was pushed near to completion. Beyond that, however, the Crown felt it had done all it could with its strained resources and Don Juan soon understood he'd have to fend for himself; there would be no warships or musketeers whipping their way from Spain. Meanwhile he was receiving reports that the pirates were building a fleet of thirty canoes for the assault. "I give you these warnings even though I know that you are a great soldier and you will not need them," the governor of Cartagena wrote to Don Juan. It was perhaps the only thing he could think to say when the news was so obviously bad.

Worse was to follow. Don Juan's informants turned out to have excellent sources in the Brethren's camp, and by June of 1670 he was told that 1,500 buccaneers were going to attempt Panama by the Chagres route. It was, for the Caribbean, an enormous number of men; Panama itself held only 6,000 residents, and just a small percentage of them would be available to defend it. The final omen came in a form that was typically Spanish: A Franciscan monk, no doubt prompted by the rumors that swept the city of a black swarm of buccaneers waiting just over the horizon, had a vision one night of what lay in store for his city. In his dream, Jamaican privateers were rampaging through Panama, murdering and looting as they went, while maroons could be spotted spreading flames from rooftop to rooftop. Panamanians lay dying in the streets, with black smoke billowing in the background. The nightmare so impressed the monk that he convinced a local painter to render his vision in oils, and the portrait was displayed at the convent. The residents came to gaze upon the apocalyptic canvas and shiver with dread; it was a scene from the future of Spanish art, from the war scenes of Goya, not their beloved Velázquez.

Slowly Panama took on the aspects of a city under psychological siege. Many believed that the only question was not would Morgan come, but when.

11

The Isthmus

Six days after setting out, Morgan's ships appeared off Providence, having covered the 575 miles in excellent time. Providence consisted of a large island connected to a smaller one, Isla Chica. The main island looked deserted as Morgan's ships pulled ashore and quickly disembarked a thousand men, and indeed it was, the Spanish contingent of fewer than 200 having decamped to Isla Chica, which Morgan soon found had been studded with castles since the last English invasion. The first one the Brethren had to face was La Cortadura, which sat between the two islands and could be approached only by a drawbridge, which was now raised.

Things began miserably. The skies opened up and poured rain on the buccaneers, who were not clothed for such weather; Roderick was lightly dressed in seaman's trousers and cotton shirt, without shoes. When the men approached the Spanish fort, the defenders "began to fire upon them so furiously that they could advance nothing that day." The buccaneers retreated and camped outside the gunners' range in the open fields. Morgan now faced a problem familiar to the commander of any large army of men: sustenance. He had no supply lines to provide meals for his soldiers; they could eat only what they carried or foraged. Shivering and gnawed by hunger,

Roderick and some mates pulled down a thatch house and made campfires. And they grumbled over the fire, with Roderick suggesting that Morgan was leading them astray. They'd voted on Panama, not this miserable piece of rock. They were sure that Morgan was not sitting out in the damp, like them. He'd probably found a warm hut to keep himself dry.

The next morning, more of the same. The rain pelted Roderick and the poor corsairs "as if the skies were melted into waters" and the Spanish peppered them with shot from behind their sturdy walls. With his belly rumbling, Roderick spotted an old nag in the nearby field and called to his friends, who chased it down for breakfast. But it was a pitiful sight: "both lean and full of scabs and blotches," Esquemeling reports. They carved up the animal and divided the tiny morsels among the lucky, who roasted the meat "more like ravenous wolves than men." The question of food was becoming critical; most of their supplies had been left on the ships. Not only that, but Morgan could now see that behind Cortadura lay a whole chain of forts; the Spanish could occupy and then abandon one after the other, killing privateers as they went. It would be a long, bloody siege. His men had come for money and glory; they hadn't asked for a miserable slog on an island in the middle of nowhere. Soon Morgan began hearing reports that some of the Brethren were planning to head back to the ships, orders or no orders. Roderick had voted with the deserters; he hadn't signed up for this mess, and he felt deceived. Who was Morgan to change their plans without a vote? With men getting ready to leave, the admiral made a snap decision and in front of his army called for a canoe to be arrayed with a white flag and sent to the castellan. His message was terse: Surrender or die.

The governor of the island requested two hours to deliberate, and Morgan agreed. He badly needed the man to surrender: He'd eventually take the island, but it could be at the cost of Panama. When the messenger returned, Morgan waited for the answer with bated breath. As the man read out the governor's words, Morgan must have smiled. The governor had written that he'd surrender, but he asked Morgan to perform "a certain stratagem of war." It was a bit of playacting designed to save the man's career and possibly his life: He directed Morgan to lead his men to Cortadura, while his ships pulled up to the gun emplacement called St. Matthew and dispatched a platoon of men. They would find the governor making his way from one fort to another and intercept him on the path. Under threat of death, they would force him to lead them into Cortadura, masquerading as Spanish troops. Once it surrendered, the rest of the island's fortresses would fall like dominoes. And one other thing: "There should be continual firing at one another, but without bullets, or at least into the air." The farce would read like a pitched battle on paper, which is all the governor cared about.

Morgan could not have devised a better solution himself; it appealed to his sense of theatrical war. That night he followed the man's instructions to the letter; the governor was surprised on his way to Cortadura, and the rest of the evening went off without a hitch. Anyone watching from seaward that night would have thought that the Spanish were defending their queen to the death, with the "incessant firing of the great guns" and the sharp reports of muskets. But the only killing took place afterward, when "the Pirates began to make a new war upon the poultry, cattle and all sorts of victuals they could find." The buccaneers feasted on the island's supplies and quickly discovered 30,000 pounds of powder and other kinds of ammunition. As to spies, Morgan found four of the "banditti" who claimed to know the intricacies of the city and a native Indian named Antonillo who had lived in the target city. Morgan offered the criminals a full share in the proceeds if they would guide his men, and the criminals cheerfully agreed. Their leader was "the greatest rogue, thief and assassin" on the island, who deserved, according to Esquemeling, to be tortured upon the rack rather than play soldier on Providence. He would fit in nicely.

※　　※　　※

Now the assault on Panama began. The city could be approached via two routes: by land or river. (Sailing down around the tip of South

America and up the Pacific coast toward Panama was out of the question for the fleet's tiny boats, and, of course, there was no Panama Canal to get Morgan's ships across the isthmus.) The first passage began at the city of Portobelo, with which Morgan was already familiar. The pirates would have to take the city, then travel due south through thick woodlands laced with vines and choked with undergrowth, tramp over five-hundred-foot mountain passes, and then travel along mule paths to the city of Venta de Cruces, where they would pick up the road to Panama. If they chose the river route, they would begin at San Lorenzo, where a large and well-armed castle guarded the entrance to the Chagres, which would take them southwest to Venta de Cruces. Halfway there they would have to abandon their canoes and complete the journey on foot. Portobelo was tempting, as Morgan knew it so well, but the Spanish had surely learned their lesson and reinforced the city after his devastating raid. All in all, Portobelo was now a completely different proposition, and a much tougher one, so San Lorenzo and the Chagres it would be. Morgan estimated that the fort could be taken with 470 men in three ships, and he assigned a lieutenant colonel, Joseph Bradley, to lead the squadron. Bradley had been raiding the Spanish since the time of Mansvelt, Morgan's predecessor; he was experienced and popular with the buccaneers, and Morgan was counting on him to open a crucial breach in the shield around Panama.

San Lorenzo was the door to the isthmus; it had been built to discourage men from thinking they could pass through it easily. It sat on the north side of the river mouth, on a high cliff that jutted out into the water, and it was really a network of defenses rather than just a single fort: two gun emplacements lower down near the water's edge, at the base of the castle walls, with six guns each; above them a tower with eight cannon that could spray oncoming ships with shot; and at the top of the peak the castle itself, its walls consisting of two rows of thick logs, between which had been packed mounds of earth, a design that made the barricade "as secure as the best walls made of stone or brick." The cliff top was divided into two sections, and the draw-bridge over a thirty-foot ravine was the only entrance to the fortress. A single set of stairs had been cut into the mountain face, allowing men to climb from the shore to the castle.

Bradley and his men arrived off San Lorenzo on December 26. The element of surprise was gone: One of the buccaneers on the Río de la Hacha raid had deserted the ranks and fled to the Spanish side; the men in the castle had been preparing for battle for weeks. There were two ways to the castle: scale the cliffs on the seaward side or go up the stairway on the landward side. Bradley quickly saw that the dizzying cliffside was a nonstarter; the "infinite asperity of the mountain" barred all but the expert climber, and his men were no mountaineers. They would have to hit the beach, absorb the fusil-lades from the gun batteries and the tower, and take the castle. It was not going to be a repeat of Providence. The Spanish held the heights and seemingly every advantage, their garrison recently sup-plied with "much provision and much warlike ammunition," as well as 164 more soldiers. "Although six thousand men should come against them," the castle's commander, Don Pedro de Lisardo, as-sured the president of Panama, "he should . . . be able to secure himself and destroy them."

Inside San Lorenzo the buccaneers' every move was being moni-tored. They had been spotted by the lookout in the castle watch-tower that very morning while four miles from the castle; as they approached, this man sent a series of running reports down to the commander: Three ships were disembarking men in six canoes, the canoes were ferrying the soldiers to the shore in shifts. When the ca-noes landed, they were observed by Spanish archers and lancers hidden in the woods. The buccaneers were not bothering to be crafty; their drummers pounded out a martial beat, their trumpeters sang of impending doom, and their color-bearers took their place at the head of the squadrons. The estimate? About 300 to 400 men, now moving off the beach and slashing their way through the jungle with machetes. The two sides would be close to evenly matched in numbers. Don Pedro dashed off a note to Don Juan Pérez de Guzmán, saying he expected the enemy within a few hours of midnight or at dawn. Three hundred men were reported to be advancing, but even if there were many more, he was confident he could smash them. "Here's a scourge for these infidels!" he wrote, bristling with confidence.

At the fort the lookout and every man at the ramparts watched the brush line. Hours went by with only the chatter of birds and the sound of the surf. Finally movement at the edge: Bradley and his men came stumbling out of the jungle; their guides had miscalculated and brought them too close to the castle onto a *campaña,* or open plot of ground. The Spanish sharpshooters on the ramparts instantly opened up on the figures below as the gunners rained shot down on the English; in the first fusillade, the Brethren "lost many of their men."

Bradley divided his men into three groups: a reserve force that would stay in the jungle and then two assault squads. In front of them lay an open stretch of bare land, where they would be vulnerable to Spanish fire, leading up to a deep crevice called the Ravine of the Slabs; only having crossed the ravine would they reach the walls of the castle. The men would have no artillery to cover their approach or armor to deflect the ball: "Being uncovered from head to foot, they could not advance one step without great danger." At last they girded up their loins and charged screaming onto the open space. As soon as they did, the sound of musket fire erupted, and the privateers ran crazily for the castle. Roderick was grazed by a Spanish ball but made it to the ravine; when he turned to look back, he saw that many of his mates lay facedown in the dirt behind him. "One could not see the *campaña* for the dead bodies of the enemy," wrote one defender with Spanish hyperbole. The survivors ran down into the ravine and then up and reached the castle walls. Now Bradley's strategy was revealed: Roderick pulled out the grenadoes he'd tied to his belt and tried to set the castle's wooden walls alight, and his comrades did the same with any combustible they carried.

But the barrage from above was too fierce; Bradley finally had to call the retreat. As Roderick ran from a battle for the first time in his life, he was startled to hear the words *"Victoria! Victoria!"* ringing out from the fort. He swore underneath his breath.

The Brethren retired to the brush, nursed their wounds, gulped down water, and regarded the castle with malice. Roderick massaged his bad leg and debated with the others "whether to forsake the Enterprise." But they decided there were things worse than death, namely "the Thoughts of Disgrace, and of being reproached by our Friends on board." Like any proud fighting force, the Brethren were intensely protective of their reputation, and the thought of losing face made them "disregard even life itself." As night fell, they charged a second time across the darkened field. The Spaniards, more confident than ever, welcomed them back: "Come on, ye English dogs," they shouted, "enemies to God and our king; let your other companions that are behind come on, too; ye shall not go to Panama this bout." Dusk provided cover, and the Spaniards fired at black shapes moving across black ground. The buccaneers dropped to their knees and raked the walls as their comrades slipped ahead and launched fireballs at the palm-leaf roof that sheltered the Spanish musketeers from rain and sun. The battle raged on until, according to Esquemeling, an act of sheer physical courage altered its course:

> One of the pirates was wounded with an arrow in his back, which pierced his body to the other side. This instantly he pulled out with great valour at the side of his breast then taking a little cotton that he had about him, he wound it about the said arrow, and putting it into his musket, he shot it back into the castle. But the cotton being kindled by the powder, occasioned two or three houses that were within the castle . . . to take fire.

The fire crept onward until it caught onto a "parcel of powder" (in Spanish reports it was a loaded bronze cannon), which exploded, raining flame and burning thatch onto the roof and the wooden walls. Other buccaneers snapped up arrows and shot them toward the looming castle. The Spanish rushed to douse the flames, but every musketeer pulled into firefighting duty was a loss to the fort's defenses, and the pirates began picking off figures silhouetted against the flames. The explosion had ripped a huge gap into the wooden palisades, and the breach became the scene of vicious, close-up fighting. Roderick found himself near the gap and blasted away at point-blank range through the gaping hole, falling back to reload while another buccaneer jumped into his spot and fired, as the Spanish tossed their combustibles at the Brethren's heads.

The palisades were now aflame in several places, and the six-inch mahogany walls began to collapse, spilling out their earthen contents and exposing the soldiers inside. The perimeter of the castle was roasting hot; the bodies of soldiers lay near the walls, terribly burned or bullet-ridden, the wounded calling out for water. The garrison's morale began to crumble; men deserted their posts and made their way down the stairway cut into the rock, escaping to boats tied along the river and then heading upstream toward Panama. The battle raged through the night, until even the privateers could no longer fight in the heat. They retreated and waited until the morning of January 6, which was a holiday known as the Epiphany of the Wise Kings. If the defenders of San Lorenzo had been back in Spain, they would have watched the burning of the Christmas tree, a tradition of the day, after children had swarmed over it and stripped it of its candies and treats. Perhaps a few remembered the date and called their minds back to happier times, for when first light came, showing jagged holes in the fort's walls, with the remaining musketeers struggling to wriggle through the gaps, they must have known that many of them were not going to live out the day.

With a yell the Brethren attacked again, "shooting very furiously" and tossing grenade after grenade. The defenders wheeled their cannons down to the breaches and fired point-blank at their attackers, the castellan having ordered his men to fight to the death. The buccaneers had rarely seen Spaniards fight with such resolve;

when their powder ran out, the Spaniards switched to lances and cutlasses and hacked at the men who attempted to slip between the splintered walls. It was now hand-to-hand, primeval war, with the castellan fighting alongside his men. When their lances broke, the Spaniards pulled out their cutlasses; when the cutlasses were knocked out of their hands, they picked up stones. Both Esquemeling and the Spanish letters written after the attack confirm that few conquistadors or musketeers in the legendary battles against the Moors had fought more bravely; the surgeon called their performance "very courageous and warlike." Roderick and the other men were impressed; they would never speak of the men of San Lorenzo except with a frank admiration. The noise of the battle was so great that it reached the ears of Francisco González Salado, the man Don Juan had chosen to defend the isthmus. The forty-year-old Spaniard had 400 to 500 men under his command and was waiting eighteen miles away at the River of Two Fathoms for news of the invasion. Hearing the cannon, he sent fifty soldiers to San Lorenzo. When they were six miles from the castle, they began meeting the desperately injured and terrified men who were running for their lives, and they relayed word of the attack back to González. The men abandoning the castle headed back toward Panama or melted away into the jungle.

At the castle, the pirates were simply proving too strong. They did not suffer deserters (or at least none are mentioned in the records), and what for the Spanish was heroic service was to the buccaneers their everyday fighting style. Eventually their numbers and their maniacal courage won the day; they streamed inside the castle and began slashing at the men with their cutlasses or executing them on the spot with their pistols. "The enemy refused quarter," Morgan reported tersely, "which cost them 360 men." As the buccaneers ran through the castle and had their vengeance on the enemy, those still at the foot of the walls looked up to witness Spanish musketeers diving from the top of the walls to the rocks below, dashing themselves to pieces rather than ask for quarter. As the buccaneers poured in, the castellan refused to yield; two cannons were wheeled in front of his position as he prepared for a last defense. But a privateer took aim with his musket and fired a shot, "which pierced his skull into his brain." The defense of San Lorenzo was over. As the deserters paddled their canoes away from the burning fort, they heard the French buccaneers break into the song *they* had sung earlier: *"Victoire, victoire."*

The pirates killed everything that moved within the fort; the Spanish had not asked for quarter, and they didn't receive it. Roderick had run out of ammunition, so he took his cutlass and chopped at the necks of the Spaniards he found cowering behind shattered remnants of the barricade. The buccaneers had lost thirty men and seventy-six wounded, including Lieutenant Colonel Bradley, who had been shot in the leg. The wounded suffered terrible agonies in the heat, their wounds festering. There is no record of whether the fleet's surgeon accompanied the San Lorenzo mission, but even if he was on the scene, one man caring for seventy casualties would have been afforded little time for niceties. One account of a shipboard operation on a pirate named Phillips reveals the level of care a patient might receive. The ship's surgeon was absent, so it was decided that the carpenter would have to remove the man's wounded leg. The carpenter fetched his biggest saw, secured the man's ankle underneath his arm, and cut off the leg "in as little time as he could have cut a . . . Board in two." There is no mention of anesthesia, and the stump was treated by heating an ax in the fire and then cauterizing the wound, but the carpenter burned the patient's flesh "distant from the Place of Amputation, that it had like to have morify'd." A patient had to pray that the surgeon was competent and sober, two attributes that were quite rare on a buccaneer ship. But most of all, he had to hope that his wounds did not get infected; once they did, death almost always followed. Bradley was an example; his wounds turned gangrenous, and he lingered in agony for ten days before succumbing to his injuries. His squadron had lost more than a quarter of their strength; if this was an omen of things to come, Morgan might run out of men before he held Panama.

Back on Providence the admiral received word of the storming of San Lorenzo. The first step was taken; now, like any smart commander, he prepared his way back from the battle. He dumped the Spanish guns into the sea and set fire to all the island's huts and most of its castles. If the Spanish wanted to take back the little isle, he'd give them no help. He left the strongest fort untouched and ordered it stocked with provisions; if he needed a place to hole up after the raid on Panama, it would be waiting for him.

Five days after Bradley's victory, Morgan sighted San Lorenzo and the English colors flying over it. Instead of looking up at the flag, Morgan's captains should have been looking down, as just below the surface of the water near the river's mouth was a notorious reef, called Laja. Morgan never saw it. Esquemeling tells us what happened next. Five of the ships, led by Morgan's *Satisfaction*, slammed into the razor-sharp coral, tearing huge holes in their hulls and throwing men into the water. A powerful north wind kept the ships impaled on the reef, raking them over the coral until they were unsalvageable. Morgan had never been much of a sailor, and now he simply moved his men and matériel off the stricken vessels and packed them into the remaining ships. As long as he had men, he could get other ships. He lost ten buccaneers in the accident, including the expedition's only female member, the much-gossiped-about witch. She failed the traditional test for enchantresses by drowning in the blue waters. Roderick and the others were actually relieved; suspected witches on board were horrible luck.

When Morgan was brought into the captured fort, "great acclamations of triumph" echoed off its walls. He supervised the last of the repairs to the castle; as on Providence, he was fortifying his escape route even as he proceeded toward Panama. But he couldn't linger; there were rumors that Spanish forces were already on the march to retake the fallen castle. Morgan left 300 men to guard it, selected seven ships from the fleet, commandeered some of the local canoes, and began the trek across the isthmus. Esquemeling noted one fateful decision the admiral made before setting out for the Venice of the Spanish Main: "He carried very small provisions with him, being in good hopes he should provide himself sufficiently among the Spaniards." It was a decision Morgan would come to regret.

The approach to Panama was, in some ways, a return to Morgan's past. In the woods ahead, along the thickly wooded banks, he knew that guerrillas were waiting silently for him. Many of them were black and mulatto soldiers, just as he'd faced back in Jamaica during the first months of the English invasion. They had lived in the woods and small towns along the Chagres for years, knew its terrain intimately, its hiding spots, its natural ambush points. San Lorenzo had been a classic storming of a stockade, a method of attack that went back to the Crusades and beyond. But now Morgan could be facing a more modern style of warfare that had devastated Cromwell's army when it settled Jamaica. The admiral had better-trained men under him than the raw youths who had fallen on Jamaica, but they were packed tightly into canoes and boats, perfect targets for hidden marksmen behind the fronds. His 1,500 men, watchful and tense, paddled down the Chagres with eyes on the brush line.

On the other side waited Francisco González Salado. Don Juan's chosen man had parceled out his 400 men to four stockades that had been built between the mouth of the Chagres and Venta de Cruces; they were lightly armed with lances, bows and arrows, muskets and pistols. He also had scouts on foot and in canoes patrolling the Chagres. González had decided to use his men not as guerrillas but in fortifications that could perhaps kill off enough of Morgan's men to prevent the invasion from reaching Panama. It was clearly a flawed strategy; San Lorenzo's 400-plus musketeers, fighting like lions, had failed to stop a small contingent of the Brethren. How could a comparable amount of men, divided into four squadrons, without cannon, protected only by thrown-up stockades, hope to do better? A shoot-and-run campaign would have been a more lethal choice, but González stood by his Spanish training.

There were guerrillas on the way, however. The president of

Panama had received an intriguing overture from three captains in the local prison: Let them out of jail, give them arms and men, and allow them to attack Morgan on the river. If they succeeded, charges would be dropped. If not, they would die in the service of Panama and their reputations would be saved. These men had grown up on the river and knew where Morgan would be vulnerable. The offer was accepted, and the three set off with 150 men; that number would double once they met up with González's forces and were reinforced. Don Juan was trying to keep Morgan as far away from the city as he could and to force the battle in the difficult, pestilent jungle rather than on the plains of Panama, where the Welshman would have the advantage.

The freed captains and their squadron made their way down to a settlement called Dos Brazos and perched along the tree line, waiting in ambush. They were expecting a force the same size that had attacked San Lorenzo, about 400 men. When the first canoes appeared on the river, the Panamanians checked their powder and prepared a surprise barrage. But then more canoes appeared, buccaneers hanging over the sides, and then small boats, and then more canoes. The vessels kept coming, an endless line of grizzled men with shiny muskets. The buccaneer army was almost four times the size of what the captains had been expecting. They wished to clear their names, but the odds of four-to-one against Henry Morgan were a dead man's bet. Instead of opening up on the English devils, the Spanish watched as a party of Morgan's men beached their canoes, foraged among the abandoned huts, and stretched their legs onshore. The lazy privateers were easily within musket range, and they were open to attack. The Spanish gaped as some of the men even lay down on the banks and fell asleep, while others sat smoking a pipe of tobacco. The Spanish sharpshooters fingered their triggers, but the names of Morgan's victories echoed in the captains' minds: Granada, Portobelo, Maracaibo. They held their fire.

Back in Panama, Don Juan was expecting to hear that the buccaneers had been attacked and their progress disrupted, or that the

Panama squadron had retaken San Lorenzo. But the captains' report filled him with disgust: "They neither fought with them nor did more than flee to the mountains," Don Juan lamented, "without trying either of the two things that they had planned." The squadron reported that they had meant to attack the buccaneers upstream, but an incompetent Indian guide had led them astray and they had missed their chance. The valor of San Lorenzo was dissolving like a mirage.

To the many reasons that the ordinary Spanish soldier was given not to fight—bad or no pay, poor equipment, legitimate fear of the pirates' reputation—was added the basic nature of the pirates' invasion. Despite Morgan's commission from the council of Jamaica, the Brethren were not there to occupy the land and enslave the people. They moved through, robbed what they could, and left. If the pirates had been traditional conquerors, settling in the territories they invaded, they would probably have met much stiffer resistance from settlers fighting for both their freedom and their land. But if you could hide from the buccaneers, you could live another day, and every soldier and militia member knew that. It was like a charging bull: You could place yourself in front of it and attempt to pierce its heart with your saber, or you could step to the side and let it brush your thigh and continue on its way. The latter choice made special sense for the poor. If you had little or no valuables yourself, why take a bullet for those who did?

Now all that stood between the buccaneers and Panama were the four lightly defended stockades. The canoes paddled up the river, while the larger ships caught breezes and sailed along. The Chagres by water was a very different prospect from the Chagres by riverbank. A nineteenth-century traveler described the pleasant scene: "In some places lofty hills, densely timbered, rose from the river banks, in others, gentle slopes of brightest green pasture terminated in white sandy shores and again impenetrable underwood, covered with ivy, formed natural arbors of every imaginable shape, abutting on the stream." Roderick spotted alligators slipping into the water at the first canoes' approach and heard parrots chattering; huge swarms of insects billowed like cumulus clouds. Even for the well-traveled pirate, there was an exotic aspect to the whole thing: three-toed sloths hammocked onto tree branches; rare nocturnal butterflies flitting by in the moonlight; anteaters, black-handed spider monkeys and howler monkeys, whose calls could be heard for miles across the treetops; the jaguar and puma stayed hidden, but their movements were heralded by a river of sound moving through the jungle, its waves overlapping onto the Chagres. The waterway was broad and tranquil (it would now be classified as a Class II) and only occasionally narrowed into churning rapids. But it corkscrewed back and forth through the landscape; a man rowing up it to Venta de Cruces would travel three times the distance as the crow flies. Still, it was one of the few moments in Roderick's life when he could be said to be sightseeing; if it weren't for the awful hunger chewing at his entrails, he could have enjoyed himself. The only worry was the low water levels in the river; even for the shallow canoes, there were toppled trees and tough mangrove roots that turned the journey into an obstacle course. The privateers wasted time paddling up tributaries that looked like the Chagres, only to have to backtrack and find the main route, or guess at it.

Unless there were rains to fill up the river, they would have to slash through the green wall of jungle sooner than they hoped. On the third day, the entire force disembarked and began cutting their way through the vines and creepers. The men left to tend the boats were warned against landing. "To these Captain Morgan gave very strict orders, under great penalties, that no man, upon any pretext whatsoever, should dare to leave the boats and go ashore." He'd learned the lesson of the early days on Jamaica all too well. Roderick disembarked and with the other buccaneers began the exhausting work of opening up a path in the jungle. After three hours, his right arm felt like lead, and the others quickly found the work so "dirty and irksome" that Morgan quickly ordered the men back to the canoes. Roderick was relieved. They would use every foot of the river they could.

On the fourth day, one of the scouts called out that they were approaching an ambuscade. Rather than go silent with foreboding, the men grew excited, as the decision to leave most of their food behind was taking its toll. The warning produced "infinite joy" among the pirates; Spanish fortifications meant Spanish soldiers, which meant Spanish supplies. Morgan's intelligence was unusually thin; he didn't know how many men were waiting behind the palisades, how they were armed, whether there were archers, cannon, battle-tested soldiers, or farmers drafted into the fight. But the men didn't care. As the attack squad approached the fortification, Roderick waited for the first shot, but as he came closer and closer without a single bullet aimed his way, he soon suspected the truth and went yelling toward the palisades, his comrades by his side. The Spanish had fled, burning their huts and taking their provisions with them. The men had obviously fallen victim to night terrors; such things as honor and duty mattered little when every snap of a twig and monkey call seemed to announce the arrival of the ravaging hordes.

The privateers' joy quickly turned to bitterness: All that the enemy had left them were a few crumbs of bread and some leather bags. Roderick was now so desperate that he began to chew at the leather, and the other men grabbed at the sacks as well, "as being desirous to afford something to the ferment of their stomachs, which now was grown so sharp that it did gnaw their very bowels, having nothing else to prey upon." As knives flashed out and the leather was ripped into portions, the Brethren smoldered. There wasn't enough of the cowhide to go around; the strongest got a piece of the bags, while others only watched them force it down. As they left the stockade and resumed their journey, Esquemeling makes a startling claim: The buccaneers were so famished that they were ready to eat their enemy. "Finding no victuals, they were now infinitely desirous to meet [the Spaniards]," he tells us, "intending to devour some of them rather than perish." The low river was complicating the mission: Morgan would have to choose what supplies to carry, as it now appeared he'd have to travel farther overland than he had first thought. To a buccaneer it was an easy choice: weapons first, food second. The beef and maize were left with one of his captains, who with 200 men would hold the stockade against any Spanish rescue party. The privateers "betook themselves to the wild wood" and came on another stockade, also deserted. The panic rose in their throats: They were fifty miles from Panama, and there didn't appear to be a rat or a corncob to eat. The leftover pieces of leather came out of the buccaneers' satchels, and they began to prepare them, smashing the cowhide between two stones to soften it, dipping it into the river, and rubbing it vigorously. By taking large gulps of water between bites, they were able to force the meal down.

The jungle was now a full-fledged nightmare. Striking off from the meandering riverbank, the men tried to cut a straight path through the undergrowth, but the vines and wait-a-minute creepers took many hacks to cut through; thorns ripped at their clothes, insects got into their boots, mosquitoes dived for their blood. Some had gone three days without anything resembling decent food. The Spanish were now an afterthought; the men prayed to be ambushed, because troops meant supplies. Finally, on the fifth day of their trek, at a place called Barbacoa, they found another abandoned stockade and this time a grotto that hid "two sacks of meal, wheat and like things" and two large jars of wine, along with some plantains. Morgan instantly ordered that the supplies be parceled out to the sickest and hungriest men. Here was a rigorous test of his leadership: His men were literally starving, and yet they were being asked to give up the food and wine so that a brother privateer could live a few more days. But Morgan was still the admiral, and the scant rations were passed down the line to those who could barely walk, who, "having refreshed themselves with these victuals . . . began to march anew with greater courage than ever." Those whom the food did not revive were placed in the canoes, and healthy men were ordered to walk. Deep in the Panamanian jungle, Morgan's discipline was still iron.

The sixth day dawned, and the Brethren started trudging forward, more automatons than men. They stopped frequently to rest, hundreds of men lying like corpses along the riverbank, too hot, hungry, and exhausted to move. The only food Roderick could find was leaves and green herbs; some of his mates were reduced to chewing grass. Their hunger curdled into bitterness against Morgan. The real question was quickly becoming, how long could he hold this rebel army together?

A temporary solution materialized. When they arrived around noon at a plantation and found a "barn full of maize," the men went wild, tearing the barn doors off, scooping up the dry kernels in their hands and eating it, without bothering about cooking the stuff. They ate their fill and distributed the rest of the maize before resuming their hike. Soon after leaving the plantation, a flurry of arrows descended on them: a minor ambush. The privateers took cover and quickly spotted the enemy: a troop of local Indians tracking them from across the river. A few of the men jumped into the river and tried to swim across and take some of the Indians prisoner. But the enemy just laughed at the white men crashing through the water; taking careful aim, they fired off a few more arrows and killed two or three of them. To the rest they cried, "Ha! Ye dogs, go to the plain, go to the plain." (The plain was the savannah surrounding Panama.) After amusing themselves with target practice, the Indians vanished into the scenery. It scarcely mattered to them whether Panama burned or not.

The fabled city seemed more and more distant. The buccaneers had imagined that once past San Lorenzo, the approach to Panama would be relatively quick, but it had turned into a grim battle against nature itself. As the buccaneers camped that night, the mood turned: "Great murmurings were heard, . . . many complaining of Captain Morgan and his conduct in that enterprize." It didn't help that many of the men had thrown away their maize when the Indians attacked; wasteful and optimistic by nature, the privateers expected to easily overwhelm the enemy and gorge on their fancier food. Now they were bone-hungry again. Roderick talked openly of returning to Jamaica with other buccaneers; others swore they would rather rot in the jungle than retrace their steps without a satchelful of silver coins. Their guides, who must have been under great pressure to lead them to a settlement, tried to convince them all that they'd soon be feasting on beef and Madeira. The stares they received in return convinced them they'd better find something, and soon.

On the seventh day, Roderick began cleaning his musket, dry-firing it to make sure it was still working. His gun had been kept coated with grease and tucked away in an oilcloth; with yesterday's ambush the weapon would have come out and been exposed to the muck of the riverbank. He checked to see that his matches were still firmly sealed in the bottle he carried and that his powder had stayed dry. Venta de Cruces was within one day's march, and it was the last key outpost before Panama; if the Spaniards were going to make a stand anywhere before the limits of their beloved city, it would be there.

The next day they crossed the river and, a new spring in their step, hurried toward their objective. When they were still "a great distance" from Venta de Cruces, they suddenly spotted smoke ahead, which apparently came from chimneys. This caused widespread excitement among the pirates; they began talking with one another about what the smoke meant, even as the pace quickened. The few clearheaded members of the Brethren must have known that the smoke was not a good sign, but the others raved on as if they were approaching an English country village on Christmas Day, where their relatives awaited them. The famished men could almost smell the plum pudding and game hen. Esquemeling recorded some of their conversations: "There is smoke coming out of every house, therefore they are making good fires, to roast and boil what we are to eat." The surgeon called these thoughts "castles in the air." It was highly unlikely the Spaniards were preparing dinner for a thousand pirates eager to despoil their town. Hunger was now causing the men to hallucinate. By the outskirts of the town, they were running.

When they burst into the settlement, "all sweating and panting," it was empty. The smoke came from the burning homes of the Spaniards, who had fled and taken everything remotely edible with them, apart from a few stray dogs and cats. After drawing all his forces to Venta de Cruces, González, who was leading the men sent by Don Juan to ambush Morgan, had lost his nerve. He told Don Juan that his men were too "useless, discontented and afraid" to face the buccaneers. *Fear* was the word of the hour; Don Juan responded that González's retreat was caused not by a reasonable estimation of troop strength and fighting capacity but by the myth of Morgan. The Spanish had passed into realms of the imagination, where pirates never lost and Spaniards were always sacrificed to the sword. "The fear that oppressed them" had defeated González's army before a shot had been fired. And with every successive collapse, the monk's vision of Panama grew more real.

Roderick did not feel like a world conqueror. The only things the Spanish had failed to remove from Venta de Cruces were sixteen jars of Peru wine and a sack of bread located in the king's stables. He and the others didn't wait to portion out the wine but guzzled it down and soon began retching. For a moment Morgan was terrified to think that the Spanish had poisoned his men—a brilliant strategy if it were true—but it turned out that the privateers' "huge want of sustenance . . . and the manifold sorts of trash that they had eaten upon that occasion" had made their stomachs unable to digest the wine. Roderick lay where he fell, too weak to move, the entire day and through the night.

At Venta de Cruces all the boats and canoes that had been paralleling the troops' progress were sent back downriver, except one, which was saved for sending messengers to Morgan's men at the first stockade. The men milled about in the empty town, searching every nook and cranny for a crumb of bread; Morgan had given orders that no one was to leave the town "except in whole companies of a hundred together." But one group disobeyed his command and snuck out of Venta de Cruces in search of food. The hungry squadron wasn't gone long. "These were soon glad to fly into town again, being assaulted with great fury by some Spaniards and Indians." They lost one prisoner to the enemy.

Panama now lay just twenty-five miles away. The men stumbled on, more dead than alive.

Day eight: Morgan sent a vanguard of 200 men to scout the route to Panama. The paths to the city were "so narrow that only ten or twelve persons could march in a file, and oftentimes not so many." It was perfect terrain for ambushes, and for all Morgan knew, the woods around him were swarming with the enemy. After the advance party had set out, Morgan rallied his main set of troops for the final push. He was rushing to get his men to Panama before they became too weak to fight, so he forced them to march ten hours that day. At the end of their trek, at a place called Quebrada Obscura, the privateers looked up to find the sky darkened by black shapes. "All of a sudden, three or four thousand arrows were shot at them, without [their] being able to perceive whence they came, or who shot them." Esquemeling was multiplying by ten; in fact, there were 300 Indian archers secreted among the rocks and hillocks, along with 100 Spanish musketeers. The countryside here was more mountainous than tropical, and Morgan's men could not see their attackers in the heights: Morgan describes how the attackers were "laying over their heads" and firing down. The buccaneers marched on through the wooded landscape, "the enemy constantly galling them with ambuscades and small parties." The admiral ordered his men into a tighter formation, four abreast, with the vanguard out front and two lines of skirmishers fending off attacks on either side. They spotted a group of Indians, who, unlike the Spaniards, stood their ground and fought "with huge courage" until their leader fell wounded. But the Indians, who had so much less to lose than the Spaniards, then gave a lesson in how to conduct battle, with their captain showing the way. "Although he was now in despair of life," Esquemeling tells us, "yet his valour being greater than his strength, [he] would demand no quarter, but, endeavouring to raise himself, with undaunted mind laid hold of his azagaya, or javelin, and struck at one of the Pirates." Rearing back for another thrust, the Indian was shot by a buccaneer. His comrades were unfazed, appearing and disappearing among the hills and calling to the pirates, "To the plain, to the plain, ye cuckolds, ye English dogs!" Finally the buccaneers emerged from the jungle onto the plains. Morgan called a halt, and the men fell out to rest. Roderick had stopped dreaming about silver and pearls and thought only of meat. At dusk a downpour began, and the men's muskets were stashed in shepherds' huts with a few men to watch over them. Everyone else lay out in the open.

At daybreak the men set off; Morgan wanted to use the morning mists to shield his men from the blazing sun. The isthmus was testing them to their limits; they hadn't eaten for five days, and now "the way was more difficult and laborious than all the preceding." Morgan's past missions each had one thing to distinguish them as extraordinary: Gran Granada was a feat of navigation; Maracaibo was a triumph of deceptive warcraft; Portobelo was noteworthy for its loot; Panama, unexpectedly, became the greatest test of endurance that any pirate army had ever undergone. And it is a credit to the leadership of Morgan, just thirty-six years old, that hardship tended to drive his men together, make them a more cohesive and determined force, as at San Lorenzo, as in countless other situations. It was success that was the true danger.

And now the march came to an end. At nine in the morning, Roderick, who was with the vanguard, crested a hill and saw the South Sea glittering in the distance. He could just make out the spars of six merchant ships in the bay. And marvel upon marvel: Lying at his feet, in the valley below him, were herds of cattle. The men rushed down the hill with their knives in their hands and began slaughtering the cows as they stood; others ran around collecting wood and building roaring fires on which to roast the meat. "Thus cutting the flesh of these animals into convenient pieces, or gobbets, they threw them into the fire, and, half carbonadoed or roasted, they devoured them with incredible haste and appetite." The valley ran red, and now the men with crazed eyes appeared to be more cannibals than former citizens of old European cities, as the blood ran down through their beards and soaked their shirts. The hill was the signal to the buccaneers that they'd beaten the isthmus. Today it's known as El Cerro de los Bucaneros.

Fortified with the desperately needed calories, the men set off on their final march. Morgan sent a vanguard of fifty men to try to obtain some information on the state of defenses in Panama; he was attacking blind at this point, having been unable to turn one informer to his side. The scouts came across a "troop of two hundred Spaniards," who shouted to the buccaneers, but the Brethren couldn't decipher what they were saying. Before they were able to gather any spies, the men saw a steeple jutting above the trees ahead of them. Forget the informers—they had arrived at their target, and the men frolicked as if the city lay undefended. "They began to show signs of extreme joy," says Esquemeling, "casting up their hats into the air, leaping for mirth, and shouting, even just as if they had already obtained the victory and entire accomplishment of their designs."

Morgan called a halt. The trumpeters brought out their instruments and began playing, with the drummers joining in. The music was both a celebration of the end to their long march and a warning to the citizens of Panama that the *corsarios* had arrived. The pirate army pitched tents and settled in for the night, knowing that the next days would decide its fortune. Roderick could not sleep with anticipation; he and the others were happy, well fed, and eager for battle.

12

City of Fire

In the city of Panama, something odd was happening to Don Juan. Just as Philip IV had seen himself as the physical embodiment of the monarchy, the president of Panama could be taken to be the manifestation of Panama in the early days of 1670: As the privateers approached, he was prostrate and feverish, his body consumed by imaginary flames that swept down his limbs and scorched his skin. He was suffering from erysipelas, or "St. Anthony's fire," an infection in which the patient feels an intense burning sensation in his limbs, where the skin turns tender and streaks with red. Fever and chills racked the president, while fatigue clouded his mind. He vomited often, and a hot, shiny rash appeared on his chest. His doctors bled him three times, with little result. It must have been cold comfort to the Panamanians, superstitious by nature, that the President's symptoms exactly mirrored the fate foretold in the portrait of the burning city that was still exhibited at the local convent. It was as if the leader's body had been transformed into a miniature metropolis, a Panama-to-be. From the beleaguered city, he sent off a quick note to Don Pedro de Ulloa. "I hope the Mercy of God shall protect us," he wrote, "and help us with the victory over these heretical dogs."

As the news reached him of Morgan's progress up the Chagres, Don Juan forced himself from his sickbed and collected what remained of his manpower out of a total population of over 6,000; there were only 800 traders, administrators, mestizos, "vassals and slaves" available to him. Everyone else had either failed to return from their postings upriver, evacuated, disappeared, or been killed. The army's departure left Panama with hardly a healthy male walking its streets. On January 20, as Morgan began his second day on the river, Don Juan marched his army to Guayabal, ten miles from Venta de Cruces, and waited for word from his lieutenants. Every successive report that trickled in over the next few days was a tale of disaster: stockades abandoned, battles avoided, troops on the run "without so much as ever seeing the Face of the Enemy." The pirate army was reported to be several thousand strong; as Morgan was unable to capture a single Spanish prisoner who could be tortured for information, so Don Juan had to depend on estimates, glimpses recorded by fleeing troops.

Clearly Don Juan would have to make a stand himself with the men he had with him; these soft-handed civilians were hardly the stuff to put against Morgan's troops, who overawed even the kingdom's best soldiers. He decided on Venta de Cruces and held a junta to confirm his intentions. But it was immediately apparent that the decision to stand and fight so far from Panama was not going to be popular: Those who had their fortunes stored in the city wanted to be close enough to protect them; those who didn't have a cob to their name wanted no part of the battle. Arguments were made for staying put and for a retreat back to Panama; Don Juan quickly countered the latter. "But it being impossible then to fortifie it, it having many entrances, and the Houses all built of Wood; so soon as the Enemy should once make a breach, we should be quickly exposed to their Fury." Finally his opponents gave up, and the exhausted, feverish Don Juan fell into bed thinking he'd at least stalled the talk of retreat.

The next morning he awoke to find his army vanished; in the

middle of the night, over 500 of his men had sneaked away back to Panama. The farce had reached its climax.

It is striking how much the collapse of the Spanish before the buccaneers mirrored, in miniature, the collapse of the Inca in the face of the conquistadors a century and a half earlier. Although the conquistadors' alliances with the Indians had a great deal to do with their success, the Inca were defeated because, in part, they believed that the Spanish were divine and destined to conquer. The Spanish, who had conquered most of the known world with steel, horses, and bureaucracy, who had created the greatest culture since Rome, would have seemed to be beyond such ghost stories; but they had slowly ceded some of the same mythic attributes to these unlettered men from Port Royal. Of course, a Spaniard could say he was rational and knew that the English walked on two legs and bled when shot — until, that is, the barbarians were camped outside *his* city. Then he became prone to the wildest superstitions, subject to every rumor and vision, a medievalist trapped in an unfolding prophecy. The empire had defeated the greatest armies on earth, driven the Moors from the peninsula, humbled France and England. But in the New World, at least, the Spanish could not help turning Morgan into a kind of deity who perhaps ate children and whose hair, it was said, brushed the branches of trees ten feet off the ground. He was evil, yes, but that was irrelevant. The point was that he was unstoppable.

Of course, the Spanish were right to fear the buccaneers; they were expert killers. And the buccaneers, without meaning to, also duplicated some of the methods that had enabled the Spanish to conquer the New World: forming alliances with disgruntled natives and carrying superior firearms, to name just two. But when perfectly capable soldiers who had faced Indians and the lethal maroons turned and ran, white-faced with terror, it was not the grudging retreat of an army who had met the enemy and found itself outgunned. It was a form of mass hysteria. Or, in Spanish terms, an enchantment.

Don Juan trudged back to the city, after leaving behind some squadrons who he hoped would pester Morgan on his approach and pick off some of his men. He arrived in Panama having done all he could with the earthly elements of battle; he'd sent troops down the river to fight Morgan, warned the healthy men of the city to be ready for service, seen that the city's armaments were in their best possible shape. But men had failed him. Now he turned to the supernatural. Sacred images were carried from the churches by the monks and the nuns of Our Lady of Rosario and others and displayed to all. The people of Panama fell in behind these processions beseeching their favored saints to strike down the *corsarios* and leave their city in peace. Masses were paid for. Relics were brought out of their cases and paraded through the streets. And Don Juan marched back into the city and on January 25 gave a rousing address to rally the citizens:

> That all those who were true Spanish Catholicks, Defenders of the Faith, and Devoto's of our Lady of Pure and Immaculate Conception, should follow my Person, being that same day at four o'clock in the afternoon, resolved to march out to seek the Enemy and with this caution, that he that should refuse to do it, should be held as Infamous and a Coward, basely slighting so precise an Obligation.

It was a speech laced with bitterness; Don Juan had been disappointed so many times he could almost believe that even with their families and fortunes in imminent danger, the men of Panama would refuse to do battle. But his words were received with a loud cheer; men swore in front of their families to fight to the death. Don Juan led the huge crowd to the church and vowed to die in the defense of the Lady of Pure and Immaculate Conception, donating a diamond ring worth 40,000 pieces of eight ($2 million) to indicate that he was serious. Other "Jewels and Relicks" were also given to the religious orders; they included fine vestments made of silk and linen laced with gold thread and weighed down with jewels embedded in the fabric; an irreplaceable necklace made of emeralds from the mines of

Colombia; diamond rings, a diamond-encrusted gold staff, and gems in bulk. Few if any Spanish governors had made such a gesture before a battle with the privateers; there was something final in the laying down of all Don Juan's earthly possessions.

The crowd chanted the same oath as their president: death or victory. In the minds of its defenders, the battle for Panama had now explicitly become the defense of the Catholic frontier against Morgan and his Protestant heathens, a religious confrontation exactly like those that rang through Spanish history. The days before the showdown heightened the symbolic dream the Panamanians were living in. In their hearts they knew that few men in the city truly lived for God the way their ancestors had, but now they convinced themselves that dying for Him would give their men the final incentive. The pirates, on the other hand, had no such illusions; they knew down to the last piece of eight what they were fighting for.

The city was frenetic: Men gathered whatever weapons they could get hold of and finalized their affairs; women and children, along with monks and nuns, boarded ships that would carry them along the coast to safety. Much of the city's wealth, including Don Juan's rich bequests to the religious orders, was being packed into the holds of ships, and Don Juan knew that with their families and fortunes safely on the waves, two huge motivations for his fighters would be gone. But he reluctantly agreed; his lawyer would later point out that Panama's open layout gave no protection to its citizens, and forcing them to stay with their plate and gems would have been inviting annihilation. He instructed that all the vessels in the harbor leave, so that the buccaneers would not be able to pursue the fleeing residents.

Now on Sunday, Don Juan marched out of the city to the savannah to meet the enemy. His army had swelled to 1,200 men, "compounded of two sorts, valiant military Men, and faint-hearted Cowards." He had three field pieces, primed for firing, but his armaments in general were "few and bad": carbines, arquebuses, and fowling pieces. But for a moment Don Juan allowed himself to believe that his army, fired by the Holy Spirit, could stand its own against the buccaneers: "The Army appeared all brisk and coura-geous, desiring nothing more than to engage," he reported. They would strike against Morgan like lightning, Don Juan thought. The old faith died hard.

The Spanish tactics were simple: The first three ranks of soldiers would wait until the buccaneers came within range and then take a knee and fire. They would retire, and the next lines of defenders would come up and discharge their arms. The wide-open plains gave Don Juan few advantages to work with, but he took what he was given, buttressing his right flank by placing it up against a small hill. His approach was drastically straightforward; his men were arrayed across the plain, armed mostly with halberds and lances and the oc-casional arquebus; many of the Indians had bows and arrows. A line of cavalry stood in front of them, and one squadron of horsemen waited on each wing, armed with lances. His only innovation was to hold in reserve a herd of fifteen hundred bulls tended by fifty black cowboys; Don Juan hoped to drive the snorting beasts into the buc-caneers' formation from both left and right, scattering them at a crit-ical moment. Don Juan had fought with the Spanish armies in the Netherlands, and he envisioned a confrontation that could have been lifted out of the European book of war: The charging bucca-neers would be fed into the center of his line, where they would be decimated by his artillery and musketeers; then the cavalry would close in from both sides, slashing at the buccaneers' flanks. Finally the oxen would stampede the survivors off the plain and send them hurtling back to the Chagres and beyond.

Two days later, on the evening of Tuesday, January 27, Morgan marched his men toward Panama. The 600 men in the vanguard were still celebrating their crossing of the isthmus with toasts of wine. The first impression of the Spanish was one of relief: One Spanish soldier called out to Don Juan, "We have nothing to fear. There are no more than six hundred drunkards." The English had not expected so many defenders of the city; Morgan, who tended to inflate the Spanish contingents at every turn, counted 2,100 foot and 600 horse. Certainly Don Juan's forces had swelled as stragglers rolled in from the Chagres, but those numbers seem a little high. Nevertheless, Esquemeling reported a crisis of faith among his comrades. "They discovered the forces of the people of Panama," he tells us, "in battle array, which, when they perceived to be so numerous, they were suddenly surprised with great fear, much doubting the fortune of the day." But after the hell they had just been through, few of the buccaneers could realistically have been thinking of retreat against a motley army such as faced them on the great plain, especially when one of the fabled cities of the Spanish Main lay before them. The Spanish reports have the buccaneers singing and dancing, which sounds more like Morgan's men. At last the buccaneers bucked themselves up "and resolved either to conquer, or spend the very last drop of blood in their bodies." One of the things that made the privateers such a fearsome enemy was that for them there was no other option. The Spanish had made the same vow, but experience showed that they were focused on survival. It was their hearts that began to fail first. In the Spanish ranks, González, the coward of the Chagres, remarked that he was keeping two horses close at hand to beat a quick retreat and that anyone with any sense would do the same. Don Juan called him a "chicken and an enemy spy" and ordered him shut away in the local jail.

The sun rose into a clear sky on Wednesday, imparting that first light brush of heat across the face that foretells a scorching day. Morgan had divided his men into three separate forces: the 300-strong vanguard, manned by the marksmen of the Hispaniola woods, would be commanded by Lieutenant Colonel Lawrence Prince, with Morgan's old ally Major John Morris as second-in-command. The right wing of the main body of 600 would be led by Morgan, the left wing by Colonel Edward Collier; the rear guard was under the command of the newly arrived Colonel Bledry Morgan (no relation to Henry). The "land" titles of major and lieutenant were now used exclusively; the North Sea lay miles behind them, and they were about to fight the kind of traditional field battle that echoed through the history of England and Spain. The ragamuffin sea bandits had transformed themselves into a classic European army. Fortified with fresh slabs of beef (some of the cattle having been brought along for sustenance), the ranks moved out to finally confront Don Juan.

It was afternoon before the privateers drew up to confront the Spaniards. Morgan took in the situation at a glance: Without any spies he couldn't know the quality of the men who faced him or the caliber or number of their weapons; he had no idea that many of the black, Indian, and mestizo troops had "never in their lives . . . seen bullets." It *looked* like a serious army; it could include reinforcements from the garrisons of any number of towns and cities. But Morgan soon spotted what he thought was a chink in Don Juan's strategy: The small hill on the Spaniard's right flank appeared undermanned. If he could take it and drive his men down it, he'd dramatically narrow the battlefield and reduce the ability of Don Juan's cavalry to maneuver. He sent Prince and his vanguard to storm the hill; hidden by a ravine, the squadron dropped out of sight, then quickly swept up the incline at the rear. Now they looked down on the right wing of the Spanish cavalry. The horsemen saw the approaching buccaneers, wheeled their mounts toward them, cried, *"Viva el Rey!"* ("God save the king!"), and charged at the figures outlined in the blazing sun.

If the cavalry was to get into the vanguard's ranks, the advantage would turn to them; the English musket and cutlass would be of little use against horsemen towering above them driving lances into their chests. But the Brethren, not panicking, dropped to one knee and took aim at the line of onrushing horses, and with a sharp crack of muskets the front line fell. The horses sprawled out on the plain, which along with the soggy ground made it difficult for the horsemen behind them to maneuver. Morgan noted an act of bravery by the cavalry's leader: "One Francesco de Harro charged with the horse upon the vanguard so furiously that he could not be stopped till he lost his life." But the advance had been quickly shattered. (The buccaneers left their mark everywhere—the hill is now known as El Cerro del Avance.)

Don Juan's brightest hope, the cavalry, had been taken out of the picture. And now the infantry made a tactical mistake; seeing Morgan's vanguard drop down into the ravine on their way to take the hill, they had assumed that the buccaneers were retreating. The left wing broke ranks and gave chase. "All of a sudden, I heard a loud clamour, crying out, 'Fall on, fall on, for they fly!'" Don Juan recalled. Their commander tried to hold the men back, but he couldn't stop the mad rush, "though he cut them with his Sword." Don Juan's hand was forced, and he wheeled his horse to the right and ordered his wing to follow the running troops as they raced toward the hill. "Come along, boys!" he cried out with a mixture of excitement and fatalism. "There is no remedy now, but to Conquer or Die. Follow me!"

Spaniards charging against buccaneers—it was a highly unusual situation. But Morgan's men, descending the hill, responded like well-oiled killing machines. They took aim at the wild-eyed infantrymen and fired. The first volley tore through the first line of onrushing Spaniards, and a hundred of them dropped to the earth dead or severely wounded, gaping holes torn in their chests and stomachs. The sight dampened the Spanish ardor. "Hardly did our men see some fall dead," Don Juan remembered, "and others wounded, but they turned their backs, and fled." A moment before, Don Juan had been riding the crest of his soldiers' courage; now he was left nearly alone, accompanied by a single Negro soldier and one servant. He watched his men run and must have wished he could have followed them. But he was an honorable man and felt *someone* had to make a show of sticking to their vow to defend Panama. Centuries of Spanish history resonated in that moment; Don Juan was sacrificing himself for a tradition his men had disgraced. "Yet I went forward to comply with my word to the Virgin, which was to die in her Defence," he wrote. A bullet barely missed his face and ricocheted off the staff he carried in his hand. Seeing how exposed he was, a priest who knew Don Juan well and even said mass in his home caught up to the president and begged him to leave the battlefield. The old warrior twice refused and "sharply reprehended" the priest for suggesting retreat. The priest wouldn't budge. "The third time, he persisted, telling me that it was mere desperation to die in that manner, and not like a Christian," Don Juan remembered. With the buccaneers charging straight toward him, in pursuit of the fleeing troops, Don Juan saw the sense of the priest's argument and relented. He was unhurt and considered it a miracle that the Virgin had protected him "from amidst so many thousand Bullets."

Don Juan wheeled his horse and saw a scene of devastation: dead horses jackknifed on the grass, bodies of men littered across the savanna, arms and legs blown off by English ball, arquebuses tossed aside in terror, wounded soldiers being chased down by the buccaneers and chopped in the back of the neck with cutlasses, the wild bulls stampeding away from the buccaneers, terrified by the reports of the muskets and the screams. (The few that made it into the buccaneers' lines merely tangled their horns in Morgan's flag before being shot down by his men.) The Spanish defense collapsed. "I endeavoured with all my industry to persuade the soldiers to turn and face our enemies," Don Juan said, "but it was impossible." The pirates were moving through the plain executing the wounded, perhaps chopping off a finger with an attractive ring or snatching off a gold necklace. In the distance were the diminishing figures of Don Juan's cavalry and infantry; as Morgan said, the retreat "came to plain running." For three miles the buccaneers chased the terrified Spaniards, who attempted to hide in bushes and shrubs; discovered by a privateer, they would clasp their hands and cry out for mercy. But there was none to be had. Anyone who made the slightest resistance died.

The devastation was not over. Don Juan had given orders to the commander of the artillery, waiting back in the city: If Morgan won the day, he was to set a match to the garrison's magazines and blow the fort sky-high. The Spanish had denied Morgan food on his trip across the isthmus; now they would deny him the means to go down the coast with fresh supplies. The commander could hear the sounds of battle in the distance, but he couldn't know who was prevailing—until, that is, he saw the first of the retreating soldiers, running with buccaneers in hot pursuit. He lit the fuse and ran for safety. When the gunpowder ignited, the almighty boom could be heard six miles away. It was the opening salvo in the destruction of Panama itself.

As survivors from the battle streamed over the Matadero Bridge, the city still had some fight left in it. Some of the streets were barricaded, others booby-trapped with two hundred kegs of powder. Snipers took the occasional shot at the buccaneers as they smashed into the city, looting houses and drinking up the stores of wine. The flat *crump* of the detonating kegs could be heard in the distance; a fuse would reach a barrel, and a house in the next street would suddenly explode. Splinters came raining down on the privateers as they ruthlessly snuffed out any sign of resistance, taking time out to pillage as they made their way across the city; burning embers touched off fires. Soon flames crackled through the wood-frame houses of the merchants. The monk, and Don Juan's fever, had been precise oracles. "Burn, burn!" cried out Spaniards in the street. "That is the order of Señor Don Juan!" The final touch came when black soldiers appeared on the streets with torches and began setting fire to the homes. If the buccaneers wanted Panama, its citizens would leave them a wasteland.

The strong winds that had swept the plains now acted as a huge bellows, blowing the fire up and arching it over the roofs. The pirates entered a city of black and orange, embers flying through the air, flames whipping from house to house, vortices of superheated air sucking the oxygen out of their lungs. Now they took on the strange role of firefighters, trying to save the city so they could pillage it. Morgan ordered barrels of powder to be detonated in lines ahead of the advancing fire, but the flames jumped the firebreaks and roared on. Valuable booty was being consumed: Silks and fine lace burned, beautifully wrought jewelry melted and streams of molten gold flowing along the floors of houses. The exhausted privateers fought throughout the day to put out the flames, "but in vain, for all was consumed by 12 at night." There were exceptions: two churches, three hundred of the outlying houses, warehouses stocked with European linen and silk garments, the imposing stone civic buildings.

Morgan had done what the illustrious Drake had failed to do: crossed the fearsome isthmus and taken Panama. Leading a band of cantankerous individualists to Panama was a major accomplishment. "The hazard, conduct and daringness of their exploits," wrote historian Robert Burton, "have by some been compared to the actions of Caesar and Alexander the Great." Now Morgan watched Panama burn, as his men swarmed over it, mad to grab all the gold and wine they could before these were destroyed by the fire. Morgan's report was touched with a sense of the scale of what he'd done; for one of the few times in his reports, a feeling for his place in history enters into the admiral's voice. "Thus was consumed the famous and ancient city of Panama," he wrote. "Which is the greatest mart for silver and gold in the whole world, for it receives all the goods that come from Spain in the King's great fleet, and delivers all the gold and silver that comes from the mines of Peru and Potozí."

The city burned through the night; it would take only thirty minutes for the flames to utterly ravage an entire street of wooden homes. Roderick lay in one of the stone monasteries and drank what wine he and his mates could find. He didn't share Morgan's sense of historical proportion; to him Panama was a storehouse of plunder, and he was anxious to begin raking in the swag in the morning. But when daylight came, Roderick and the others awoke to find Panama a place of cinders and ash. One of the few structures to survive was the stone tower of the cathedral. The tower had been transformed from the premier showpiece of a Christian civilization in its new frontier to what it would be for decades to come: a blackened, bitter landmark for Spanish mariners lost in coastal storms.

The dead city was only the outward manifestation of what had been lost. The illusion that the Spanish in the New World were crusaders cut from the old cloth had fled along with the ranks of fleeing soldiers. They would apparently no longer fight for God. They certainly wouldn't die for their king. The buccaneers had torn away the illusions on which the kingdom had survived for so many years.

❋   ❋   ❋

In full control, the buccaneers methodically searched Panama for swag. Morgan posted guards in key sectors and used the rest of his men to extract the remaining treasure from the hollowed-out city; the privateers sifted through the ruins of the finer homes. Roderick lowered a lighter comrade down a well where the water had been turned to mist by the raging fires so he could hunt for dumped plate and gems and helped rip apart the foundations and walls of buildings, looking for hidden stashes of gold and jewelry. Citizens unlucky enough to be caught up in the privateers' dragnet were treated to hard questioning. Roderick had heard so many stories of Panama's wealth that he found it difficult to believe that there were not piles of silver bars secreted somewhere in the city. He found melted blobs of gold here and there, but never the shining vaults packed tightly with plate that tortured his imagination. The interviewees paid heavily for their city's reputation. There was one rumor in particular that haunted the buccaneers: There was said to be an altar made of gold that had been painted black to keep it out of the hands of the *corsarios*. It was never found. Instead of a torrent of loot, there was a slow, steady trickle of trinkets and chains tossed into piles and watched over jealously by the privateers.

The buccaneers didn't restrict themselves to the city limits; realizing that the merchants and traders who hadn't sailed out of the bay would be on the trails leading from Panama, they sent out squads of men to track the escapees down. "The men marched out in parties," reported buccaneer William Fogg, "sometimes 100, sometimes 40 and 10, and took prisoners every day." Morgan reported that they made "daily incursions on the enemy for 20 leagues without having one gun fired at them in anger." Three thousand prisoners were brought back for interrogation and to be held for ransom. One triumph came with the capture of a bark that had run aground and been partially burned by its crew, who didn't want it to fall into the privateers' hands. Morgan desperately needed a boat to take command of the waters around Panama, and this modest vessel served his purpose. His men cruised the coastline and sailed to the nearby islands of Perico and Taboga and Taboguilla, capturing other traders and taking prisoner the fleeing Panamanians onboard. The trickle of loot grew into a modest stream. But the prize that would have made them all wealthy came within a hair of capture: Before Morgan reached the city, a ship called *La Santíssima Trinidada* had left Panama loaded down with "all the King's plate and great quantity of riches of gold, pearl, jewels and other most precious goods, of all the best and richest merchants of Panama." Not to mention a tremendous hoard of ecclesiastical treasures being transported by a group of nuns. The value of the loot easily ran into the millions. This was what the buccaneers had come to Panama for, but they let it slip through their grasp. When some of the Spanish crew left the ship to fill their water casks, they were captured and brought to the bark's captain, Robert Searle, who soon learned that the *Santíssima* was loaded with booty. He ordered his men to take the Spanish ship, but by that time Roderick and the others were well oiled on "several sorts of rich wines" they'd confiscated, and they yawned in the captain's face. Instead of boarding the *Santíssima*, the buccaneers watched through bleary eyes as it sailed away, and then went back to drinking themselves into a stupor. When Morgan heard about the fortune that had just escaped his clutches, he sent four boats looking for the galleon. The little fleet spent eight days searching for the *Santíssima*, without result; they did, however, stumble across a different vessel near the islands of Taboga and Taboguilla and found aboard "cloth, soap, sugar and biscuit, with twenty thousand pieces of eight in ready money." A meager consolation prize.

✝ ✝ ✝

The buccaneers first took out their frustration on the prisoners. Some, according to Esquemeling, "were presently put to the most exquisite tortures imaginable": cutting off ears and noses, woolding, burning, and being put to the rack. The reports of cruelty were heard as far away as London, but the surgeon Richard Browne later gave a different account, in which he strongly defended Morgan's conduct. His letter was shot through with a common soldier's complaint: Civilians could not begin to understand the nature of battle, he wrote, denying that there were atrocities. His version had no pirates forcing themselves on the captive women and only one questionable action on the battlefield, a captain executing a friar after quarter was given. "For the Admiral," Browne said, "he was noble enough to the vanquished enemy."

As Don Juan's Panama breathed its last (it would be rebuilt in a new location, where it stands to this day, and the old one abandoned forever), the president was in the town of Nata, seventy-five miles away. The contagion of fear had reached even this distant village. "I found not one soul therein," Don Juan remembered, "for all were fled to the mountains." Indeed, many of the rich merchants and administrators and church authorities were deep in the hills of central Panama, where they now faced the same privation through which Morgan and his men had suffered; starvation was a real threat, and the trader who had been used to earning a fistful of silver cobs for a week's trading now had to forage through the jungle looking for fruit and roots.

Once he was safely in Nata, Don Juan tried one last time to rally the locals and the dispersed Panamanians to take up arms. Those who refused were milquetoasts who would "bear the infamy and stain for ever." But there was little chance that men who did not have their life's savings tied up in the great city would go to defend it when its leading citizens had run from the battle. Even the fact that many thought that Morgan had come to conquer Panama for England didn't light a fire under the Spanish. "The pirates had brought with them an English Man," Don Juan wrote, "whome they called The Prince, with intent there to Crown him King of Terra Firma." The reference was probably to Captain Prince, who fought under Morgan, or to the still-fresh legend of Prince Rupert coming from over the seas. In any case very little was done to impede the buccaneers' looting. The English scoffed at the Spanish defense of their jewel; when asked who had burned Panama, the buccaneer Bartholomew Sharp said that it couldn't have been Don Juan, as he was miles away "saving his bacon." Don Juan was philosophical about the defeat he'd just suffered; for a Spaniard, nothing so momentous as the destruction of a city could be achieved without being part of God's plan. "This . . . has been a chastisement from Heaven," he wrote. The same might have happened to any great Spanish commander, Don Juan thought, "as did to me, if his Men had deserted him, for one Man alone can do little."

This was a comfort provided by the Spanish mind-set: The individual could never truly be responsible for disaster, as they didn't have the power to turn history one way or the other. The lone Spaniard need not despair: defeat was part of a larger pattern.

As to why Panama had been lost, the Spaniards looked deep into themselves and acknowledged what they saw. "Fear has taken hold of the men of this Kingdom," wrote a soldier from the castle of San Felipe. "to whom every single Englishman seems to be a strong squadron and it is for this reason, due to weakness, that the enemy is able to accomplish its plans to perfection." This virus of terror was the result of decades of military neglect, underfunding, bureaucratic infighting, the huge territories to be protected, and Madrid's indifference—in other words, all the ills of an empire that had shrunk within its enormous shell. But Don Juan was right: If all the Spaniards Morgan faced had fought like the heroes of San Lorenzo, he probably would have gone home without ever seeing Panama. The Spanish had let a myth get out of control.

Instead of an army, the Spanish sent a letter to Morgan. It came from the governor of Cartagena, the other rumored target of the privateers, and it recounted his exploits before making a ridiculous demand: "You should give satisfaction for the very serious damage that you have done and restore everything that you have robbed." The letter did refer to one thing that had changed since Morgan set out from Jamaica: A peace treaty had finally been signed. The governor even included a copy of it with his rather whiny letter. Spain had made huge concessions; it now recognized Jamaica and the other English territories in the Indies and consigned to the past all the raids and outrages of the privateers against the Spanish Main. In turn, England agreed to stop its undeclared war against the kingdom and to bring in the privateers. The opening up of Spanish ports was not addressed, but there was a loophole that accomplished the same thing: English ships would now be allowed to enter Spanish harbors to get wood, water, and the other necessities of sailing life. In two quick strokes, Spain had renounced two founding principles of its empire in the New World: that the territories there belonged to them by divine right and that foreign trade would be outlawed forever.

Morgan had played no small part in this. His provocations had helped to force the Spanish to renounce their exclusive rights to the Spanish Main. The pressure from his relentless raids, the interruption of trading routes, the fact that their best-fortified cities were no longer safe from the admiral helped force the Spain into accepting that the New World had to be shared. Some officials saw the capitulation as a disaster. When the peace treaty was read in Lima, Peru, the viceroy wrote to the queen, "The Indies are lost, since there is no defence in the ports of this realm to resist them if they want to make themselves masters of the region where they come ashore."

The Treaty of Madrid had been signed on July 21, and the English were given until November 28 to ratify it. Once that was done, there was a grace period of eight months in which both governments would inform their far-flung citizens to stop all hostilities against the other nation. The treaty finally put the relationships of the great powers in the Indies into black and white; the Caribbean would now cease to be a Wild West. The grace period introduced the only notes of gray—who was informed when could be argued forever. And now Morgan had just conducted the greatest raid in the history of buccaneering under the treaty. He'd helped create the pact; now he'd be the first to test it.

⁜ ⁜ ⁜

Morgan spent twenty-eight days raking over the coals of Panama. Before he left, he had to face down the first real mutiny he'd ever experienced. As the buccaneers prepared to leave Panama, the money had not yet been divided, but the buccaneers sensed that it was not the fabled sum they'd hoped for. Roderick was among a small group of pirates who formed a plan to steal away from Morgan and "go and rob upon the South Sea until they had got as much as they thought fit." Morgan's authority was gone. Like prisoners of war in a German camp, Roderick and the others had secreted away provisions, ammunition, powder, and muskets, even a cannon to load onto a ship they had commandeered. The extensive planning only pointed up how disgruntled the men had become. Morgan found out about the plans and had the mainmast of the ship cut down and burned; the renegades now had nothing to sail away on and so stuck with their commander. The admiral might need them to fight his way out of Panama, and who knew how many had emeralds or pearls sewn into their clothes?

Finally, on February 24, the occupation of Panama ended, and Morgan marched out the way he'd come in. Along with him went 175 mules loaded with "silver, gold and other precious things" and six hundred prisoners who had not been able, or willing, to raise the ransom price of 150 pesos. Morgan had sent scouts ahead of the main party so that he'd flush out any dead-enders and ambush squads in the treacherous jungle. But there was one good piece of news, at least: Heavy rains had fallen, and the Chagres was back to its normal levels; the ships he had left at San Lorenzo could make it all the way to Venta de Cruces and were waiting for him. In his absence, with their food running out, the crews had gone buccaneering themselves and captured a Spanish vessel packed with rice and maize. They would have plenty to eat on the way home. Panama had proved a brutal city to approach but a very easy place to leave.

At Venta de Cruces, the army paused. Morgan wanted to give

the remaining prisoners a chance to cadge the ransom money from friends and relatives or retrieve it from hiding places. He also announced that his own men would be searched for any undeclared treasure. Every buccaneer was forced to swear that he hadn't pocketed any of the loot, "not even so much as the value of a sixpence." That would usually have been good enough for the Brethren, but Morgan now called for the men to be inspected from head to toe, their satchels turned over, their shoes taken off and shaken. It was a sign of the suspicions and rumors that raged through the buccaneer camp that even the admiral allowed himself to be patted down. The camaraderie that had brought them so far was gone.

Just as it had exposed the Spanish system, Panama revealed a great deal about the pirates. As soon as the dream of great riches evaporated, the buccaneer army atomized into a thousand separate pieces. The pirates would never threaten the systems they destabilized with a nation-state of their own, because they had no faith, no laws, no institutions that would hold them together beyond the next raid. A force powerful enough to make kings tremble, the Brethren imploded, and individual members split off on their own, available to be hunted down by those they had offended.

Now the Brethren became nautical again. The leaders regained their maritime titles, and the privateers floated down the Chagres to San Lorenzo. Morgan picked up the garrison he'd installed there and attempted one last bit of extortion. He sent a ship to Portobelo and demanded a ransom for the fort; either the Spanish pay up or he'd raze San Lorenzo to the ground. The Portobellans were past caring: "They would not give one farthing toward the ransom of said castle, and that the English might do with it as they pleased." True to his word, Morgan loaded the cannon on board his ship—they would become part of the defenses of Port Royal—and torched the fort. Like any good Lucifer, he was leaving the isthmus trailing the smell of smoke.

Before the ships sailed from the mouth of the Chagres, the spoils had to be divided. The mistrust was palpable as jewels and plate and ransom money and gold doubloons were brought forth and tossed into the common pile. Each piece was weighed and appraised. How much the buccaneers came away with has been disputed ever since the raid; the estimates range from 140,000 pieces of eight ($7 million in modern dollars) to over 400,000 pieces of eight ($20 million). Most evidence points toward the lower estimate as being the more accurate. It was a significant sum, but it had been taken by an enormous army, and after deductions were made for the wounded, the brave, the surgeons, the carpenters, and the officers, the ordinary buccaneers received a share of 80 pieces of eight each, or $4,000 in modern dollars. When Roderick heard the share, his face twisted with bitterness. It was not enough. For the death march up the Chagres? For nearly starving to death and taking the capital of the Spanish Main? To Roderick it was a derisory amount, especially alongside Morgan's cut — 1,400 pieces of eight, or today's $70,000 — and he let his commander know it. "So it was that the rest of his companions," Esquemeling wrote, "even of his own nation, complained of his proceedings in this particular, and feared not to tell him openly to his face, that he'd reserved the best jewels to himself."

Did Morgan cheat Roderick and the rest of his foot soldiers? Many of his underlings felt he did. But the admiral would have been taking his life in his hands; on the slightest evidence of double-dealing, his men would have slashed his throat. It seems unlikely that he'd risk death or permit his belongings to be searched if he was really hiding an enormous diamond or a sackful of plate. The problem was not only the light haul; it was the number of men. The privateers had taken more swag than they'd extracted from Portobelo, but now it had to be split among four times as many buccaneers. In his report to Modyford, Morgan showed that he was aware of the controversy by devoting the final sentences to refuting the charge; he "had it from the prisoners that the reason there was no more wealth was because [the Spanish] had two months' notice, and laded two great ships of 350 and 700 tons with money, plate, gold and jewels." The light payday gave birth to a thousand legends. Treasure hunters off Haiti and elsewhere still talk about the famous golden altar of Panama City, painted black and smuggled out of the city by Morgan (or by the Panamanians — there are several versions). Talk of buried treasure is a must in all pirate legends, but it is rare that an expedition's own crew begins the gossip.

Morgan took no risks. He'd already heard about the possible peace with Spain, bringing with it a new era for Port Royal. There was no time to waste; he had to make his case to Modyford and the Crown as quickly as possible. And he had to avoid being garroted by his men. Without calling a council, as was customary, he slipped away with just four ships and no advance notice. The other vessels split off for Tortuga, Costa Rica, or other hideouts. England and Spain were at peace; the Brethren were now public enemies.

The raid had shattered the Spanish idea of a Catholic kingdom built on faith and the bureaucracy that supported it. But it also marked the last gasp for the Brethren; they had become almost too successful. Nothing but the capture of a galleon's load of treasure would have satisfied the pirates, and that had not been found. Now Morgan and the others would have to face the fact that there was no loyalty between pirates beyond the search for gold. The dispersal of Morgan's fleet into small convoys foreshadowed the blood-letting to come.

13

Aftermath

The news of the destruction of Panama filtered across the Atlantic in rumors and wild tales told tenth-hand on ships and in waterfront taverns. Finally, on June 5, a ship arrived in Lisbon with an authoritative report of the invasion. The news shook the Continent. Englishmen living abroad, at least those not in the pro-Spanish wing of the government, took great relish in the sacking of Panama. The distances covered and the fame of the target seemed to indicate London's widening reach and power. "They say the King of England may conquer the whole world," crowed the English consul in Portugal, "for nothing can be too difficult for Inglishmen to undertake." Even those ministers who were aghast at the diplomatic implications of the raid could not help but acknowledge that it was an "unparalleled exploit" in the history of the nation. "Such an action had not ben done since the famous Drake," wrote the Restoration diarist John Evelyn, and Drake was the standard for all such expeditions. The reaction was far different on the other side of the Treaty of Madrid. The Spanish went beyond strategic horror; it was as if their faith in the world had been given a hard wrench. "The sacred knot was untied," wrote the Venetian ambassador to Spain, "and the laws not only of friendship but of nature were broken." The Spanish court felt it had been tricked; the duplicity of Charles II and his ministers was beyond fathoming. To the Spanish there was no possibility that the invasion could have gone ahead without approval at the very highest levels of English government. The queen reacted violently, falling victim to "such a distemper and excess of weeping and violent passion as those about her feared it might shorten her life." The Conde de Peñaranda, who had negotiated the treaty that was supposed to make Morgan's type obsolete, demanded satisfaction from the English, after wiping away his own tears. The English said the right things: King Charles even claimed that he objected to the invasion as if it had been made on English soil, but the Spanish could not, at first, be appeased.

When the total costs of the raid were added up, the loss of Panama had cost between 11 and 18 million pesos, or between $550 and $900 million. A portion of the costs for rebuilding the city and its fortifications would have to be borne by the Crown, adding hugely to its expenses, drastically reducing its ability to expand or fortify the rest of its holdings in the New World. The flow of trade was interrupted, and whatever claims Spain had to enforcing its will in the New World were now largely in shreds. Losing a galleon could be explained by simple bad luck. But losing Panama was a systemic failure on a huge scale.

A war council was called, and it began its deliberations by emphasizing how important Panama was to Spain. "It has been considered in detail the great importance of that population for it is the throat of the Realm of Peru and the wall that defends it," the ministers wrote, "on whose restoration depends the conservation of the Catholic religion, and . . . the interests of the Spanish monarch and its trade." The councilors, including the Conde de Peñaranda, knew the Crown's history in these matters and urged haste; "too much dallying" would render the whole effort useless. The men suggested an ambitious response: 4,000 men, including 600 or 700 of the Royal Guard, along with cavalry and ten ships. But the costs were added up and passions inevitably cooled, although from white-hot levels, and the forces were eventually reduced to only three vessels with

550 men, which set out in the middle of August. Part of the reason for the tempered response was that the English had made real gestures toward their new friends: The first step came with a private meeting between the English diplomat Godolphin and the queen, in which he apologized profusely and swore that the king did not know of Morgan's plans. Then Modyford's son was tossed into the Tower of London, not for any crimes of his own but as collateral for his father's arrest. An order had been issued calling the governor of Jamaica an enemy of the state.

Modyford waited anxiously back in Jamaica. He'd heard nothing from England about the treaty; rather awkwardly, he had to wait until the Spanish governor of Puerto Rico sent him a copy of the accord, as a sign of the new atmosphere of friendship and cooperation. It didn't take an exquisitely tuned weather vane like Modyford to realize that the winds from Europe were stiffening against him. Days before his replacement, the rigid and humorless Sir Thomas Lynch, sailed into the harbor, Modyford decided to punch up a memo to Arlington detailing exactly why the raid on Panama was justified. Gone was his insinuating style, replaced by fourteen quick bullet points, listing his reasons for war: the "violences" of Rivero; His Majesty's permission to counter any Spanish outrages; the "fears of the planters, the cries of the women and children"; and so on. His final statement had a touch of his boldness: Even if he'd known of "all the trouble which now threatens me" because of the Panama raid, Modyford stated, he wouldn't have called Morgan back. Anything else would have caused "the manifest ruin of this island." The document lacked Modyford's usual polish; worry clearly cramped his hand.

At last, on the first of July, Sir Thomas Lynch sailed into Port Royal harbor to relieve him of his duties. Tucked away among Lynch's linen shirts and talcum powder was an order to arrest Modyford. The lingering mystery that surrounds the document centers on the fact that it was dated well before reports of the Panamanian invasion reached London. Does this mean that Charles II was secretly hoping the Jamaicans would make one last strike before the treaty went into effect—and kept the arrest order on hand to show the Spanish he was serious about reining them in once that last raid was done? Or was the warrant issued for the general crimes of the privateers, committed under Modyford's watch, an insurance policy to get him out of the way and the pro-trade Lynch more easily into office? Or was the fact that the document was left to gather dust just evidence of London's scandalous inattention to Jamaica? The truth is unclear, but the combination of silence and treachery practiced by London against its own colonial governor make Modyford's efforts at dissembling seem almost naïve by comparison.

Lynch was in an awkward spot; he was here not only to replace Modyford but to put him in chains. Cautious to a fault, he wanted to test the air before spiriting Modyford away, and so he spent weeks as the governor's guest, staying in his house (where an attack of gout laid him up), then attending parties thrown in his honor by Mody-ford, who was punctilious to the last. Eating the man's beef, drinking his rum, and accepting his health tips, even the harsh-tempered Lynch must have felt like a cad at times. Still, he started setting the trap, telling the leading lights of Jamaican society that the privateers and those who supported them were in bad odor in London. The whisper campaign got a boost from the grumblings of the privateers, who were returning to Port Royal from Panama ship by ship. Lynch reported to London that the buccaneers' unhappiness was working in their favor: "They would take it as a compliment to be severe with Morgan whom they rail horribly for starving, cheating and desert-ing them." Soon Lynch felt comfortable enough to spring his trap. He invited Modyford and some members of the council aboard his ship, the *Assistance*, for a sumptuous dinner. Once he had the gover-nor there, safely under the eyes of his loyal crew, he broke the news: Modyford was a prisoner of state. The crime? That "contrary to the King's express commands," Modyford had "made many depreda-tions and hostilities against the subjects of His Majesty's brother, the Catholic King."

That fact is, Charles's commands had been anything but "express";

when he did issue one, it was often as opaque as a Spanish pearl and soon to be countermanded. Lynch softened the blow by telling the shocked governor that his "life and fortune were in no danger. . . . There was a necessity of the King's making this resentment for such an unseasonable irruption." In other words, Modyford was to be the fall guy for Panama.

Morgan was now under a black cloud for the first time in his career; he retired to his plantation, where he fell ill with a fever. The jungles of Panama had a long reach, and they'd dosed Morgan's blood with one of their many contagions. While Modyford was sailing for England as a prisoner, his ally sweated and tossed in his bed at home, subject to nightmares. The news of what he'd done was spreading Morgan's name further. Panama would seal his reputation among historians of Jamaica as "the one great man, the one figure of heroic proportions" in the nation's history (Williams); the man whose "master mind rendered Jamaica English" (Hodgetts). But in 1671, Morgan knew he'd gone too far. Although he liked the insurance of the commissions he received, he'd acted as if the Old World did not exist. The pirates had thrived in a vacuum, like men stranded on a desert island who made up new laws for themselves. That idyll was about to end.

The other privateers began trickling into Port Royal from all points of the map. Roderick sneaked in at dusk with twelve others on one of the smallest ships and, avoiding the waterfront, slipped off to his rooms. Esquemeling returned from adventures on an unnamed island, where, after a hot skirmish with some natives, the buccaneers found two bodies on the beach, one of them with "a beard of massive gold," a kind of sash of fine beaten metal that was hung from holes pierced in the man's lips. Finally he returned to Jamaica, and his old obsession: Morgan. Esquemeling takes his last look at the man he would make famous, and despite the many glories he'd attributed to the admiral, his eye was now jaundiced by disappointment. "Morgan left us all in such a miserable condition," he wrote in one of the few self-incriminating passages in his memoir, "as might serve for a lively representation of what reward attends wickedness at the latter end of life." Esquemeling was not alone in his complaints. Even Browne, the surgeon general on the Panama expedition who had always spoke admiringly of the Welshman, took his shots. "There have been very great complaints by the wronged seamen in Sir Thomas Modyford's time against Admiral Morgan . . . ," he reported. "Nothing was done, but since Sir Thomas Lynch's arrival they are left to the law." Indeed, Lynch was making it clear that Port Royal's time as a pirate haven was over. He'd received "strict and severe orders" to keep the privateers from molesting the Spanish. The news seemed all bad for the Brethren. Those, like Esquemeling's crewmates, who were not starving were shipwrecked; an untold number of vessels wrecked on the reefs of Central America as they sought fresh victims. Others of the ex-Morgan forces attacked a town in Cuba and fell into torturing and robbing again, ignoring the noises Lynch was making in Jamaica. The new governor reacted quickly, pardoning all the privateers who had taken part in the Panama expedition, so long as they reported to Jamaica for absolution. But he went after the recent offenders. He caught some of the "chief actors" in the Cuban atrocities and had them hanged at a place called Gallows Point, or simply the Point. It was a shocking sight: the bodies of the guardians of the island, the heroes of Jamaica, swinging from a scaffold in the town they had shielded for decades.

It makes one wonder how much of Henry Morgan's illness was bacterial and how much the result of foreboding. Or perhaps the old commander was simply planning his next step, watching where the bodies fell.

In Panama the Spanish were returning to a city that looked as if it had been hit by an earthquake and a firestorm. The interim governor, Don Francisco de Marichalar, arrived back in the smoldering ruins on June 9, and "found nothing but disgraces, sorrows and misfortune." The rich merchants and their wives were near-naked and living in crude huts on the outskirts of the city formerly inhabited by their slaves. The English invasion had humbled the moguls of the New World with a biblical thoroughness; their homes were rubble, their bodies were racked with fevers, their trade was gone, and they had nothing to do but "watch their people die." Every sliver of wood had been consumed in the fire, which had even reached into the stone buildings and burned out the wooden beams, leaving the shells vulnerable; the soaring walls of the convents were now blackened monoliths that jutted up here and there like rotten teeth. Marichalar could hear them crash to the ground throughout the day, the impact of the falling stone startling the officials who were trying to get a head count and organize some sort of defenses, in case the English should return. The entire city would have to be razed; the foundations of the remaining buildings were so damaged that "nothing could be built on them."

Calamity or no calamity, this was still the Spanish Empire, and a full-fledged inquiry into the events of the past few months had to be undertaken. Marichalar made his rounds of the flattened metropolis and interviewed relevant witnesses in their pathetic homes, with acrid smoke still flavoring the air; he had no fewer than fifty questions to ask, most of them focused on Don Juan's performance leading up to and during the attack. The evidence pointed to a huge calamity, with 3,000 people, half the city's population, dead (that would translate into the loss of 250,000 people in present-day Panama City). The men who had run from Morgan and the soldiers who refused to fight now testified that in fact Don Juan had been the real traitor; he'd mismanaged the garrisons, failed to take the battle to Morgan on the Chagres, and committed one tactical mistake after another. It was, of course, completely untrue: If his subordinates and his superiors had responded to Don Juan's requests with even a modicum of vigor, Panama might have been saved. The paper trail and a good lawyer vindicated Don Juan: The barrister produced Don Juan's many letters asking for reinforcements and reams of testimony that directly contradicted the portrait of the old man as a failed leader. He was acquitted and returned to Spain, where he died three years later. The true criminals of the Panama episode on the Spanish side were never brought to justice.

The destruction of Panama was so complete that the old site of the city was abandoned and a new location six miles away was found for the inevitable rebuilding. This is where the modern city of Panama grew, with its bone-white skyscrapers. The ruins of the old cathedral and a few other buildings still stand and are a minor tourist attraction; a foreigner visiting La Vieja will hear a few legends about Morgan's raid, including the old canard that he burned down the city, and slightly more bizarre additions—such as the notion that the privateers entered the city singing "There'll Be a Hot Time in the Old Town Tonight."

The Panamanians never got their revenge on the infidels of Port Royal, but a fuller justice did come in a way they understood. For that they would have to wait twenty-one years.

Charles II had given up Modyford, but Madrid pressed for more. Master bureaucrats that they were, the Spanish had always blamed Modyford and the anti-Spanish lobby in London, rather than Morgan himself, for most of the admiral's mayhem in the West Indies. In the Spanish system, a lone commander making up his own rules, attacking his own chosen targets, was unthinkable. Their world was so regulated from top to bottom, so bound together with affidavits, hearings, councils of war, and miles of parchment, that they could hardly imagine the free hand Morgan was given. Although he always obtained the cover of commissions, Morgan's exploits were largely his own. The Spanish simply could not get their minds around that fact—until Panama. Trekking across the isthmus and holding 1,500 privateers under his sway was clearly not the act of a faceless cog; the Spanish finally recognized that the Welshman was greater *"en audaciay en el fortuna"* than anyone else who threatened them in the New World.

King Charles did not want further complications with the Spanish; tensions with Holland were ratcheting up, and he needed the Catholic power on his side in any possible war. The year before, Charles had signed the secret Treaty of Dover with the French, who would provide him with support against the Dutch in the event of a war, in return for his secret conversion to the Catholic faith. Everything Thomas

Gage had worked for was in jeopardy: The king was making peace with the hated Catholic empire in the New World, allying himself with the rising Catholic power of Louis XIV in the Old World, and facing off against those good Protestants, the Dutch. In this intricate game of kings and queens, Henry Morgan became an easily sacrificed pawn. The Spanish clamored for more evidence of English regret, and so orders were issued: Arrest the admiral.

Ironically, the arrest warrant arrived in a Jamaica that was again besieged, and from the old enemy. Lynch had received information that a fleet sent from Madrid to avenge Panama and retake Jamaica was under sail, with 5,000 soldiers aboard. The governor was skeptical but worried; he called a council of war and put the island on battle footing, but still he could not believe that the Spanish would attack. "I cannot think it is for the Spaniards' interest to break [the peace]," he wrote. "Lest we should bring the war again into their own quarters." Modyford was whiling away the days in the Tower of London; under his rule, the news of a fleet on the way would have been cause to bring the privateers roaring out of Port Royal. But Lynch kept his powder dry. When the letter arrived ordering him to arrest Morgan, however, he now saw his old nemesis in a fonder light. "To speak the truth of him, he's an honest, brave fellow," he wrote. He even wavered for a second on the arrest: "The sending home of Morgan might make all the privateers apprehend they should be so dealt with," Lynch admitted. But there was no thought of refusing London. "I shall send him home so as he shall not be much disgusted, yet the order obeyed, and the Spaniards satisfied."

A proper vessel for the prisoner's return was found, the *Welcome*, an ancient frigate that had once lain at the bottom of the Thames as a barrier to Dutch marauders but was later reclaimed and sent to Jamaica. It was a junker hardly fit for a person of Morgan's standing, but it told his current fortunes well enough. In April of 1672, at age thirty-seven, he was finally brought aboard as a prisoner of state, and the last of the true founders of Jamaica and the English empire in the West Indies disappeared into the stinking hold. One

Jamaican wrote of the islanders' feelings about their old protector, now in chains on his way to London: "I know not what approbation he may find there, but he received here a very high and honorable applause for his noble service. . . . I hope without offence I may say he is a very well deserving person, and one of great courage." But others, like Roderick, were glad to see him go. They still believed he'd buried their gold somewhere on his estate, and the admiral could burn in hell for all they cared. Roderick felt that the great man had let him down, that the thing that had come to replace the family he'd left behind—the Brethren—was now in shreds because of Morgan. Roderick spent most of his time drinking in Port Royal, sleeping with his prostitute girlfriend, and working the pirate grapevine for news of upcoming missions. He was not fit for returning to England or for starting another kind of life. He'd done great things, and the life back there would be too strange to him.

⁜   ⁜   ⁜

Morgan sailed to England, getting sicker as he got closer to the seat of his troubles. On the voyage he commiserated with Captain Francis Witherborn, a pirate who had been condemned to death. The mood for the Brethren could not have been darker: Back in Jamaica, Morgan's second-in-command on the Panama expedition, Edward Collier, quietly sold his plantation and attempted to leave the country before the garrison came looking for him. In Port Royal some of the merchants and planters breathed a sigh of relief. Their spokesman, Lynch, expressed what the buccaneers had done to Jamaica:

> People have not married, built, or settled as they would in peace; some for fear of being destroyed, others have got much and suddenly by privateers' bargains and are gone. War carries away all freemen, labourers, and planters of provisions, which makes work and victuals dear and scarce. Privateering encourages all manner of disorder and dissoluteness, and if it succeed, does but enrich the worst sort of people,

and provoke and alarm the Spaniards, constraining them to arm and fortify. . . .

It was an analysis that went all the way back to the buccaneers' rowdy male-only club, where women were banished and a kind of bestial party atmosphere reigned. Pirates were just not good for good bourgeois family values, and now that they were out of favor, the bourgeois were sticking their heads up and saying so. With Morgan and the boys prowling outside your windows, there was an atmosphere of lawlessness, always a hint of threat in the scented air. Civil society couldn't flourish where they held so much power.

Now Jamaica had gotten rid of the outlaws. Or so Lynch thought.

❖   ❖   ❖

After a rough passage, the admiral arrived in London in August 1672. He must have wondered if he'd join his friend Modyford. The wily governor was still in the Tower of London, where Walter Raleigh and Thomas More had spent their last days. Actually a series of buildings, the Tower had been founded almost six hundred years before by William the Conqueror and its expanding collection of structures had served as a castle right up until 1625. Its many uses had included an observatory, a zoo for the royal menagerie, and a mint. But it was as a jail that the Tower had become famous, and Modyford was in illustrious company: Princes had been murdered here, the treasonous Duke of Clarence was drowned in a barrel of wine, Elizabeth I plotted behind its walls, and Guy Fawkes's screams echoed off the stones as his torturers softened him up before his court date. Although Modyford was not whipped, he knew that the atmosphere behind the thick stone walls of the Tower was subject to every change in the diplomatic weather. The lives of rightful heirs to the throne had been snuffed out here; executing a mere colonial governor would hardly cause the king to lose a moment's sleep.

Morgan, on the other hand, was allowed the freedom of London.

If he'd landed in Cromwell's tight-lipped, Puritan England, the buccaneer king would surely have found it tough going. But Restoration
London was piratical in its outlook — hard drinking, displayed
wealth, luxurious dress, dubious morals were all in favor. If it were
only thirty degrees warmer, Morgan would have felt right at home. He
arrived in a country where religion and war were once again on people's minds. Charles II had cemented an alliance between England
and France, which gave the always strapped king access to some of
Louis XIV's ready cash and included a notorious clause stipulating
that the English monarch would declare himself a Catholic "as soon
as the welfare of his kingdom will permit"; all of this had tilted the nation toward France and against his fellow Protestants in the United
Provinces, who had become England's great competitors for world
markets. Indeed, everywhere he turned, the Londoner saw signs of
the current fetish for things Catholic: their new St. Paul's Cathedral
was practically a duplicate of St. Peter's in Rome; the aristocrats
marched down Oxford Street in French wigs, gripping the latest
Gallic novel, speaking French to their chambermaids and delighting
in the latest Spanish-influenced play. The old, tramped-down vine of
Catholicism was sprouting new leaves in England. And any alliance
with Catholic powers was bad news for Modyford and Morgan, as it
would always bring with it a consideration of Spain's desires. So
Modyford shivered in the cold lodgings of the Towers while Morgan
sank deeper into a heavy tropical fever.

Why did Morgan remain free? Because even before he arrived,
the political situation was shifting in his favor. The war with the Dutch
was not going well; the enemy had outwitted its larger, clumsier opponents with a combination of guerrilla warfare and unconventional
tactics, including opening the dikes and flooding their own countryside to stop a French advance. The English commoners were growing weary of battle, and with weariness came irritation: Why was the
nation expending its money and the lives of its youth on fighting
good Dutch Protestants? Here the ancient hatred of France played to
Morgan's favor. When it was revealed that Charles's newest mistress

was a Catholic and that others in his immediate circle had recently converted, the English hysteria raised its head again. Jailing Morgan would only have incensed Charles's anti-Catholic critics, and so he stayed out of prison. Even Modyford benefited: After two years in the Towers, he was released.

The admiral walked the London streets as a free, if deeply annoyed, man. A contemporary painted a picture of a frustrated Morgan, paying for lodging, food, and new clothes while he waited for his case to be decided, while his plantations were neglected back in Jamaica. "Under those difficulties and the perpetual malice of a prevailing court faction, he wasted the remaining part of his life, oppressed not only by those but by a lingering consumption, the coldness of this climate and his vexations had brought him into, when he was forced to stay here." But he enjoyed himself, too, going to parties and regaling the scandalized socialites with tales of plunder, sea battles, and nights in Jamaica's finest holes-in-the-wall.

There is evidence that Morgan fell in with a raffish, even dangerous crowd. His newest friend was the nineteen-year-old Christopher Monck, one of the princes of the realm, the son of Charles's redoubtable and rich general George Monck. The son was hotheaded and impetuous. Before meeting Morgan, he'd been cavorting in the red-light district of London with two highborn friends; when the beadle (or sheriff) of the district had stepped in to protest their drunken outrages, the young men killed him in the street. The locals wanted to lynch the trio, but their names saved them. Henry Morgan found young Christopher's wild ways to his liking; it was the closest thing to being in Port Royal after a rich haul.

It is odd how much of what we know of Morgan's three years in London retraced the rise of Thomas Gage. At a party attended by the best and brightest of English society, the diarist John Evelyn records the only sighting of the famous privateer and the now-released Modyford. He characterized Morgan as the man "who undertooke that gallant exploit from Nombre de Dios to Panama" and reported that the admiral estimated it would take only 10,000 men to conquer the Indies. He also reported that Morgan bragged about the "great booty" they had taken, surely a required note in any buccaneering tales told in London drawing rooms. Twenty years after Gage had spread the word of immense riches in the Spanish New World and the ease with which they could be extracted, here was Morgan saying the same thing. Morgan's estimate of the manpower needed was much more realistic than the pastor's, but Gage's dream of New World domination had not died. Nor had his avarice. By now it was practically the national credo of Jamaica.

And then, a final echo from the past: The king asked Morgan to draw up a memo with his ideas on Jamaica's protection, just as his old nemesis Cromwell had done with the pastor from Deal on the subject of the New World. The wars with the Netherlands meant that Jamaica faced new enemies: Dutch warships sailed out of Curaçao; the unappeased Spanish were still a threat; even the French could not be trusted. But with Morgan thousands of miles away, the privateers could no longer be called on to defend the island, as Lynch had so alienated the Brethren that they would not come to the country's defense. The governor asked the king for "a frigate or two" to protect his shores from invasion, but Charles was hard up, barely able to sustain his war against his Protestant rivals, and in this situation Lynch's pacifism looked increasingly like weakness. Morgan's stock rose by the week; say what you would about the buccaneer, he'd held England's enemies in check. After reading his memo, Charles called him in and they went over his points: More guns and ammunition for Port Royal led the list.

From arriving in London in the company of a doomed man, Morgan was being consulted by his king. It was a delicious turnaround. The meeting went so well that he was later presented with a snuff box bearing the king's profile done in small diamonds, a few extra required for Charles's long Gallic nose. Finally, on November 6, Morgan received word that he'd been named deputy governor of Jamaica, "his Majesty reposing particular confidence in his loyalty, prudence and courage, and long experience of that colony." With the job came a knighthood, and Morgan, dressed in the finest suit a London tailor could cut, attended the ceremony and felt the royal sword touch his clavicle. With clouds gathering on the horizon again, the rulers of England had finally clasped Morgan close; he was now one of theirs.

Cynics would have laughed at the ceremony; Morgan had almost been stuffed away in a dungeon by the same people who were now making him a knight. But one can be sure he was not among the scoffers: Morgan was a Royalist to the bone. It was certainly one of the happiest days of his life.

※　　　※　　　※

In London, Morgan had returned from the jungles to a brawling, febrile city that still thought of itself as in the forefront of new thinking in natural philosophy (that is, science), astronomy, and other disciplines. One tiny offshoot of this scientific revolution was a fresh look at the perennial scourge of Port Royal, the shaking of the earth, which had for centuries been attributed to one thing: God's wrath. There were dozens of theories as to what caused these tremors, some dating back centuries, some brand-new. The Greek Thales of Miletas proposed that the earth's crust floated on an ocean whose waves and gales caused the ground to heave up and down, while Descartes believed that subterranean gases shot out of their dens and sparked the tremors. Steam vapor caused by underground rivers flowing onto hot rocks was another hypothesis, while one famous London expert on earthquakes came down on the side of "eruptions of fiery Conflagrations inkindled in the Subterranean regions." A shift in the earth's core, the influence of passing comets, and—from the director of the Royal Observatory in London—"an explosion of nitreous and sulphurous particles in the air" were also suggested. In the *General History of Earthquakes*, published in the late 1600s, the author began with this statement: "An earthquake is a shaking of the Earth occasioned by Wind and Exhalation inclosed within the Caves and Bowels of the Earth." When the winds were out of balance, they found a gap in the earth's surface and proceeded to "rendeth and openeth" the ground. There were four kinds of quakes, and all were related to the movement of air:

1. A lateral quake, in which "the whole force of the inclosed wind and vapors [are] driven to one place and there is no contrary motion to preserve it." This represents an early attempt to describe how land actually moved during earthquakes, which the author compared to "a man shaking in an ague [fever]."

2. The explosive upward event, where "the earth is lifted up with great violence so that the buildings are like to fall and instantly sink down again." These kinds of tremors, it was believed, were caused by the earth actually collapsing into the cavern that had once been supported by the pressure of the escaping wind.

3. A split in the earth, "when the sea in some places has been drunk up so that people have gone over on foot." This accounted for the phenomenon of disappearing lakes and rivers so common to powerful quakes.

4. The reverse, quakes that caused mountains "to arise out of the Earth."

✤   ✤   ✤

Morgan was appointed deputy governor of Jamaica, second-in-command on the island. The new governor and Morgan's new superior was one Lord Vaughan, five years younger than the thirty-nine-year-old Morgan, a man of letters who had some claim to "discovering" the poet John Dryden. He was a fitting emissary from Restoration London: an aristocrat with a satyr's face whom Samuel Pepys once called "one of the lewdest fellows of the age." Still, he was no match for a veteran like Morgan. The young lord warned the buccaneer to stick close to his vessel on the voyage from England to Jamaica and under no circumstances set out ahead. If Morgan arrived first, he'd be acting governor of the island until Vaughan made it ashore. The admiral agreed and then completely ignored Vaughan; he set out in the *Jamaica Merchant* under the command of Captain Joseph Knapman, but there is some evidence that Morgan himself whipped the crew on to leave Vaughan in his wake. Knapman later said that some evil genius had plotted the *Merchant*'s route, and "never was any man more surprised considering the course they had steered."

If past performance is any clue, Morgan was the evil genius in question, because the *Merchant* crashed into a coral reef off Île-à-Vache, the buccaneers' old meeting place off the southern coast of Haiti. Morgan treated ships like disposable objects, to be wrecked, sunk, rammed, or turned into blazing weapons whenever necessary, and the *Merchant* was no different: The ammunition and cannon that he'd brought with him, as per his memo to the king, sank straight to the bottom of the ocean. Morgan had not been humbled by his time abroad; he reported solemnly to London that "they had all perished had Morgan not known where he was." Undaunted, he soon caught a ride with a privateer who happened by and was brought in his old style to Port Royal on March 6. The parties commenced immediately; those who had been pining for a resumption of the town's notorious ways and a strong man to face down all comers stood drinks for their returned hero. His wife, Elizabeth, fell into his arms, his nephews and nieces crowded around him, planters pressed invitations on the admiral, and all in all the wide-open spirit of the buccaneer paradise seemed ready to whir up again to its old dizzying heights.

His enemy, Lynch, was waiting for him with a scowl on his face. The governor had in November written to London to warn them that Morgan's second coming would only lead to more bloodshed in the West Indies. The Spanish were reportedly sending a fleet of galleons, "biscaniers, Ostenders and Flushingers, which are likely to clear the Indies of all that Infest them," adding with a sting, "one of the reasons of their coming is, the noise of Admiral Morgan's favour at Court and return to the Indies, which much alarmed the Spaniards, and caused the King to be at vast charge in fortifying in the South Sea." Morgan's old cronies, including Roderick, who had lost two fingers in a grenado accident, were sailing under French commissions out of Tortuga and keeping to their old style of "rapine and libertinage." Time had sweetened their memories somewhat, that and the fact that they had yet to hit a payday equal to the admiral's best. If Morgan could promise another rich target, they might be ready to take up with him. It seemed like the old wars were about to begin again.

As he'd arrived before Vaughan, Morgan assumed the office of governor until his superior landed. He immediately took charge of the island's defenses, which he found in a deplorable state, with only fourteen barrels of powder available for the fortress guns. He accused Lynch of selling the king's supplies to the Spanish, a fair indication of the nasty tone of Jamaican politics that Morgan would help ramp up. Increasingly, as he grew older, Morgan needed enemies; he thrived on controversy and in-close fighting. "Nevertheless that shall not daunt him," he wrote to his superiors in London on April 13, only five weeks after arriving and referring to himself in the third person, "for before he will lose his Majesty's fortifications, he will lose himself and a great many brave men more, that will stand and fall by him."

Even as he knocked heads together, the return of the rugged Morgan disguised the fact that there had been a fundamental change in his life. Over the next few years, he had a career that was marked by a series of long and bitter feuds, and he was a lively figure in domestic politics. There is little that compares in viciousness to the backbiting and infighting that goes on in a colonial council, especially when ambitious men are left to fight over the reins of power, and Morgan joined in with gusto. He stayed on as deputy governor, made enemies, and wrote suave, violent letters back to London reporting and complaining about everything from taxes to slanderous colleagues and the logwood trade. He built up Jamaica's defenses, feuded with Lynch, drank like a pirate, and extended his holdings in the Jamaican countryside to include another fine plantation (his third), four thousand acres in the parish of St. Elizabeth's. But it was a different kind of life, a far more ordinary one. The diversions of local politics are simply not as exciting as those that take place on blue waters when the course of empires is at stake. The first part of his life could have been written by Dumas, the second by Orwell, in a bleak colonial mood. There was, in fact, only one remarkable and revealing thing that Morgan did that sets him apart from the thousands of bureaucrats who underpinned the English empire in the next two hundred years, sweating and growing old in places from Bombay to the Falklands, and it had to do with his old comrades, the buccaneers.

Morgan was charged with exterminating piracy from Jamaica and the surrounding waters. He did it, as always, with a style balanced somewhere between mockery and brutality. Morgan most likely wrote a 1679 report that laid out the Jamaican government's policy on pirates: They were "ravenous vermin" who used any Spanish cruelty against English sailors as justification for their raids on the enemy, thereby wreaking havoc on trade. Morgan kept up a constant stream of letters to London on his efforts against the pirates, issued arrest warrants, and sent squadrons of militia out into the surrounding waters to chase down suspicious ships. When one sloop anchored in Montego Bay and the sailors stayed aboard, his suspicions were aroused; only buccaneers uncertain of their reception acted in this way. Morgan invited the seventeen men aboard to King's House in Port Royal (which Morgan preferred to the governor's mansion in Spanish Town) and served them red snapper, lobster, beef, fruit pie, and goblets of the best local rum. As the alcohol worked through their veins, the men dropped their pretenses and admitted that they were indeed pirates. Morgan roared with laughter, and the party continued; for the younger men, it was like being feted by their boyhood hero, the greatest buccaneer who had ever lived. After a long night of storytelling and carousing, Morgan sent the boys to their beds. The next morning he greeted them, and with reluctance they strolled out the door. Waiting on the steps were members of the local garrison, and the confessed pirates were clapped in chains.

The seventeen were brought before the Admiralty Court, and there they found a far less jovial Henry Morgan, staring down at them from the bench, where he sat as chief judge, and regarding the crew as if he'd never seen them before. There is a portrait of Morgan in his later years that has never been found, but Charles Leslie, who saw the painting in 1740, gave a description of it. "There appears something so awful and majestick in his countenance," he wrote, "that I'm persuaded none can look upon it without a kind of veneration." This is the Morgan whom the pirates met that morning; this is the man who conducted a quick, businesslike trial and sentenced them to death. The unlucky crew were marched out of the courts and handed over to the "finisher of the law," the hangman. It is moments like this that make one wish Morgan had written his memoirs; the sheer enjoyment he got out of being a ruthless bastard could have made him one of the great seventeenth-century characters. One of the maxims he used in later life was "Nothing but a diamond can cut a diamond," and Morgan was certainly hard enough to deal with the average pirate.

The separation between Morgan and his former mates was now complete. The admiral had seen the future, and it was trade, not pillage. Privateering had given him estates and status, but he knew that only a rational system of trade and a lasting peace could ensure his family's position for generations to come. Morgan's writings never betray a flicker of doubt about his actions; he believed he'd turned privateer for the benefit of his family and his country. Now he was hunting pirates for the same reason. Morgan proved more inventive and flexible than the Rodericks of the world; he'd made the final turn that they were not capable of. The Brethren were a passing phase; he wanted to join that which would last.

Without hesitation the admiral terrorized his former comrades, whom he now described as "a dangerous pestilence." Although with tongue in cheek he claimed to "abhor bloodshed," he didn't shy away from it when dealing with pirates. "I have put to death, imprisoned and transported to the Spanish for execution all English and Spanish pirates that I could get," he wrote his masters in London. The fact that he was accused of secretly encouraging the pirates and taking a cut of their profits only increased his severity; any whiff of scandal weakened his position with London, and he was not going to have that. His letters to his superiors were filled with reports of "bloody and notorious villains" he'd sent soldiers to capture, "a powerful and desperate pirate" prowling out in the North Sea. When London pressed for even more action, he acidly replied that piracy could no more be ended in the West Indies that the brigands who terrorized people on the highways of London could be wiped out. Morgan spent five years hunting down buccaneers. Some he pardoned (if they returned to Jamaica and renounced their former lives); many others he hanged.

Pirate trials the world over tell us what kind of things happened at Port Royal. Outlaws were encouraged to confess before dying and to cleanse their souls of their many, variegated crimes. Some were broken by their impending doom, cried out for mercy, found Christ, or at least mumbled an apology and blamed their wrongdoings on drink. Asked what had drawn him into the life, one pirate recalled, "I may begin with gaming! No, whoring, that led on to gaming. . . ." There were scenes of quite heartfelt regret and penance. Others reacted differently. "Yes, I do heartily repent," one told the judge. "I repent that I had not done more Mischief, and that we did not cut the Throats of them that took us, and I am extremely sorry that you an't all hang'd as well as we." These kinds of mocking confessions run through the transcripts of pirate trials, and many a judge was incensed to see the condemned corsairs cracking jokes, laughing at the crowd, and generally living as they were about to die.

Another incident caused Morgan to further distance himself from his past: the publication of Esquemeling's *The Buccaneers of America*. The book was an immediate sensation. "No other book of that time . . . ," wrote one observer, "experienced a popularity similar to that of *Buccaneers.*" It spawned a thousand imitators: Every fictional buccaneer from *Treasure Island*'s Billy Bones to Johnny Depp's very postmodern Captain Jack sprang from its overheated pages. Originally titled *De Americaensche Zeerovers*, it was a smash success and would soon be translated into Spanish (where Morgan's name was blackened even further by the translators) and then English. The book depicted Morgan as a bold and at times brilliant leader, but it also painted him as a rampaging, torturing, thieving pirate. The Spanish editors described him acidly in their preface, failing even to get his name right: "the English of Jamaica, under the command of the intrepid and valiant John Morgan, who would have gained greater honour for his skilful management and daring, if his tyrannical cruelty to the conquered had not blotted out all the splendour of his glory." Morgan was livid. He sicced lawyers on the Dutchman and his publishers, and the libel suit produced intriguing testimony from Morgan. "The Morgan family had always held due and natural allegiance to the King," he wrote, "were both by sea and land of good fame, and against all evil deeds, piracies, &c, had the greatest abhorrence and disgust, and that in the West Indies there are such thieves and pirates called bucaniers, who subsist by piracy, depredation and evil deeds of all kinds without lawful authority, that of these people Henry Morgan always had and still has hatred."

Was Morgan a hypocrite? The line between pirates and privateers is a thin one to modern eyes; they often behaved exactly alike, and to their victims there was no difference whatsoever. But to Morgan those commissions with the king's blessing were everything. A Welshman to the bone, he craved respectability, or at least respect, for his clan (notice that Morgan mentions his family in the testimony above). Esquemeling had cut him to the quick not by describing the lines of Spaniards that fell under his men's swords but by classifying himself as a renegade and a criminal. Morgan got his revenge, however, by winning the suit; abject apologies soon followed from the publishers, along with heavily edited versions of *The Buccaneers*, which did not sell very well.

Morgan saw things in stark black and white. One was either with him, and England, or against them. To the admiral it was not he but the pirates who had betrayed the cause—the cause of getting rich while at the same time serving their country.

The realities of life in the Caribbean, where piracy still offered a chance at quick wealth possible in few other trades, kept the corsairs' flag flying. Roderick sailed with a small, international outfit, attacking settlements along the coast of the Main and making only enough to sustain a regular drinking schedule. He still dreamed of hitting a galleon, but like many pirates he was reduced to hand-to-mouth living. The stories of Panama and Portobelo got told and retold.

Morgan was not sentimental about the past; he was now hunting all the Rodericks he'd helped create. Not only were many of the veterans who had studied buccaneering under him in his great raids now sailing under French commissions and passing along the lessons of his leadership to their acolytes, but the stories of his success echoed around the West Indies and even through the harbors of England and France, keeping the new recruits flowing in. The next generation of pirates would often be straight outlaws, not sanctioned by the English king. And they'd add new dimensions to the pirate life, just as Morgan had built on Drake's example and made the privateer, in the words of one historian, into "that raffish instrument of foreign policy."

❋   ❋   ❋

To find out what happened to Morgan's former enemies, we must skip ahead. By the late 1600s, the empire Morgan had fought was reeling; Queen Mariana had died in 1696 of breast cancer, after her doctors had given up and called in a *santiguadore*, a faith healer from La Mancha, the seventh son of a daughterless couple. This unlettered peasant was rumored to have miraculous powers, and he'd hurried to Madrid to work his art. But when he arrived, the man simply produced a crucifix, stood holding it over the royal patient, and chanted "I cross thee, God heal thee" over and over. The queen's enormous, melon-size tumor showed no change, and soon she was dead. The devastated Carlos II, the last of the Spanish Hapsburg kings, was left alone. In 1679 he'd married Marie Louise, the niece of Louis XIV, but he had proved impotent, and the deeply depressed queen ate herself to an early death, passing away at age twenty-seven. The race for an heir became even more urgent: Carlos the Be-witched had then married a neurotic German queen, Maria Ana, whom he openly hated. Their unfortunate marriage produced no heirs, and Carlos spent his last years as a weakling sitting atop a golden chest, with the great powers of Europe waiting impatiently for him to die so the spoils could be distributed. He began to suffer from the death obsession that ran through his family's history, even to the point of ordering his ancestors' bodies exhumed so that, like his father before him, he could sit and contemplate the illustrious corpses. For a Spanish king, it was not as macabre a thing to do as it would be for an Englishman or a Frenchman, and for Carlos it made a special kind of sense. In many ways his dead ancestors were the only ones who could truly understand his dilemma; even the de-formed, impotent Carlos considered himself to be a divine prince, without equal on earth. Only death would release him from the monstrous body that disgusted his wife and made a mockery of his greatness. It comforted him to know that he'd soon join his family and meet the Lord he'd striven so hard to serve.

Month by month he grew sicker, more spectral. The English am-bassador wrote that the king was so weak he could barely lift his head to feed himself and that he was "so extremely melancholy that neither his buffoons, dwarfs nor puppet shows can in the least divert him from fancying everything that is said or done to be a temptation of the devil." The king's bewitchment was now regarded as official fact; his inability to produce an heir was, in fact, taken as a sign that Carlos was possessed by the devil. The court was convulsed with talk of witches, charms, and ciphers with the king's name written in diabolical code. The exorcist assigned to the case conducted interviews with the devil to find out how the king had been enchanted, and he reported that it had been "done to destroy his generative organs, and to render him incapable of administering the kingdom" and that the enchantment had been achieved using "the members of a dead man" mixed into a chocolate drink. Carlos was paraded before the public, staggering and pale as a ghost, with one eye sunken into its socket; he was clearly failing. On his sickbed freshly killed pigeons were laid on his head to ward off vertigo, and the entrails of slaughtered animals were placed on his stomach to warm it. But nothing could save him, and on November 1, 1700, Carlos died, and his body was placed alongside the other descendants of Juana the Mad. Despite much back-channel negotiation and maneuvering by all the major powers, the question of who would get Spain had not been settled, and so the War of Spanish Succession was joined in 1702, with England and Holland battling France and Spain over who would rule in Madrid and lay claim to the wonders of Potosí and the rest of the American treasure. The Treaty of Utrecht in 1713, in which Spain lost Portugal and its territories in the Netherlands, marked the nation's retirement from the ranks of first-tier world powers.

Morgan had helped, in his own way, point a path toward the future. Some historians have even argued that without Morgan the Spanish would have been able to settle and defend Florida more vigorously and even extend their control along the Gulf Coast, creating an impregnable empire stretching to Texas. Without him who knows what the map of the Caribbean and even of the United States might look like? He battled a divine empire on behalf of men interested in trade and gold and rational society (but certainly not freedom for every member, as the pirates had insisted on). The next great world empire, the British, would be a mercantile, not a religious, one. The world had turned Morgan's way, and he'd nudged it along.

✠   ✠   ✠

We have skipped ahead of the final chapter of Morgan's story. As his inheritors sailed to every corner of the known and unknown world, Henry Morgan was back in Port Royal. He'd grown increasingly cantankerous against his enemies, including Sir Thomas Lynch, who returned to the island in 1682 to serve as governor and resumed his duel with the Welshman. The sickly Lynch reported to London that Morgan, although friendly in the beginning, had soon shown his deep enmity and in fact was "mightily elated by the hopes of my death." Old sea captains do not make good followers, and old buccaneers make even worse ones. Over the years the stories had become memorized, the rum had become a necessity, the glory of fighting the Spanish was whittled away to battles between planters and merchants. In his forties Morgan developed a heavy paunch and could be found any night of the week drinking himself into a stupor with a passel of cronies who treated him as a vilified hero. Lynch petulantly wrote of his rival that he sat in his regular haunts drinking for days on end with the "five or six little sycophants" with whom he traveled. "In his drink," Lynch wrote, "Sir Henry reflects on the government, swears, damns and curses most extravagantly." The thing that finally caused Morgan's downfall was almost ridiculously petty: Leaving a tavern one night, he was heard to say, "God damn the Assembly." The ex-buccaneer denied it, but he was removed from the council and from public service in October 1683. He was forty-eight and had five years to live.

If a pirate's life was about excess, it could be said that Henry Morgan died of it. Long years of alcohol abuse had weakened his system; his stomach grew to an enormous size so that his tailor could not even design a coat that would button over it, his appetite disappeared, his legs became swollen and painful. The admiral was suffering from dropsy, in which the body's tissues retain excess fluid. The doctors who treated him were using concepts of the body that went back fifteen centuries to Claudius Galen, who was physician to the gladiators and, later, to Marcus Aurelius. The medical care that was directed at Henry Morgan was little different from that which would have been received by a Roman warrior clawed by a captive lion in AD 190. Galen took Aristotle's theory of the four elements—earth, water, fire, and air—and developed them into the corresponding theory of humors. Health depended on a correct balance between the humors at work in the body: blood, phlegm, yellow bile, and black bile. Each humor had a condition linked to it (dryness, heat, cold, wet) as well as an organ (liver, kidney, gallbladder, and spleen). Balancing these competing elements was the physician's delicate work.

Morgan was lucky enough to have one of the best doctors in the West Indies, perhaps even in the world, attending him. Dr. Hans Sloane was a rising physician and naturalist who would go on to treat the royal family. He arrived in Port Royal in 1687, accompanying the star-crossed Duke and Duchess of Albemarle; the duke was assuming the governorship of the island. The new arrival was the same young rake who had murdered a beadle in London and later escorted Morgan through the delicious byways of Restoration vice. Now he was married to the ex–Lady Cavendish, a shopper of epic proportions who was showing signs of mental instability, while he himself was deteriorating from the effects of years of riotous living. One of their initiations into Jamaican life came on February 19 of that year, when a minor earthquake struck. "It was felt all over the island at the same time," wrote Sloane. "Houses were near ruin with few escaping injury." The tremors seemed to be getting more frequent: Just about a year later, Sloane reported three short shocks over the span of a minute, with the sounds of thunder that seemed to be coming from under the ground. Two years later a quake rocked the eastern Caribbean, with a huge chunk of a rock formation on the island of Redonda splitting off and crashing into the ocean. Sugar mills were swallowed up on St. Kitts, and people died on Antigua. The governor of the island of St. Thomas reported that the sea withdrew, and townspeople could walk out onto the seabed and collect fish flopping on the dry land.

Modern seismologists use the Modified Mercalli Intensity Scale to measure the "shaking severity" of an earthquake (the more popu-

lar Richter scale measures magnitude). Invented by the Italian vul-
canologist Giuseppe Mercalli in 1902, its grades range from I to XII.
A Value I earthquake would not even be felt by humans standing
on affected areas; a Value IV would cause chandeliers to swing,
wooden walls to creak, and glasses to clink in the cupboard. It is the
earthquakes at Value VIII and above that are the great ones. At
VIII, towers and chimneys can collapse, poorly built houses suffer
severe damage. At X, most buildings are completely destroyed and
landslides add to the devastation. In recent times the Northridge,
California, earthquake in 1994 registered scale values from the extremely mild I to the devastating IX rating at the epicenter. The
1906 San Francisco quake reached a value of IX to X. Anything
above X is an apocalyptic quake. The tremors shaking Jamaica
month after month were nothing close to that. Not yet.

✤　　✤　　✤

Back in Port Royal, few thought about the inner workings of the
earth; people focused on their daily lives. Dr. Sloane was concerned
about Henry Morgan, a rare colonial species in decline, and the
young doctor studied him with an exacting eye. Sloane's writings,
which are admirably precise and alive, would later become the basis
for the British Library and would form its first collection. In his
words the old privateer was

> lean, sallow-coloured, his eyes a little yellowish and belly jutting out
> or prominent. . . . He complained to me of want of appetite for victuals,
> he had a kicking or roaching to vomit every morning and generally a
> small looseness attending him, and withal is much given to drinking
> and staying up late, which I supposed had been the cause of his present
> indisposition.

Sloane prescribed a thin gruel and a feather (for sticking down
Morgan's throat), so that he'd vomit and bring up the fluids in his
stomach. Once that had been done, Morgan tried some "Madeira

wine in which roots of gentian, tops of centaury had been infused with Mich.Vomit." What Morgan really needed was rest and a different lifestyle, but he refused to change. He spent his days lolling in a hammock, his bloated body straining against the cords, and received friends, who could not be turned away without a drop of rum. The nights were the worst: The heat, the buzzing insects (but not a guilty conscience) kept him awake; he could not pass water and croaked like a night frog, belching to relieve his stomach of the intolerable feeling of swelling. Finally he'd reach, against Sloane's express orders, for the liquor bottle and drive away the boredom and the more unpleasant memories with a long pull. Sloane despaired of his muleheaded patient: "Not being able to abstain from company, he sat up late at night drinking too much." Morgan grew tired of hearing the young Englishman chide him about the rum and called for another doctor. Sloane's rival diagnosed timpany, or an excess of wind in the belly; the contrary opinion must have pleased Morgan, who one can imagine repeating it to Sloane with a broad smile on his face, as it meant he could keep on drinking.

Morgan must have known he was dying. In one of his last public outings, he returned to the Council of Jamaica, which by permission of the king he'd been allowed to rejoin. The summer heat was roasting, but Morgan was transported in his carriage and made it to his seat with the help of a cane, and there he heard a last valedictory by the Speaker of the assembly. Morgan's time as lieutenant governor was described as a golden age. "His dispensations of favour and kindness were great and many," the Speaker said, "even to those who, true hornet like, lay buzzing about him during his government."

But finally Western medicine could do him no more good, and Morgan went to the black doctor the local slaves depended on for cures. He was given urine enemas and covered with clay plasters, but the treatment only gave him a persistent cough. He moved on to another. What other remedies the folk doctor prescribed have not been passed down, or if a desperate Morgan in fact consulted with an obeah man, spirit doctors who used ghosts as assistants for their curing, bribing the shades with doses of rum and offerings of silver. But all measures failed, and on August 25, 1688, at about eleven in the morning, Henry Morgan died at age fifty-three.

In his will the admiral revealed himself as he rarely did in his letters. His holdings were valued at 5,000 pounds, or $1.2 million in today's dollars. He left the bulk of his sprawling estates to Elizabeth, whom he described with uncharacteristically tender language as "my very well and intirely beloved wife Dame Mary Elizabeth Morgan." She'd be the caretaker of his wealth until her death, when the lands would pass to his nephew Charles — on one condition. Charles would have to change his last name from Byndloss to Morgan "and always go thereby." Morgan's almost desperate desire to continue his line had extended even after death. There is no doubt that Henry wished to be remembered: He left mourning rings not only to his godsons and nephew but to his friends and secretary and even his servants.

His funeral proceeded along the lines of any farewell for a major government official, with one twist. The governor of the island quietly issued a twenty-four-hour amnesty for anyone wishing to attend the ceremony; soon ships flying no flag were arriving in the harbor and discharging groups of men into the evening gloom, men with no fixed address who were now making a living raiding ships of all nations as they caught the trade winds on the North Sea. Armed as always with pistols, their faces scarred and grim, on any other day they'd have been met by members of the local militia, who could spot their kind on sight and would have clamped them in irons and marched them off to hear their death sentences. But Morgan's day was a one-of-a-kind legal holiday, and so they made their way along the pier toward King's House, the home of the governor and the official seat of government on the island, where Morgan lay in state until the funeral on August 26. Every sort of person passed by his lead-lined coffin and stood to regard the face of the man who had made Jamaica: French corsairs, fantastically wealthy merchants, madams, tavern owners, skilled tradesmen, Morgan's cousins and drinking mates, prostitutes, government officials. Morgan was by no means an uncontroversial figure in the city; there were certainly men who came to look on his face with barely concealed satisfaction; there were buccaneers from the Panama mission who still could not forgive him for, they believed, violating their trust and stealing their silver plate. But Panama had been fourteen years ago, and Morgan was, in death, bigger than any single expedition.

Roderick came. Now forty-seven, he'd survived two recent bouts of malaria and was living in Nassau. The teeth were rotting in his head, he was lean, he had new scars on his face (some martial, some nightlife-related), and, to judge by his general appearance, it didn't seem he'd outlive his leader by many months. Why had he come? Because the raids with Morgan now seemed like his halcyon days; he'd never been involved in anything on the same scale again, nothing so daring or rich. The fact that Morgan the governor would have hanged him didn't bother Roderick; he'd accepted years ago that the world wanted him dead. Pirates recognized that self-interest was at the bottom of most things. Many of them didn't bear the admiral a grudge—that is, after the bitterness about the Panama money had gone, which had taken a few years. Still, Morgan had brought things off with style. He'd made the world take notice of the Brethren, and pirates had a love of the world's regard. They sought it out. And here was the man who had spread their name to every corner of the earth. Roderick took his hat off at the coffin, tilting slightly as he did (he was not entirely sober), and studied the admiral's face. He was in many ways the sum of the urges that had brought white men like Roderick to the New World, minus any spiritual ones, and the qualities that had allowed the hugely outnumbered English to battle the Spanish Empire to a draw. Roderick had come because, despite it all, he was proud to be a pirate, proud of the unconventional and wicked life he'd led. The Brethren had been his family, and Morgan was the greatest of his kin.

As the time for the ceremony approached, Morgan's old partner in crime, the Duke of Albemarle, arrived, looking anything but healthy himself (he'd be dead in two months, the victim of the same ills that killed Morgan). The pallbearers carried the coffin to a gun carriage, the conveyance that would be used for royal funerals such as Queen Victoria's, and the procession wound its way to St. Peter's Church, where the funeral mass was said. The mourners then marched to the cemetery on the Palisadoes, where the coffin was interred in the sandy ground. The ships in the harbor fired a twenty-two-gun salute, one more than even Albemarle would receive at his death. Governors came and went. Morgan's passing was unique.

Perhaps there were other ceremonies that were never recorded. Morgan's estate included 109 slaves, and he was said to have fathered children by several of them; today there are even rumors of his descendants living near Montego Bay, though no ancestry can be proven. One colonial administrator in the early 1900s reported that the wild behavior of a number of Jamaican families in the Yallahs Valley proved they were descended from the Welshman. If Morgan did indeed have family, whether by force or through a relationship, however oppressive, it's likely his passing was marked with a ritual. The slaves in Jamaica believed that hotheaded people were survived by like-minded ghosts, or duppies, who would go through the world causing havoc if measures were not taken to stop them. There were several methods available to restrict the duppy's progress: sticking pins into the dead man's feet, so that the ghost could not walk without pain, and cutting out the pockets in the burial suit, so that the duppy would not have rocks to throw at his enemies. The slave family would not have had access to Morgan's body, but there was one rite that could be performed without it: nine days of singing, followed by a banishment ritual on the ninth night, expelling the duppy forever.

If the banishment was performed, it didn't take. Morgan had one final appearance to make in the story of Port Royal.

14

Apocalypse

The day of June 7, 1692, came in hot and airless. As the lamplighters moved through the blue-and-violet dawn, snuffing out the streetlights, there wasn't a breath of wind or a cloud in the sky to give the promise of rain. It was growing unbearable. For the last five months, the weather had continued in this nervous-making pall of heat. A sharp burst of rain in May had served only to increase the mosquito population, which was now feasting on pale English skin. The lack of wind was not only annoying, it was bad for business: The ships waiting in the harbor with their holds full of logwood and sugar couldn't exit Port Royal and sail out to the open seas to markets in Europe and North America. Nor could the merchant ships loaded with the latest Parisian brocaded dresses and fine linens make the dock and unload the European trade goods that Port Royal was rich enough to buy. The term "earthquake weather" had not yet been coined, but the townspeople would have understood it instinctively.

The stifling heat was connected, in locals' minds, with the tremors that had shaken the town every year of its brief history. The smoldering air also tended to agitate the more sensitive members of the population; doctors were kept hurrying from home to home to minister to the neurasthenic wives of merchants who could not leave their beds because of black moods and bouts of low energy. Many of that morning's patients had their conditions worsened by the latest gossip. An astrologer had visited the island weeks before and left it with a prediction: There would be a major earthquake in the near future. Four years earlier another mystic had given a similar reading, and a quake followed, strong enough to topple some of the brick-and-mortar buildings constructed in English style (the residents living as if they were on a floating remnant of Sussex or Coventry and building their homes accordingly). The sick were prone to rumors, of which Port Royal had plenty. The crazed-looking men who strode up and down Market Street loudly proclaiming that "judgment was at hand"—did the doctors think they knew something? The physicians tried to comfort the patients, but, sweating and wild-eyed, they broke in with the latest gossip: Dr. Heath in his sermon that Sunday had reminded his congregations about the wife of his colleague John Taylor. She'd suddenly quit Jamaica, left Port Royal and her husband behind, because she could no longer stand "the badness of this place." It was not as if she were being original: Ever since its founding, Port Royal had been the scourge of religious men and women, who were constantly predicting, even praying for, its destruction. "Port Royal could not stand," went the refrain, "but would sink and be destroyed by the judgment of God." It was just that all the signs— religious, astrological, meteorological—were now conspiring to make the nervous women call for the rum punch and the doctor. The physicians came promptly and soothed their patients, dispensing advice and "cooling, diluting drinks," but not what the women truly wanted: the Bolus of Diascord, an elixir that contained one-tenth of a grain of opium. The merchants' wives were high-strung enough; all they needed was a dose of it, and a rumor of unrest in the slave quarters, for pandemonium to infect the white community of Port Royal.

Down by Fishers Row, the markets were open. Meat in the tropics spoiled within hours, so fish and fowl were brought fresh and slaughtered just before cooking. In the fish market, the huge local tortoises swam placidly in the "turtle crawl"; June was the month when they emerged from the sea to climb onto the beaches and lay their eggs, only to have them snatched up by local fishermen. Along with turtles, there were lobsters and crabs and manatee and snapper and eighteen other varieties of fish for the servants coming down from High Street to choose from. Out in the harbor, the water was as smooth and reflective as a pane of silvery glass; the only ripples came from porpoises surfacing to snipe at a school of minnows or sharks snatching the offal thrown into the water by the butchers and fishmongers. Everyone glanced occasionally at the horizon for unfamiliar shapes against the sky; England and France were at war again, and the French had in late May swooped down onto the north of the island, sacking and torching sugar plantations and killing anyone they came across. The next logical step was a strike at Port Royal itself, especially as one of the town's two guard ships, the HMS *Guernsey*, was becalmed to the east and couldn't reach the port in an emergency. Port Royal lay open to any strong force. The lieutenant governor, John White, had scheduled an assembly of the Council of Jamaica to assess the threat, but there was little one could do; this was Jamaica, a jewel envied by foreign powers. Martial law had been declared, and the local garrisons had been called to arms in Port Royal, Liguanea, and Spanish Town. Lookouts at the town's formidable military forts—including Morgan's Fort, finished in 1680 and named after the great Welshman—watched the horizon.

Just the night before, a strange ship had been spotted lurking at the eastern end of the harbor, flying no flag. Was it a pirate—or a scout for a fleet waiting over the horizon? The commander of Fort Charles had sent an armed squadron to investigate; as they had approached the vessel, the soldiers were on standby with their muskets. But it was just a merchant ship out of Bristol that had coaxed enough speed from the occasional breeze to make it this far and was waiting for dawn to unload its goods and passengers. The commander reminded the ship's captain to have the newcomers brought to the King's Warehouse to sign the register; if they refused, they'd be thrown into the prison as suspected spies or provocateurs. If they signed, they'd be handed a certificate giving them each fifty acres of land; the interior needed fresh men—white men, that is—and Port Royal was their entryway into the dream they had nourished back in England. Soon they would most likely be either building their fortunes or dead from malaria.

The men who had made it in Jamaica emerged from their brick homes dressed as any London gentleman would be; when a fashion was all the rage in London, it was all the rage on the streets of Jamaica. In the 1670s, down the paths of this steamy tropical town, you might find a man striding toward his offices dressed in "a Turkish garment of black watered chambles lined with crimson taffety, a black cloathe coat lined with blew sarconet, creeches, black silke stockings and a pair of garters with christial stones, a Turkish capp of crimson velvet, a silke crimson Turkish sash, a pair of Turkish shoes, gloves and a periwig, . . . a sealed gold ring, a silver ring with a blew stone in it and a pair of silver buckles." What a sight he must have been, every fold and stitching in his clothes brought into sharp focus by the Jamaican sun! It didn't matter that such an outfit was far better suited to chilly London than to sweltering Port Royal; the Turkish outfit was based on the wardrobe of Charles II, and thus one wore it. There was so much money flowing through the town, licit and illicit, that it had to be spent. The merchants did their level best, living "to the height of splendour, in full ease and plenty, being sumptuously arrayed, and attended on and served by their Negro slaves, which always waits on them in livereys, or otherwise as they please to cloath them." The traders' wives were not left behind. The local shops carried a full line of materials—Persian silks, fine serge—ready to be whipped into a ball gown or a fashionable tucked-up skirt. Unlike their predecessors, their men did not get rich off the privateers' spoils. Port Royal had become a hub of the West Indies plantation economy, a huge trading post, and an important slave mart. Between 1671 and 1679, nearly 12,000 African men and women had emerged from the holds of ships in her harbor and taken their miserable place as slaves on the vast sugar plantations that now covered the island. It was a different sort of pillaging, but Port Royal had found it just as lucrative.

For the pirates and their brethren, at least those who had not made the switch to farmer or merchant, the dawn found them still drinking in the malodorous taverns or unconscious in local alleyways, knocked senseless by round after round of Kill Devil, the "hot, hellish" rum made from the plantation molasses; it got its name from the belief that it was potent enough to kill Satan himself. Some had attempted to reach their homes on horseback, but the black liquor was so potent it was known to drop men from their mounts and leave them unconscious in the street, where they would "lie on the ground sometimes the whole night exposed to the injuries of the air." There were two captured ships in the harbor, legally taken under commissions against the French, and many of the matelots were guzzling their part of the proceeds. With the whores draped over them in repose, they could have been Parisian dandies after a long night of slumming—that is, if you didn't study their hands or faces too closely. Like marauding bears, they'd sleep for a day or two, then wake up penniless and brain-coshed and clamor to their captains for another mission. Roderick had made his way back to Port Royal, working the logwood boats and taking a privateer mission whenever one came around. He was yellow-eyed, his blood coursing with malaria, and his body had been racked by years of alcohol intake that would have killed most civilians. He lived with a whore and took part of her earnings when things were tight.

Nearby were the two prisons, the Bridewell, home to the "lazie strumpets" who had run afoul of the law, and the Marshalsea, where the more violent criminals were housed. Also close at hand were the courts where wrongdoers were tried; as the sun rose higher in the sky, the first prisoners of the day emerged, those who had not escaped the eyes of the militia on their regular tours. By midmorning the prisoners had already been sentenced and were being marched to the prison to be whipped or dunked. Then they'd spend the rest of the day in the stocks, broiling under the merciless sun, with passersby tossing rocks and garbage at their heads. There were more serious cases, too: The courts tried runaway slaves, and the guilty were ushered out to the gallows, followed by their owners. The luckier ones avoided the penalty for rebellion: being nailed to the ground with crooked sticks and having fire applied first to the hands, then the legs, then the head. ("The pains," Sloane reported, "are extravagant.")

There were places of worship dotted through the town for Quakers, Jews, Anglicans, Catholics, and Presbyterians, and the town's leaders liked to believe that it was a tolerant place. But, even in this small corner of the world, the old bacilli of Europe had found a home in Protestant hearts, and bitter jealousies and hatreds ran through Port Royal society, sharpened by competition. The Jewish residents were hidden away in their own precinct and were active in business—far too active, according to some. Just weeks before, the council had written to England a petition, saying that Jewish merchants "eat us and our children out of all our trade" and were an evil spreading itself across the islands.

The pastor of St. Paul's Cathedral, Dr. Heath, began his day by reading prayers at the church, which he did every day "to keep some show of religion among a most ungodly, debauched people." Afterward he strolled over to meet with the lieutenant governor, John White; they had been friends for years, and Dr. Heath allowed himself a glass of wormwood wine "as a whet before dinner" (which, in Jamaica, was taken just after noon), while White puffed on a pipe filled with tobacco. Some West Indies planters had tried to compete with the American colonies and planted the addictive weed, but the soil did not produce a leaf anywhere near as rich and flavorful as that grown by the planters up north. The tobacco in White's pipe came directly from Virginia, part of the triangular trade that kept Port Royal humming. The two men talked about the heat, about business, and about the French.

For all the signals and portents that people the world over would later point to, it was really an ordinary day. Disaster would subsequently etch significance into each everyday thing, but Port Royal was simply living its remarkably successful life as it always had.

Everyone was merely waiting for noon, when the three-hour siesta, one of the few concessions to the latitude in which these expatriates dwelled, would begin and the town would drop off into a fitful sleep.

⁂

Seventeen minutes before noon, the ground started to roll gently under the feet of the townspeople. "It began with a small trembling," wrote Hans Sloane. People froze and marveled at the feeling of the earth turning oceanlike, but they were not panicked; the town had suffered these rollings ever since the English had been on Jamaica. Dr. Heath asked White, "What is this?" "It is an earthquake," White said. "Don't be afraid, it will soon be over." The ground swelled and dipped slightly like a wake under a ship, but the buildings stood. Then a second, stronger heaving motion rolled in from the north, and they heard a crash as St. Paul's collapsed to the ground, followed quickly by a huge metallic clang; it was the church steeple, the pride of the town, slamming into a crowd gathered at its foot and snuffing out the lives of twelve townspeople. The tower bell shuddered out a strange ring, but it was quickly swallowed up in the sounds now vectoring in from all directions: the screams of men, the bomblike thud of three- and four-story brick buildings imploding, and a strange "hollow rumbling Noise." The second wave had given way to a third tremor, which dwarfed the others in its ferocity. Terrified, Heath and White ran into the street and were instantly separated in the noise and chaos.

Heath ran toward Morgan's Fort, and the scenes that greeted him along the way were a combination of Jules Verne and Hieronymus Bosch. The tremors had literally liquefied the earthen streets on which the townspeople were fleeing for their lives; with its surface gleaming as water saturated the sandy soil, earth became water, and the streets rose and fell in nauseating ripples. People were swept along like corks tossed on a wave, and some clutched at the gables of buildings that went past like boats; one doctor snatched at a passing chimney with his two children around his neck and miraculously survived. But most did not. "While they fled from the Sea, the Earth devoured them in her gaping Jaws," said Heath. "Or they were knockt on the head with their houses falling on them . . . or the Sea met them and swept them away." Men and women were pulled down into the sand and then cemented there, as the quake caused all the water that had surged up into the now-briny earth to be sucked away just as quickly. Some stood trapped in the earth up to their necks, crying for help. One observer reported:

> That watery haitus closed again the next moment, catching hold of some people by a Leg, of others by the middle of the Body, and of others some by the Arm, etc., detaining them in dismal torture, but immovably fixed in the ground, till they, with almost the whole Town besides, sunk under Water.

The hardening sand squeezed the captives until they suffocated or until wild dogs swarmed on them and ate their heads. A drawing of the calamity shows women's heads sticking out of the earth like cauliflowers, with dogs poised nearby, as well as a woman and her daughters who were "beat to pieces" by smashing into each other during the quake. "Others went down," Sloane wrote, "and were never more seen."

As he ran toward the fort, Heath looked up to see a sight he'd never forget: water cresting over the fortress's three-story stone walls. Clearly this was Judgment Day, and the deluge would now follow the first catastrophe. Strangely, the fact that he believed that hope was now gone calmed Heath; he was certain he'd die, and so the pastor turned and ran back toward his own house. "I then laid aside all thoughts of escaping," he remembered. "And resolved to make towards my own lodging, there to meet death in as good as posture as I could." Heath hurried through narrow lanes that separated him from his home on Market Street; as he ran, the walls and houses on each side of him collapsed, spraying bricks and timbers across his path like props in a Buster Keaton film. "Some Bricks came Rowling over my shoes," he said. "But none hurt me." Dr. Sloane reported that "the Ground heaved and swelled like a rolling swelling Sea"; people who had been tripped up lay facedown on the ground, their arms and legs spread out and their hands digging into the sand, trying to hold on to it as one would a raft in a plunging river. The violence of the rippling earth astonished those who saw it; one said the earth in the town of Liguanea moved "as a man would shake a twig."

When the rector reached his lodgings, he was stopped by another bizarre tableau: The home sat there pristine, unmarked, as if it were just an ordinary day. The street had not been touched. "Not a picture, of which there were several fair ones in my chamber," was even a half inch out of place, he reported. Rushing to his balcony, Heath threw open the doors and looked out over the town. His immediate neighborhood was intact down to the panes of glass, while over the roofs he could see a picture of utter destruction: homes, warehouses, and townspeople being flung up into the air or dropping into the open maw of the earth. Spotting the pastor at his window, men and women in the street began shouting to him; they, too, were convinced the Rapture had arrived, and they wanted to pray with him. (The minister later said that even some of the Sephardic Jews called him to their side and were eventually converted to his faith.) Heath must have hesitated a fraction of a second: His survival had been nothing short of miraculous; why tempt God? But he turned and went down, with the roar of the earthquake still deafening. "When I came down," he wrote, "every one laid hold of my clothes and embraced me, that with their fears and kindness I was almost stifled." These men and women did not believe they were witnessing a random natural event; for them it was the Day of Judgment unfolding just as the Bible said it would. Didn't they live "in the very place where Satan's throne is erected," as they had been warned many times before? And so the quake signaled the breaking of the Sixth Seal, as described in the Book of Revelation:

When I saw the Lamb break open the Sixth Seal, there was a violent earthquake; the sun turned black as a goat's-hair tentcloth and the moon grew red as blood. The stars in the sky fell crashing to earth like figs shaken loose by a mighty wind. Then the sky disappeared as if it were a scroll being rolled up; every mountain and island was uprooted from its base.

The devout could expect only one thing to follow: the breaking of the Seventh Seal, followed by a half hour of silence and then the approach of the Four Horsemen of the Apocalypse, their breastplates the colors of fiery red, deep blue, and pale yellow, riding horses with heads like lions spitting sulfur and smoke and fire, and then the seven-headed dragons with diadems, and then unthinkable things. The rector, whose calm had returned after his panicked moment with White, spoke to his fellow citizens gently and urged them to kneel down in a circle around him. Expecting the final crack of doom at any moment, he prayed in a loud voice, his eyes closed, his face tilted up toward the cloudless sky.

All around the circle of men and women, oddities of nature that would rarely be seen again were unfolding. Geysers erupted from the ground and arched towering plumes of water into the summer sky; some opened beneath men's feet and shot them a hundred feet in the air until gravity caught up with them and they began to fall on the descending pillar of water, down to the ground and then into it, as they disappeared into the holes that had caught them unawares. Thousands of these "sand volcanoes" were reported throughout the island. "In Clarendon Precinct, the Earth gaped and spouted up with a prodigious Force great Quantities of Water into the Air, above Twelve Miles from the Sea." The vicar of Withywood reported that "dire Chasms spew'd out Water to a considerable heighth above ground." People running for their homes dropped away into "the Pit," tumbling into an infernal washing machine filled with sand, water, and flotsam; a lucky few hit subterranean rivers that had been born just minutes ago and were carried horizontally under the earth at great speed, whipping beneath the feet of their fellow residents, only to crash into another geyser moving upward and so shoot back to the surface a half mile from where they first went down into the earth, drenched but unhurt. One woman ran out of her house into the street and saw the sand before her "rising up"; she clutched her black servant, and they dropped together into the earth, "at the same instant the Water coming in, rowl'd them over and over," until in this sunken world they saw a beam from a house passing and grabbed on to it and were saved. A merchant named Lloyd gave his story: He'd been in his shop when the "earth opened and let me in." He was carried along in an underground channel until he was pushed up through a wooden floor and found himself lying with other victims, many of them critically wounded. He himself was nearly unhurt, but his house had disappeared completely into the muck that had swallowed him up. One French refugee, Lewis Gauldy, was sucked down and released not once but twice, popping up at various points in the landscape like a target at a shooting gallery. The next day he announced that he'd found God.

With the ground turning to mush, the living ran in terrified packs toward the harbor but were thrown down as they fled. Many of them jumped into the water and swam for the surviving ships that bobbed there in the chop, where six-foot waves swept over them. Stray timbers, canoes, and other refuse from the ruined city swept by in the strong current, braining some of the swimmers as they tried to escape. Soon the boats were crowded, and men fought for space on the decks. There were scenes of memorable courage, including that of a slave saving a white man and then drowning while trying to save his master, and another of a bondsman who dug a Colonel Beckford out of the sand before it crushed him. Depravity would soon overwhelm the memories of kindness.

The earthquake tore the city apart. But it was the tsunami that followed hard upon it that proved lethal. Sweeping in, three stories high and traveling at sixty miles an hour, the great wave carried on its back the HMS *Swan* from the harbor, which "by the violent motion of the Sea, and the sinking of the Wharf," reported one resident, "was forced over the tops of many Houses; and passing by that House where my Lord Puke lived, part of it fell upon her, and beat in her

Round House." The frigate stayed upright and later served as a life raft for over two hundred people. The foamy top of the inrushing water was even with some of Port Royal's tallest structures as it came toward the town, then smashed buildings to pieces and carried off citizens back toward the harbor. The enormous surge of water bore away carts, cannon, fishing boats, wooden homes, and hundreds upon hundreds of men, women, and children, depositing their naked bodies miles away or, as it drew back, taking them out to the ocean, never to be seen again. One resident wrote home about the horrors but could not express them to his satisfaction: " 'Tis impossible for my pen to write, or tongue to relate ye horror and terror of that daye."

As the wave rippled across the landscape, sections of the smoky blue mountains that had framed the town's horizon dropped away like children's blocks; one landslide dammed the river that supplied the town with drinking water (which would soon be selling at exorbitant prices in the postdisaster city). The drought lasted sixteen hours, until the runoff from the mountains could cut new paths down their sides and onto the plains. Many believed that the earthquake was even more intense in the blue hills than it had been in the towns. The sounds that rumbled in from their direction testified that tremendous natural forces were at work; the mountains "bellowed forth prodigious, loud, terrible Noises and Echoings," and the rich forest that used to cover their sides was stripped away in places from peak to foot so that it looked as if they had been peeled clean. Hans Sloane wrote a long letter in 1694 filled with accounts of the earthquake, and his contacts from all over the island reported that the earth had acted in unaccountable ways. In Yallahs, west of Port Royal, "a great Mountain split, and fell into the level land, and covered several Settlements, and destroy'd nineteen white People." The locals believed it was a judgment on the victims' evil ways, and the place is now known as Judgment Hill. A man named Hopkins rushed home to his plantation, only to find it gone, the entire mass of earth, sugar crop, and house, and all having moved half a mile from its original spot. New lakes appeared where there had been only dry fields; a thousand acres of forest near the French settlement of St. Ann's Bay disappeared underwater, taking fifty-three settlers with it. The seventeenth-century mind groped for words to describe the unsolid earth they now inhabited; it had become animated, even willful. A section of one mountain, "after having made several Leaps or Moves," proceeded to track down and "overwhelm" a family, having traveled more than a mile to snuff out its victims.

Four of the town's five forts dropped into the harbor with their heavy guns, leaving only Fort Charles standing. Which of the ordinary citizens survived depended in most cases on what kind of house they lived in. The poor and piratical fared best: The huts that the slaves and the very destitute inhabited were made of thatch and wood held together with dried mud or mortar. The Spanish-built dwellings were the next step up in the social ladder. These low-slung houses, with their wall beams driven deep into the ground, withstood the earthquake very well. It was the rich merchants' houses, which had been constructed to resemble the middle-class dwellings back in England, that proved to be death traps; they were three and four stories high, built of bricks, with tile roofs and glass in the windows. Heavy and rigid, they collapsed en masse, killing everyone inside. All the structures built of brick or stone—churches, warehouses, sugar works, and homes—were affected. The vicar of Withywood, whose parish lay thirty-five miles inland from Port Royal, wrote that the buildings "are now either leveled with the ground, or standing Monuments of the Wrath of God, . . . so shattered and torn that they are irreparable." Those neurasthenic wives who could not escape from their beds were among the first to die, while tiny huts that housed black slaves easily withstood the shaking of the earth. It was an early lesson in the earthquakeproofing of houses.

✤　　　✤　　　✤

The echo of the original, enormous boom faded away, and soon the sound of seabirds could be heard above "the wailing and the screaming." The quake had lasted approximately six minutes. In that time

90 percent of the town's homes, its warehouses stuffed with goods, and the main pier for the city had been destroyed or simply vanished into the sea. Two thousand people died from the combined effects of earthquake and tsunami; another two thousand would die in the coming weeks from injuries and disease. The death toll was twice that of the San Francisco calamity of 1906, but that had occurred in a city of hundreds of thousands. The Great Earthquake of 1692 took more than 70 percent of Port Royal's 6,500 residents; it would stand as the most lethal quake until the 1868 Peru-Ecuador disaster.

Professor George R. Clark of Kansas State University, who has studied the 1692 quake intensively, has rated it between values X and XI over the majority of Jamaica, with spots of Value XII intensity in isolated spots. A Value X earthquake involves the destruction of most buildings and foundations; in a Value XII, objects are thrown into the air and the ground moves in waves. The Port Royal was one of the strongest earthquakes ever to hit the Western Hemisphere. It was accentuated by the formation of the land beneath the city. The sand that Port Royal stood on was loosely packed and saturated with water before the tremors struck. As the earthquake hit, violent seismic waves rippled through the sand and literally changed the granular structure of the soil. The shaking caused the sand molecules to sink downward, where they were met by water rushing up to fill the empty space; this caused the layers of sand to lose their stiffness and strength. Very quickly the sand stopped acting as a solid and began behaving as a viscous liquid, and the ground beneath the residents' feet changed from solid earth to quicksand in an instant. People and buildings dropped down into the watery mush and were lost. As to the tsunamis that Heath and others reported seeing, they may have been classic tidal waves caused by the violent buckling of a tectonic plate offshore or simply the result of the ocean's flowing in to fill the space once occupied by the plunging surface of sand. Only those buildings, such as Heath's home, which happened to sit on a solid base of limestone or gravel, were saved.

Looking over the ruined city, one of Hans Sloane's correspondents grew somber:

Indeed, 'tis enough to raise melancholy thoughts in a Man now, to see
the Chimneys and Tops of some Houses, and the Masts of Ships and
Sloops, which partak'd of the same Fate, appear above Water; and
when one first comes ashore, to see so many Heaps of Ruines, many
whereof by their largeness shew, that once there had stood a brave
House; to see so many Houses shatter'd, some half fallen down, the rest
desolate and without Inhabitants, . . . there, where once stood brave
Streets of stately Houses stood, appearing now nothing but Water, except here and there a Chimney, and some parts and pieces of Houses,
surviving only to mind us of their sad Misfortune, Habitations for Fish,
contrary to the Intent of the first Builders.

Sometime during the six minutes, Henry Morgan's coffin erupted
from the sandy ground of the cemetery and was spewed out into the
churning waters of the Port Royal harbor, never to be found again. At
11:49 the great pirate city that he'd helped create ceased to exist.

⚜   ⚜   ⚜

In Port Royal the geological quake triggered a social one. The richest survivors were set upon by looters and, in some rare cases, slaves
who had seen their chance for freedom. Men died in revenge attacks
or simple robberies; in fact, what happened after the disaster might
be described as a class war: A minority of the town's despised lower
orders, including those pirates who remained in Port Royal, rose
and began robbing the upper-crust stalwarts who had tried to ban-
ish them from the town. "No man could call any thing his own," a
minister wrote. "The richest are now the poorest. . . . The strongest
and the most wicked seized what they pleased, and where they
pleased and when they pleased." The old nightmare of the rebellious
buccaneers had finally come true. Poor men and criminals broke
into shops and battered down the doors of rich men's homes, carrying away gold and jewels and plate pillaged in Morgan's raids.
Roderick was among them. Asleep on the beach, he'd awoken during the earthquake from a rum-induced sleep, turned over, and
grabbed at the earth as it rolled beneath him. When the quake had

passed, he'd run into his mates and formed a plan. They began breaking into the warehouses that had not sunk underwater and pilfered whatever they found. When one roof collapsed, he saw two of his friends crushed beneath the falling timbers, but he didn't stay to pull them out. Slaves joined in, since, according to one writer, they "thought it their time of Liberty, wherein they committed many barbarous Insolencies and Robberies," until arrests of some and the killing of others quelled the revolt. Traders who had for so long depended on the buccaneers' violent natures when they were unleashed on Spanish cities now found the same hands raised toward them. If the irony of Port Royal was that it had grown fabulously wealthy on the backs of the men it at least in part despised, there was a measure of divine justice in what happened.

The receiver general of Jamaica, Edward Ellyn, wrote to a colleague about the behavior of the local sailors, a significant portion of whom would likely have been ex-buccaneers:

> That afternoon most of the seamen, English and Spaniards, contented themselves with what was floating on the water, tho' some instantly entered and riffled standing houses. But the following nights and dayes those villains, more savage and cruel than any Indians and Negroes, robbed all houses, broke in pieces all scriptores, boxes, trunks, chests of drawers, cabinets and made spoil of all of value in the town, threatening to kill several inhabitants, if any durst be so hardy as to say, "This house is mine." Our enemies could not have treated us worse than the seamen.

Dr. Heath was more precise. He called the marauders "a company of lewd rogues whom they called Privateers" and reported that they had proceeded to pillage their own town even while the earthquake was shaking the ground. Roderick took the loot he'd gathered and began celebrating among the ruins with the local whores, who were just as "Impudent and Drunken as ever." As slaves said after the American Civil War, the bottom rail was now on top. Some of that old feeling, of being one of the great men of Port Royal, came back to Roderick that day. He drank and danced with his friends, robbed any civilian who happened past, while the scene around him prompted him to tell stories of old Panama and how they had left it. He departed the town the next day and was sighted in Nassau two years later. In 1695 he was lost at sea while chasing a French trader with a crew of Dutch and English pirates off Hispaniola. He left nothing to anyone.

With law and order vanished, the poor sold the goods they had managed to extract from the sunken buildings, most of Port Royal now resembling a kind of Atlantis, with streetlamps, benches, and shops sunk to between eighteen and thirty feet of seawater. The survivors dived down like pearl fishers and extracted the good Spanish silver that had been displayed in every respectable home. Some of the former owners of the brick homes were still trapped in their rooms, their eyes goggling, their hair waving gently in the current. Heath reported that many of the town's most wretched citizens, "by watching opportunities," had grown rich. A Quaker citizen, John Pike, wrote a sibling:

> Ah, brother, if thou didst see those great persons that are now dead upon the water, thou couldst never forget it. Great men who were so swallowed up with pride, that a man could not be admitted to speak with them, and women whose top-knots seemed to reach the clouds, now lie stinking upon the water, and are made meat for fish and fowls of the air.

Port Royal was forced to relive the fate that had come to Panama after Morgan's raids. With only a tenth of the houses remaining habitable, the wealthy traders returned to their homes to find them heaps of brick and mortar, and so they were forced to seek accommodation in the thatched huts of the black slaves. "Here you see colonels and great men bowing their bodies to creep into this little hutch," wrote John Pike, "who before had houses fit not only to receive but to feast in an extraordinary manner a prince or King, as great as England's monarch. . . ." Although some slave owners did rent "Negro quarters" instead of evicting their servants, others threw their slaves out of their huts and moved their families in. The gentry had always feared a slave uprising more than an earthquake; their dreams were filled with Negro butcheries and rapes, and as they surveyed the ruined city, their thoughts quickly turned to rebellion. "Our first fears were concerning our slaves," wrote one merchant. "Those irreconcilable enemies of ours . . . who seeing our strongest houses demolished, our Arms broken . . . might in hopes of liberty be stirred up to rise." There were some incidents of slaves' joining in the robberies, but in the end it was the gentry who turned on the Negroes and cast them out of their humble shacks.

The most immediate problems for the townspeople were disease and supplies. One observer recalled looking out into the harbor and seeing corpses packing the water's surface from one end of the harbor to another, like logs on a Wisconsin river. The bodies "caused such an intolerable stench, that the Dead were like to destroy the Living." The corpses that had been expelled from the graveyard mixed with the cadavers of the newly dead, and in the heat their flesh roasted and blistered. Inevitably they became carriers of diseases that struck the survivors with shocking force.

To get away from the spreading plague, some Port Royalists moved their shelters across the bay, thereby founding the city of Kingston. Others began to rebuild on the narrow strip of land where the old town had stood. A year later the survivors were still struggling to reestablish their society. "The island is in a very mean condition," wrote Sir William Beeston nine months after the calamity. "The earthquake, sickness and desertion of discontented people have carried off so many as to leave the island very thin of people."

In the face of the disaster, people ignored faddish scientific theories and thought only of God. Natural disasters were seen as divine warnings by the vast majority of people. The London earthquake of 1580 prompted the writer Thomas Twynne to publish his *Discourses of the Earthquake*, in which he stated that each man was being warned to "call himself to an accompt, and look narrowly into his own life." Another treatise linked the severity of the earthquake to debauched living: The quake had been a reaction to "the horrid Enormities that are boldly committed amongst us." This was the dominant theme of the commentaries on the Port Royal catastrophe the world over. The news of the earthquake reached London, Boston, and New York within weeks. The disaster had immediate ramifications for the English empire, and especially the colonies of Virginia and Massachusetts; in the short term the lucrative trade with Port Royal was completely disrupted, and in the long term the Americas vaulted ahead of their West Indies neighbor. "Never again before American independence," wrote one historian, "did any Caribbean community rival the five cities on the continent of America." The events in Jamaica seemed to inaugurate a series of disasters around the world: There was a strong quake in England on September 8 that, according to John Evelyn, "greatly affrighted" the people and led to rumors of the coming Armageddon; hoping to defray the Lord's anger, authorities began cracking down on drunkenness and other public vices immediately afterward. Along with the Salem witch trials in the Massachusetts colony, the quake spread a mood of divine retribution throughout the English-speaking world. Pamphlets and books were published warning that the destruction of the Sodom of Jamaica was a message from above. "Behold an accident speaking to all our English America," wrote Boston's famous preacher, Cotton Mather, of the quake. Priests and ministers through the civilized world spoke of Port Royal as an omen. "To the inhabitants of that Isle," wrote one commentator, "has the Lord spoken terrible things in righteousness." Even the people of the island accepted the quake as a sign of their own sinfulness. "I shall only instance myself for one," wrote one resident, "who have lost my ship, and very considerably other ways but I am very well satisfied because it is the Lord's Doings." Of course, if it was a sign of divine punishment, in retrospect men insisted on reading it selectively. The slave empire was just beginning to take hold in places like Port Royal, but it was the venal sins that obsessed the chattering classes: Port Royal had surely been struck down because of whoring and booze. The possibility that it was the sugar plantations where Africans were burned alive for attempting to escape that was the source of God's displeasure was not mentioned in a single letter or sermon.

The calamity put a hard stop to the golden era that Port Royal had embodied. The city was rebuilt, but it never again rose to the heights of the glory days. Pirates continued to cruise the waters off the city, and some were occasionally hung on Gallows Point during fits of law and order, including the randy and dashing "Calico Jack" Rackham, in 1720. His lover, the rare female pirate Anne Bonny, and her widely feared friend Mary Read, escaped the noose by "pleading their bellies" (both were pregnant). Bonny's reprieve was short; she died of a fever in a Port Royal jail, while Read disappeared off the face of the earth. Officials in Jamaica and Tortuga often looked the other way when pirates strolled through town, as many of the locals had a soft spot in their hearts for the old Brethren, but the pirates no longer ruled the town and the entire region as they once had. Those privateers who had earned enough pieces of eight from Morgan's raids and managed not to relinquish them to the Port Royal vice economy settled onto their estates and emulated the admiral's final years. Jamaica, however, no longer belonged to them.

No longer would the city shelter large numbers of the men who had made it rich and infamous the world over. No longer could a buccaneer organize the largest army in the Western Hemisphere, made up of trash tossed out of half a dozen European countries, plus runaway slaves and restless servants, and roam far and wide over half a continent, facing down an empire and stealing its riches. The Royal Navy stationed warships at Port Royal; Admiral Lord Nelson did a tour of duty at Fort Charles, and the English fleet took over from the Brethren the role of naval enforcers. The remaining pirates often restricted themselves to small lightning attacks on merchant vessels, instead of the audacious land attacks on major cities that

Morgan had perfected. In the 1700s the sugar-and-slave economy came into its own, and more and more Port Royal became a traders' town where it paid to be good with an abacus and not a musket. Not long after Morgan's death, young men clambered out of ships arriving in Port Royal no longer dreaming of pirates. They wanted to own plantations and as many Africans as possible to work them. A different kind of cruelty won out.

But somehow over the years, the exquisite cruelties of the pirates' expeditions were forgotten, their exploits resonated louder, and they became romantic figures. Crazy, yes, but romantic. Perhaps the traders' world was simply too boring and too successful to compete with the story of the flaming arrow at San Lorenzo, the Maracaibo fireship, and all the rest. Morgan would not have understood it; he wanted to be bound more closely to the king and the English empire that he loved. He was never a wild-eyed revolutionary; far from it. But the superoxygenated air that the pirates seemed to carry with them over the Atlantic, in which any act of barbarity or valor was possible at any given moment, stamped the image of the buccaneer indelibly on the imagination. The pirate can seem at times like the freest man who ever walked the Americas, freer even than the Carib or the Arawak.

If it's a myth, and it partly is, the world will take the myth. But you can't attempt to do what Morgan and his men did without seeing yourselves as a prince of the New World, deserving of every wonder it possesses. Men like that do not live very long, but they are not easily forgotten.

Glossary

Ambuscade: An ambush launched from a concealed fortification.

Arquebus: A heavy, notoriously inaccurate matchlock gun that first came into use during the fifteenth century. Also spelled *harquebus*.

Ball: A bullet.

Boucan: The tangy smoked meat produced and traded by the buccaneers of Hispaniola.

Buccaneer: A pirate, especially one who operated against Spanish shipping and settlements in the West Indies during the seventeenth century.

Castellan: The military officer in charge of a castle or fort.

Colors: A flag.

Commission: Also known as a letter of marque, this was a document authorizing a private citizen to wage war on a nation's enemy.

Corsaro: A pirate.

Doubloon: A gold coin used in Spain and Spanish America.

Galleon: A large three- or four-masted sailing ship used from the fifteenth to seventeenth centuries, especially by Spain, as a war and treasure ship.

Grandee: The highest-ranking noble in the Spanish hierarchy.

Hispaniola: The Caribbean island now divided between Haiti and the Dominican Republic.

Logwood: A spiny tropical American tree whose heartwood was used to make a purplish red dye.

Low Countries: A region in northwestern Europe consisting of Belgium, the Netherlands, and Luxembourg.

Maroon: A fugitive black slave in the West Indies during the seventeenth and eighteenth centuries; also, the descendant of such a slave.

Matelot: Literally, "bedmate," but most often used to mean companion, or friend. Used by the early buccaneers to describe the man they paired up with in the jungles of Hispaniola.

Mestizo: A person of mixed race, especially of mixed Native American and European ancestry.

New Spain: Present-day Mexico.

New World: The lands of the Western Hemisphere.

North Sea: The present-day Caribbean Sea.

Piece of eight: A common Spanish silver coin used widely in the New World. Also known as a peso or a cob.

Purchase: All monies and goods obtained during a raid. The commonly used phrase "no purchase, no pay" meant that the buccaneers would depend solely on the booty they recovered on an expedition for their pay.

Roundshot: A cannonball.

South Sea: The present-day Pacific Ocean.

Spanish Main: The Spanish-held mainland of North and South America.

United Provinces: The present-day Netherlands.

Woolding: A commonly used form of torture in which a knotted cord was tied around a victim's head and then twisted with a stick until the eyes popped out.

General Bibliography

Allen, H. R. *Buccaneer: Admiral Sir Henry Morgan.* Arthur Baker Ltd., London, 1976.

Aveling, J. C. H. *The Handle and the Axe: The Catholic Recusants in England from Reformation to Emancipation.* Blong & Briggs, London, 1976.

Bassett, Fletcher. *Legends and Superstitions of the Sea and of Sailors.* Singing Tree Press, Detroit, 1971.

Bennassar, Bartolomé. *The Spanish Character: Attitudes and Mentalities from the Sixteenth to the Nineteenth Century.* University of California Press, Berkeley, 1979.

Black, Clinton. *Port Royal: A History and Guide.* Bolivar Press, Kingston, Jamaica, 1970.

Bradley, Peter. *The Lure of Peru: Maritime Intrusion into the South Sea, 1598–1701.* Macmillan, Hampshire, U.K., 1989.

Bridenbaugh, Carl and Roberta. *No Peace Beyond the Line: The English in the Caribbean, 1624–1690.* Oxford University Press, New York, 1972.

Carr, Raymond, editor. *Spain: A History.* Oxford University Press, New York, 2000.

Coote, Stephen. *Royal Survivor.* St. Martin's Press, New York, 2000.

Cordingly, David, consulting editor. *Pirates: A Worldwide Illustrated History.* Turner, Atlanta, 1996.

———. *Under the Black Flag: The Romance and Reality of Life Among the Pirates.* Harvest Books, San Diego, 1997.

Cruikshank, Brigadier General E. A. *The Life of Sir Henry Morgan.* Macmillan, Toronto, 1935.

de Madariaga, Salvador. *The Fall of the Spanish American Empire.* Collier, New York, 1963.

Earle, Peter. *A City Full of People: Men and Women of London 1650–1750.* Methuen, London, 1994.

———. *Pirate Wars.* Metheun, London, 2002.

———. *The Sack of Panama: Sir Henry Morgan's Adventures on the Spanish Main.* Viking Press, New York, 1982.

———. *Sailors. English Merchant Seamen 1650–1775.* Methuen, London, 1998.

Elliott, J. H. *Imperial Spain 1469–1716.* St. Martin's Press, New York, 1964.

———. *Spain and Its World, 1500–1700.* Yale University Press, New Haven, 1989.

Fraser, Antonia. *Cromwell, the Lord Protector.* Knopf, New York, 1973.

Galvin, Peter. *Patterns of Pillage: A Geography of Caribbean-Based Piracy in Spanish America, 1536–1718.* Peter Lang, New York, 1998.

Gohau, Gabriel. *History of Geology.* Rutgers University Press, 1991.

Haring, C. H. *The Spanish Empire in America.* Peter Smith, Gloucester, U.K., 1973.

Honigsbaum, Mark. *The Fever Trail: In Search of the Cure for Malaria.* Farrar, Straus and Giroux, New York, 2002.

Hume, Martin. *The Court of Philip IV: Spain in Decadence.* Eveleigh Nash, London, 1907.

Jackson, Stanley. *J. P. Morgan.* Stein and Day, New York, 1983.

Jenkins, Geraint. *The Foundations of Modern Wales, 1642–1780.* Clarendon Press, Oxford, 1987.

Jenkins, Philip. *A History of Modern Wales, 1536–1990.* Longman, London and New York, 1992.

Johnson, Charles. *The History of the Lives and Bloody Exploits of the Most Noted Pirates, Their Trials and Executions.* The Lyons Press, Guilford, U.K., 2004.

Kamen, Henry. *Empire: How Spain Became a World Power, 1492–1763.* HarperCollins, New York, 2003.

————. *Spain in the Later 17th Century, 1665–1700.* Longman, London and New York, 1980.

Kietzman, Mary Jo. *The Self-Fashioning of an Early Modern Englishwoman: Mary Carleton's Lives.* Ashgate, Burlington, U.K., 2004.

Lane, Kris E. *Pillaging the Empire: Piracy in the Americas, 1500–1750.* Sharpe, Armonk, N.Y., 1998.

Langdon-Davies, John. *Carlos the Bewitched: The Last Spanish Hapsburg, 1661–1700.* Jonathan Cape, London, 1962.

Marx, Jennifer. *Pirates and Privateers of the Caribbean.* Krieger, Malabar, Fla., 1992.

Marx, Robert. *Port Royal Rediscovered.* Doubleday, Garden City, N.Y., 1973.

McCullough, David. *The Path Between the Seas: The Creation of the Panama Canal, 1870–1914.* Simon & Schuster, New York, 1977.

Newton, Arthur Percival. *The Colonising Activities of the English Puritans.* Kennikat Press, Port Washington, N.Y., 1966.

Newton, Norman. *Thomas Gage in Spanish America.* Faber, London, 1969.

O'Laughlin, K. F., and James Lander. *Caribbean Tsunamis: A 500-Year History from 1498–1998.* Springer, New York, 2003.

O'Shaughnessy, Andrew Jackson. *An Empire Divided: The American Revolution and the British Caribbean.* University of Pennsylvania Press, Philadelphia, 2000.

Parry, J. H. *The Spanish Seaborne Empire.* Alfred A. Knopf, New York, 1966.

Payne, John. *History of Spain and Portugal.* University of Wisconsin Press, Madison, 1973.

Peterson, Mendel. *The Funnel of Gold.* Little, Brown, Boston, 1975.

Petrovich, Sandra Marie. *Henry Morgan's Raid on Panama—Geopolitics and Colonial Ramifications, 1669–1674.* Caribbean Studies Press, Volume 10, Edwin Press, Lewiston, N.Y., 2001.

Pope, Dudley. *The Buccaneer King.* Dodd, Mead, Mellen, New York, 1977.

Pringle, Patrick. *Jolly Roger: The Story of the Great Age of Piracy.* Dover, New York, 2001.

Rappaport, Angelo S. *Superstitions of Sailors.* Gryphon, Ann Arbor, Mich., 1971.

Roberts, W. Adolph. *Sir Henry Morgan, Buccaneer and Governor.* Pioneer Press, Kingston, Jamaica, 1952.

Stevens, John Richard, ed. *Captured by Pirates.* Fern Canyon, Cambria Pines by the Sea, Calif., 2003.

Taylor, S. A. G. *The Western Design.* The Institute of Jamaica, Kingston, 1965.

Thornton, A. P. *West India Policy Under the Restoration.* Oxford at the Clarendon Press, Oxford, U.K., 1956.

Todd, Janet, and Elizabeth Spearing, eds. *Counterfeit Ladies.* Pickering & Chatto, London, 1994.

Ure, John. *The Quest for Captain Morgan.* Constable, London, 1983.

Volo, Deborah Denneen, and James M. Volo. *Daily Life in the Age of Sail.* Greenwood Press, Westport, Conn., 2002.

Winston, Alexander. *No Man Knows My Name: Privateers and Pirates 1665–1715.* Houghton Mifflin, New York, 1969.

Primary Sources

Barlow, Edward. *Barlow's Journal of His Life at Sea in King's Ships*. Transcribed by Basil Lubbock, Volume II. Hurst & Blackett, London, 1934.

Carleton, Mary. *News from Jamaica in a Letter from Port Royal Written by the Germane Princess to Her Fellow Collegiates and Friends in New-Gate*. London, Printed by Peter Lillicrap, for Philip Brigs Living in Mer-maid Court near Amen Corner in Pater-Noster Row, 1671.

de Lussan, Raveneau. *Journal of a Voyage into the South Sea in 1684 and the Following Years with the Filibustiers*. Translated by Marguerite Eyer Wilbur. Arthur H. Clark, Cleveland, 1930.

Dunlop, John. *Memoirs of Spain 1621–1700*. Neill & Company, Edinburgh. 1834.

Esquemeling, John. *Buccaneers of America*. Dover, New York, 1967.

Gage, Thomas. *The English-American*. George Rutledge, London, 1648.

Johnson, Captain Charles. *A General History of the Robberies and Murders of the Most Notorious Pirates, May 1724*. Carroll and Graf, New York, 1999.

Rogers, Woodes. *A Cruising Voyage Round the World*. Cassell, London, 1928.

Sloane, Hans. *Voyage to the Islands of Madeira, Barbados, Nieves, S. Christopher and Jamaica*. Self-published, London, 1707.

Wafer, Lionel. *A New Voyage and Description of the Isthmus of America*. The Burrow Brothers, Cleveland, 1903.

Notes

The titles of the sources are listed in the bibliography. The notes are given by chapter and page and indicated by the last words of a sentence or phrase.

The main sources for research are the Archivo General de las Indias, Seville, Spain, and the British Library and Public Records Office in London. The following abbreviations are used: CSPWI (Calendar of State Papers, Colonial: North America and the West Indies); CSPD (Calendar of State Papers, Domestic); COP (Colonial Office Papers, British Library) Panama (the Panama Section of the Archivo General in Seville); IG (the Indiferente General Section of the Archivo); Escribiana (Escribiana de Cámara section, Archivo); Contratación (Contratación section, Archivo); Add Ms. (Additional Manuscripts, British Library).

1. "I Offer a New World"

6. "on a secret mission": Thompson, p. xliv.

6. "by order of the Protector": CSPD, December 20, 1654, p. 586.

6. " 'many secret conferences' ": quoted in Newton, p. 190.

7. "blush to behold": quoted in Thompson, p. xv.

7. "across the oceans to drown them": Bassett, p. 108.

8. "I offer a New World": Gage, intro, p. xxvi.

8. For the preparations for the Hispaniola expedition, see Taylor, p. 1.

9. "rather to die than to live": quoted in Taylor, p. 94.

10. "fetch their pedigree": quoted in Cruikshank, p. 1.

10. "measuring, uninnocent": this portrait can be viewed at: www.data-wales.co.uk/morgan.htm.

10. "even more tedious pedigrees": Jenkins, *Foundations*, p. 213.

10. "surrounded by goats and unpronounceable names." Jenkins, *A History*, p. 19.

11. "used to the pike than the book": Morgan to Lords of Trade and Plantations, February 24, 1680, CSPWI item 1304.

11. "the daily prayer of Henry Morgan": Morgan to Leoline Jenkins, August 22, 1881, CSPWI item 208.

14. "who would kill her": Gage, intro, p. xiii.

15. "acquainted with gamblers' oaths": Gage, p. 40.

16. "leaving Gage in despair": Newton, p. 164.

16. "sounded like 'an Indian or a Welshman.' " Newton, p. 178.

16. "until the moment of his execution": Newton, p. 184.

18. "within two years": Fraser, p. 523.

19. "the great enterprise you have in hand": quoted in Fraser, p. 526.

21. "on the shores of Hispaniola": Pope, p. 72.

22. " 'turned into dross' ": quoted in Newton, p. 194.

22. "many of these were already failing": Turner, p. 92.

23. For the history of tsunamis in the Caribbean, see O'Laughlin.

2. The Tomb at the Escorial

25. "wear black from head to toe": Hume, p. 447.

26. "where his own body would lie." Hume, p. 449.

27. "the rest of mankind are mud": quoted in Kamen, p. 8.

28. "180 tons of gold flowed through the official port of Seville": Kamen, p. 287.

28. "16,000 tons of silver": ibid.

28. "a minting machine": Peterson, p. 42.

29. "to his country": quoted in Kamen, p. 292.

29. *"in unadjusted dollars"*: Peterson, p. 38.

29. "totaled nearly 74 million": Carr, p. 144.

29. "93 percent of the budget": ibid., p. 155.

30. "and the Calle Mayor": Hume, p. 439.

31. "Blessed be his holy name!": quoted in ibid., p. 439.

3. Morgan

32. "cartridges on an infantryman": Newton, 192.

32. "to light their muskets": ibid.

33. "They grow bold and bloody": Sedgwick to Thurloe, March 12, 1655, quoted in Taylor, p. 102.

37. "only 4 percent had taken a wife": Cordingly, p. 69.

37. "strange countries and fashions": Earle, *Sailors*, p. 18.

37. "the longer and more dangerous, the more attractive": du Lussan, p. 33.

38. "where we rob at will." The original reads: "We might sing, sweare, drab, and kill men as freely as your cakemakers do flies . . . when the whole sea was our empire where we robbed at will." Quoted in Earle, *Pirate Wars*, p. 25.

40. "4,500 white residents and 1,500 Negro slaves": Pope, p. 80.

40. "three hundred more than its competitor, New York": Roberts, p. 10.

46. "by faithful Protestant hands": Cootes, p. 40.

46. "in both marriage and war": ibid., p. 40.

46. "life-bitten": ibid., 176.

47. "the great Spanish treasuries in America": Thornton, p. 71.

48. "for a decade": ibid., p. 14.

50. "nothing new in the English situation": quoted in Langdon-Davies, p. 12.

51. " 'I am thine' ": quoted in ibid., p. 54.

4. Into the Past

53. "built to fly." For a discussion of the pirate ship, see Konstam, Angus, *The Pirate Ship 1660–1730*. Osprey, Oxford, 2003.

54. "gleamed like porcelain": For examples of the seventeenth-century French musket, see Grancsay, Stephen, preface and notes. *Master French Gunsmiths' Designs of the XVII–XIX Centuries*. Facsimile. Winchester Press, New York, 1970.

55. "in the style of Sir Francis Drake": Pope, p. 115.

56. "a diamond cross hanging around it": Cordingly, p. 12.

57. "searching and purging": quoted in Cordingly, p. 95.

59. "10 pounds." The compensation rates come from Esquemeling, p. 59.

59. "toward the Yucatán Peninsula": The main source for Morgan's first raid is the "Examination of Captains John Morris, Jackman and Morgan," included in a letter from Modyford to Albemarle, March 1, 1666, CSPWI item 1142, volume 5 (1661–1668), pp. 359–61.

60. "lead them to land": ibid., p. 62.

62. "to their approach": ibid.

62. "gathered a few hundred prisoners": ibid.

63. "to every day's distance": Pope, p. 112.

64. "when they would have meat": Gage, p. 67.

67. "set course for Jamaica": The account of Morgan's raid is taken from Mody-ford to Albemarle, March,-1, 1666, CSPWI item 1132.

5. Sodom

70. "fell and died": Report by Colonel Cary, CSPWI item 1086.

71. "nor trade but privateering": Lynch to Bennet, May 25, 1664, CSPWI item 774.

71. "liable to turn on their own": from "Mr. Worsley's Discourse on the Privateers of Jamaica," Add Ms. 11410, pp. 623–45.

73. "beneath which lay coralline limestone": "The Port Royal Earthquake of June 7, 1692," unpublished, by George R. Clark, Department of Geology, Kansas State University.

74. "for many weeks": For an account of Juana's bizarre procession, see Langdon-Davies, pp. 24–27.

75. "neither Jewish nor Muslim": Langdon-Davies, p. 45.

76. "and so on with the rest": Payne, p. 299.

77. "the Christian Algiers": quoted in Cordingly, *Pirates*, p. 55.

78. "from the Portuguese or French": Modyford to Albemarle, March 1, 1666, CSPWI item 1142.

79. "the council declared": Minutes of the Council, CSPWI item 1138.

79. "gone to the French": Modyford to Albemarle, August 21, 1666, CSPWI item 1264.

81. "very narrowly concerned here": quoted in Esquemeling, p. 125.

81. "lose their lives": quoted in Esquemeling, p. 127.

82. "battered with the irons": Deposition of Robert Rawlinson, October 5, 1668, CSPWI item 1851.

82. "to his wicked life": Esquemeling, p. 125.

6. The Art of Cruelty

84. "new insolences": Modyford to Arlington, July 30, 1667, CSPWI item 1537.

86. "commerce of the region": letter from Don Francisco Calderón Romero, April 4, 1668, IG 2541.

88. "some pieces of cannon": Esquemeling, p. 134.

88. "very dextrous at their arms": ibid., p. 135.

89. "come to their aid": ibid., p. 137.

91. "full of danger": Morgan's report, September 7, 1668, CO 1/23.

91. "where he was raised": For an account of L'Ollonais's career, see Esquemeling, pp. 79–119.

94. "vile crew of miscreants": quoted in Cordingly, *Under*, p. 93.

94. *"forget who he was"*: Johnson, p. 69.

94. "than the rest": Johnson, p. 101.

95. "a silence followed": Stephens, p. 219.

7. Portobelo

101. "way of conversing": Roberts, p. 219.

104. "in the spoils": Esquemeling, p. 141.

105. "seriously undermanned": Earle, *Sack*, p. 57.

106. "to attempt that place": Morgan's report, CO 1/23.

107. "with the usual ceremonies": du Lussan, p. 187.

108. "pay for the expedition himself": Earle, *Sack*, p. 54.

109. "marching over land": ibid., p. 69.

112. "formerly brought from Puerto Rico": Morgan's report, CO 1/23.

112. "charged each gun anew": Esquemeling, p. 144.

112. "ascend by them": ibid.

114. "at Portobelo on Saturday": quoted in Earle, *Sack*, p. 81.

115. "It was very possible": ibid., p. 76.

115. "a thousand lives": Bennassar, p. 214.

116. "the Province of Panama": Morgan's report, CO 1/23.

117. "in this place": The letters are collected in Panama 81, (III), fos. 40–46, 1669.

118. "you to do it": ibid.

118. "as the Spanish are used to doing": ibid.

119. "with considerable damage": Morgan's report, CO 1/23.

119. "whichever way we went": quoted in Earle, *Sack*, p. 86.

120. "silver cobs": Panama 81, 1669 (III), "Inventory of the Treasure."

121. "achieved at Portobelo": Both letters are quoted in Esquemeling, p. 148–49.

126. "on February 17, 1669": The report of the council is addressed as a letter of March 16, 1669, to the queen and is contained in the file "Original Consultations" in IG 1877.

8. Rich and Wicked

129. " 'rushing through' its streets": quoted in Bridenbaugh, p. 380.

131. "a Law to your self": quoted in Bridenbaugh, p. 384.

132. "for married women": Crespo's "declaration," dated June 12, 1669, is found in IG 2541.

132. "on a river barge": for Mary's testimony and glimpses of her later career, see Todd and Spearing, *Counterfeit Ladies*; and Kietzman, *The Self-Fashioning of an Early Modern Englishwoman*.

133. "Seamen of the Ship": The quotations from the letter are from Carleton, *News from Jamaica*, 1671.

134. "her intended designs": quoted in Black, p. 22.

135. "and more corruption": see Black, epigram.

137. "returned again to sea": Dunlop, p. 37.

140. "a better sort of folk": quoted in Marx, *Port Royal,* p. 2.

9. An Amateur English Theatrical

144. "hunting licenses": Pringle, p. 84.

148. "to port": The English version of the Maracaibo raid is included in Esquemeling's account and Morgan's report, contained in A. P. Thornton's article "The Modyfords and Morgan," from *Jamaican Historical Review*, 1952.

149. "to staff it": The Spanish perspectives on the Maracaibo raid are taken from the testimony of Captain Juan de Acosta Abreu and Gabriel Neveda of June 20, 1669 (Escribiana 699A, part I, fos. 39v–40, 44), in "Information concerning the loss of the Armada of Barlovento at the Lagoon of Maracaibo" (Contratación 3164).

149. "in their peaceful cay": Abreu testimony, point 4, Escribiana 699A.

151. "do not eat me!": de Lussan, p. 22.

151. "left him alone": Captain Juan de Acosta Abreu and Gabriel Neveda of June 20, 1669 (Escribiana 699A, part I, fos. 39v–40, 44), point 5.

151. "Realm of Spain": ibid., testimony of Gabriel Neveda.

157. "law and reason": Morgan to Jenkins, March 8, 1682. CSPWI item 431, pp. 203–5.

158. "spotted the pirate's flag": The story of Alonzo's itinerary and his views of the confrontation with Morgan are from Contratación 3164.

160. "all sorts of ammunition": Esquemeling, p. 167.

161. "all manner of hopes": ibid.

162. "a parcel of cowards": The correspondence between Morgan and Alonzo is contained in Esquemeling, pp. 168–78.

165. "everything was ablaze." Contratación 3164.

165. "hands of their persecutors": Esquemeling, p. 172.

167. *"by Captaine Morgan"*: The illustration can be seen at Esquemeling, p. 170.

167. "to do it withal?": Esquemeling, p. 176.

169. "of this New World": ibid., p. 173.

172. "in my favor": Contratación 3164.

10. Black Clouds to the East

175. "befall the vessel": quoted in Volo, p. 155.

175. "into a foam": Bassett, p. 115.

176. "by a whistling sound": quoted in Rappaport, p. 57.

177. "indeed invaded": IG 1877.

177. "passivity of Her Majesty's subjects": ibid.

177. "and spying on their fortifications": White's hugely entertaining demands are contained in a letter of December 4, 1671, from the Count of Medellín to the queen, IG 1877.

178. "with love and respect": Arlington to the queen, February 23/5, 1669. IG 1877.

178. "put an end to it": Arlington to Modyford, June 12, 1670, CSPWI item 194.

180. "in his Majesty's men-of-war": ibid.

180. "of the Indians": quoted in Earle, *Sack*, p. 145.

181. "or set up for themselves": Modyford to Arlington, August 20, 1670. CSPWI item 237.

182. "ready to serve us": quoted in Cruikshank, p. 127.

185. *"Happy victories"*: CO 1/25. Translated by M. Isabel Amarante.

186. "by these Pirates": letter from Don Pedro de Ulloa Riva de Neira, April 24, 1670. IG 2542.

187. "since it is the source": letter of April 9, 1669. IG 1877.

189. "Dated 5th of July, 1670": CSPWI item 310.

189. "everlasting renown": from *Don Quixote de la Mancha,* Cervantes, translated by Tobias Smollett. FSG, NY, 1986, p. 30.

189. "commissions against us": from "Extract of a Letter from Port Royal," June 28, 1670. CSPWI item 207.

191. "account of your fleet": Governor Modyford's instructions to Admiral Henry Morgan, July 2, 1670. CSPWI item 212.

193. "said to be a sorceress": "Declaration of Juan de Leo," February 14, 1671. Panama 93, fos. 11–14.

193. "as successful as expected": Browne to Arlington, October 12, 1670. CSPWI item 293.

194. "much care and watchfulness": Morgan to Jenkins, June 13, 1681. CSPWI item 138.

195. "a final answer from Spain": Arlington to Modyford, June 12, 1670. CSPWI item 194.

196. "sociableness of man's nature": Modyford to Arlington, August 20, 1670. CSPWI item 237.

197. "here to reunite": letter of Salvador Barranco, November 11, 1670. Panama 93, fos. 11–14.

197. "a thousand cursed things": ibid.

199. "to Admiral Morgan": Browne to Arlington, October 12, 1670. CSPWI item 293.

202. "audacious character": from *Fragment of a Voyage to New Orleans (1855)* by Elisée Reclus. Translated by Camille Martin and John Clark, published in *Mesechabe* 11 (Winter 1993) and 12 (Spring 1994).

203. "an enemy position": The contract terms can be found in Esquemeling, p. 189.

205. "take this one": quoted in Ure, p. 180.

206. "beyond description": ibid.

206. "to stock the garrisons": Some of the correspondence relating to the improvements made for the defense of Panama is in Guzmán's letters of October 29 and November 3, 1668, Panama 87.

207. "and you will not need them": letter from Don Pedro to Don Juan, January 7, 1670, Panama 93, fos. 34v–36.

11. The Isthmus

209. "Things began miserably": The main English sources for the Panama mission are Esquemeling and "A True account and relation" by Morgan, August 20, 1671, CSPWI item 504.

212. "stone or brick": Esquemeling, p. 198.

213. "infinite asperity of the mountain": ibid.

213. "and destroy them": letter from Don Pedro de Elizalde to Don Juan, Panama 93, fos. 112v–113.

215. "and the wooden walls": Among the most complete Spanish accounts of the battle is the letter from Don Miguel Francisco de Marichalar to the queen, October 25, 1671; and the "Declaration of Fernando de Saavedra," Panama 93, fos. 11–14.

217. "to defend the isthmus": "Declaration of Fernando de Saavedra," Panama 93, fos. 11–14.

222. "they had planned": A copy of Don Juan's report was also captured by the English and sent to Morgan, and later reprinted in Bartholomew Sharp's *Voyages*.

12. City of Fire

233. "seeing the Face of the Enemy": Don Juan's report, from Sharp's *Voyages*.

233. "to their Fury": ibid.

235. "so precise an Obligation": ibid.

237. "nothing more than to engage": ibid.

238. "in their bodies": Esquemeling, p. 219.

239. "drew up to confront the Spaniards": The main English accounts of the battle come from Esquemeling and from Morgan's report, "A True account and relation," April 20, 1671. CSPWI item 504.

239. "till he lost his life": Morgan, April 20, 1671. CSPWI item 504.

240. "Follow me!": Guzmán, February 19, 1671. Panama 92, fo. 5.

241. "so many thousand Bullets": ibid.

241. "it was impossible": ibid.

243. "Alexander the Great": quoted in Petrovich, p. 38.

243. "Peru and Potozí": Morgan, April 20, 1671. CSPWI item 504.

244. "took prisoners every day": from "Copy of the Relation of Wm. Fogg concerning the action of the privateers at Panama, taken the 4th of April 1671," CSPWI item 483.

245. "richest merchants of Panama": Esquemeling, p. 225.

246. "to the vanquished enemy": Browne to Williamson, August 21, 1671. CO 1/27, fo. 69v.

246. "fled to the mountains": Guzmán, February 19, 1671. Panama 92, fo. 5.

247. "of the men of this Kingdom": letter from Don Juan Olivares Urrea, February 25, 1671. Panama 93, fos. 129, 129v, and 130.

248. "where they come ashore": quoted in Bradley, p. 104.

13. Aftermath

254. "were broken": quoted in Petrovich, p. 94.

254. "11 and 18 million pesos": Earle, *Sack*, p. 255.

254. "and its trade": This quotation and the details that follow are from the council's letter to the queen, June 13, 1671. Panama 93.

255. "cries of the women and children": This and the following quotations are from "Considerations from Sir Thomas Modyford which moved him to give his consent for fitting the privateers of Jamaica against the Spaniard," June ?, 1671. CSPWI item 578, pp. 237–38.

256. "cheating and deserting them": Lynch to Arlington, July 2, 1671. CSPWI 580.

257. "an unseasonable irruption": ibid.

258. "left to the law": Browne to Williamson, August 21, 1671. CSPWI 608.

258. "sorrows and misfortune": Don Miguel Francisco de Marichalar to the queen, October 25, 1671. Panama 93, fos. 11–14.

261. "the Spaniards satisfied": Lynch to Arlington, December 17, 1671. CSPWI 697.

262. "one of great courage": Bannister to Arlington, March 30, 1672, quoted in Pope, p. 285.

265. "forced to stay here": quoted in Pope, p. 289.

269. "where he was": Morgan to Williamson, April 13, 1675. CO 1/34, no. 55.

270. "in fortifying the South Sea": Lynch to Williamson, November 20, 1674. CSPWI item 1389.

270. "and fall by him": Morgan to Williamson, April 13, 1675. CO 1/34, no. 55.

272. "a kind of veneration": Roberts, p. 274.

272. "can cut a diamond": Morgan to Jenkins, August 22, 1681. CSPWI item 208.

273. "that I could get": Morgan to Jenkins, April 9, 1681. CSPWI item 73.

273. "led on to gaming": quoted in Cordingly, p. 239.

273. "as well as we": Johnson, p. 26.

280. "with an exacting eye": Sloane's account of Morgan's illness is included in his *Voyages*, pp. xcviii–cxix.

14. Apocalypse

285. "hot and airless": For the circumstances of life in Port Royal, I am indebted to Marx's wonderfully detailed *Port Royal Rediscovered*, especially pp. 1–12; and to Black's *Port Royal*, especially pp. 99–119.

291. "a small trembling": from "A Letter from Hans Sloane . . . ," reprinted in *Philosophical Transactions*, volume XVIII, S. Smith and B. Walford, London, 1695. Sloane was not present on Jamaica for the earthquake but collected letters from actual eyewitnesses. It will not be referenced here again.

291. "It will soon be over": from Heath's "A Full Account of the late dreadful Earthquake at Port Royal in Jamaica," June 22 and 28, 1692. Printed in *A True and Particular Relation . . .* , second edition, T. Osborne, London, 1748. Heath's entire account is contained here and will not be referenced again.

292. "sunk under Water": quoted in Clark, p. 16.

294. "above ground": from *The True and Largest Account of the Late Earthquake in Jamaica*, J. Butler, London, 1693.

296. "nineteen white People": quoted in *Judgment Cliff Landslide in the Yallahs Valley*, by V. A. Zans, Geonotes, volume II, p. 43. 1959.

297. "snuff out its victims": ibid.

297. "they are irrepairable": ibid.

298. "before the tremors struck": I am indebted to George Clark's research on the earthquake, referenced above.

301. "fowls of the air": Pike's letter of June 19, 1692, is reprinted in "Quakers and the Earthquake at Port Royal," 1692, by H. J. Cadbury, *Jamaican Historical Review*, volume VIII, 1971.

Acknowledgments

I'd like to thank my researcher in Seville, Yolanda Morillo, who searched through miles of documents to find the relevant papers. Her sister, Maria, helped enormously in coordinating the Spanish research. My translators, Ana Triaureau and M. Isabel Amarante, turned seventeenth-century Castilian longhand into legible English, for which I'm grateful. Fact-checker Miriam Intrator combed the manuscript with her sharp eye for historical detail. Ken Kinker read the manuscript and offered valuable comments. I'd also like to thank the staff at the British Library in London and the Public Record Office for their assistance in tracking down Morgan-related papers. Professor George R. Clark of Kansas State University graciously provided me with his research on the Port Royal earthquake.

My agent, Scott Waxman, helped focus my original idea and found the right home for the book. Farley Chase carried the manuscript to foreign shores and placed it with sympathetic editors abroad. And my editor at Crown, Rick Horgan, sharpened the original narrative and undoubtedly made *Empire* a better book.

My lovely wife, Mariekarl, was an inexhaustible source of humor and love when they were needed most. And finally, my son, Asher, born during the revisions, did nothing at all, except arrive safely.

Index

About the Author

Stephan Talty is a widely published journalist who has contributed to *The New York Times Magazine, GQ, Men's Journal, Time Out New York, Details,* and many other publications. His book *Mulatto America: At the Crossroads of Black and White Culture* was published to critical acclaim in 2003.